Essential Readings on Struggling Learners

Compiled and introduced by Richard L. Allington

International
Reading Association
800 Barksdale Road, PO Box 8139
Newark, DE 19714-8139, USA
www.reading.org

Executive Editor, Books Corinne M. Mooney
Developmental Editor Charlene M. Nichols
Developmental Editor Tori Mello Bachman
Developmental Editor Stacey L. Reid
Editorial Production Manager Shannon T. Fortner
Design and Composition Manager Anette Schuetz

Project Editor Wesley Ford

Cover Linda Steere

Library of Congress Cataloging-in-Publication Data

Allington, Richard L.

Essential readings on struggling learners / Compiled and introduced by Richard L. Allington.

p. cm.

1. Reading--Remedial teaching--United States. 2. Students with disabilities. I. International Reading Association. II. Title.

LB1050.5.A4495 2010

372.43--dc22

2010009199

Contents

Comprehension: The Reason for Reading

Introduction

Richard L. Allington

Addressing the needs of struggling readers is a relatively new idea. In the United States, for example, struggling readers have been on educators' minds for less than a century, and there has been a national effort to address their needs only since the passage of the Elementary and Secondary Education Act of 1965.We have, however, made enormous strides—especially in the past decade—in understanding just what it is we need to do to eliminate reading difficulties.

I suggest that we can do this with no more money than we currently spend. But we have to use that money in new and different ways to fund the efforts that are needed.

Currently, in too many, if not most, schools, we spend almost no money on intervention programs for kindergarteners. At the same time, we have good evidence that even modest kindergarten interventions can reap big rewards. It isn't that we don't know which students are at risk for reading difficulties on the first day of school—because typically we do (McGill-Franzen, 2006). They are the children who arrive for kindergarten knowing the names of fewer than five letters. Of course, letter-name knowledge is only one thing these students know less about than is typical of children who are entering kindergartener. But knowledge of letter names is a good, simple predictor of who will need help in kindergarten to avoid struggling and ultimately experience retention in grade or classification as a pupil with a disability.

Students with little knowledge of letter names also know a lot less than their peers about reading, so we cannot expect them to catch up simply by teaching them the names of the letters. These students have fewer concepts about print, less knowledge of books and stories, and often smaller oral vocabularies than the students who arrive at the beginning of kindergarten knowing most, if not all, of the letter names. Addressing the needs of students at risk of reading difficulties means we must provide each of them with more intensive and more expert early reading instruction (McGill-Franzen, Allington, Yokoi, & Brooks, 1999; Vellutino, Scanlon, Zhang, & Schatschneider, 2008). And we must begin to provide this during their kindergarten year.

But kindergarten support will not ameliorate learning difficulties for all students at risk. Some students will need more intensive and more expert reading instruction after kindergarten. This additional help may be needed for only another semester or less, at which point most of these students will have caught up with their classmates and will likely never again fall behind. A few will need longer periods of support, perhaps across first grade and into second grade. But we have good evidence that 98% of all children entering kindergarten can be at grade level by the end of first or second grade (Allington & Walmsley, 1995; Mathes et al., 2005; Vellutino et al., 1996).

Currently, we have few studies focused on older readers as opposed to studies of early literacy attainment, but we have what seems a sufficient research base to assert that we can also eliminate reading difficulties with older readers (Torgesen, 2004). However, the later we wait until intervening, the further behind struggling readers fall; the further behind readers are, the longer it takes them to catch. Schools in the United States have not seemed especially interested in mounting the effort required to catch those eighth graders reading at the fourth-grade level up with their peers. Schools would have to quadruple these students' rate of reading acquisition, from a half-year to two-year growth per year, and would have to continue to offer instruction that powerful across all the high school years to ensure these learners are at grade level before they leave school.

At its simplest, students at risk for reading difficulties need more expert and more intensive reading instruction than that which is normally provided. It seems quite clear from the long-term outcomes of special education programs—and, in the United States, of Title I—that these students do not benefit much from instruction focused primarily on basic skills or from instruction that is different from that offered in the classroom (Cohen & Moffitt, 2009). The several evaluations of the federal Title I program indicate that while participating students make small gains, most never achieve grade-level reading status (Borman & D'Agostino, 1996).

Special education reading outcomes in general are not so positive compared to Title I (Denton, Vaughn, & Fletcher, 2003). In the United States, as elsewhere, current federally funded programs for addressing reading difficulties are failing. It's not that the programs don't help, because they do. But they are not designed to provide both more expert and more intensive reading instruction. As they say, "You can look at the research" (e.g., Allington & McGill-Franzen, 1989; Vaughn and Linan-Thompson, 2003) for evidence that Title I students and pupils with learning disabilities typically receive fewer and lower quality reading lessons than do their achieving peers.

I cannot tell you just how this happened, but it has. Given what most schools currently have in place to address the needs of students with reading difficulties, it is not surprising that we continue to have struggling readers. Too often the programs we have add no reading lessons to the school day; they simply replace part of the classroom reading instruction with other reading instruction. Too often the adults providing the reading lessons under the federal programs are not very expert: In the majority of cases, the providers are less expert than the classroom teachers whose instruction they are replacing (Allington, 2009). And most of the supplementary reading lessons provided in Title I or special education classrooms are focused on low-level mastery of basic skills, not on engaging reading lessons.

In short, what most schools have to offer their students with reading difficulties is not what these students need.

What Struggling Readers Need From Their Schools and Their Teachers

Struggling readers do not need new commercial reading programs, print or electronic—although this is what most schools spend the available money on. What struggling readers need are schoolwide efforts to provide them with more expert and more intensive reading lessons.

The effort must begin in the general education classroom. We know too well that classroom teachers vary in the quality and quantity of reading lessons they offer struggling readers. Some classroom teachers feel it is not their responsibility to teach reading to their struggling students (Scharlach, 2008). Others feel that, if their job is to teach fourth grade, then they should provide fourth-grade–level instruction. The truth of the matter is that struggling fourth-grade readers need a full classroom reading lesson offered at their level every day, and it is the classroom teacher who must provide this. But these readers need *additional* reading instruction, perhaps another 30–45 minutes per day, of reading lessons.

We have large-scale research indicating that roughly one quarter of primary grade teachers effectively teach virtually all of their students to read (Pianta, Belsky, Houts, Morrison, & National Institute of Child Health and Human Development Early Childcare Research Network, 2007). That same study indicates that half of our primary grade teachers can teach some of their students to read—in this case, those students we would expect to become readers. These teachers provide high levels of social and emotional support to their students but not very effective reading lessons. The result is that readers experiencing difficulty often do not receive the quality of reading lessons that they need to exhibit accelerated growth (more than one year of growth per year). Finally, the study indicates that almost 25% of primary grade teachers offer reading instruction unlikely to benefit most students in their classrooms.

According to this study then (Pianta et al., 2007), the problem lies in the fact that 75% of classroom teachers are not very expert at teaching students to read. These teachers follow the directions in a commercial reading package but are not very adept at modifying those directions when students are not benefiting. This is a problem we can solve but only if we admit this is the problem. Scheduling students with reading difficulties for an additional 30 minutes of reading instruction from someone else will not likely lead to accelerated reading growth unless the classroom instruction is improved first.

So the first step schools must take is ensuring the quality of classroom reading instruction. At its most basic, this means gathering evidence that all students are receiving reading instruction at their current instructional level rather than on grade level. We have strong evidence of just how important matching a student with books of appropriate difficulty is if learning is the goal (Betts, 1949; O'Connor et al., 2002).

By saying appropriate difficulty level, I am suggesting that most students benefit most from having texts they can read with 99% accuracy in their hands for almost all of the school day. This is high-success reading. During small-group guided reading, slightly more difficult texts can be used, but the best evidence here is for texts students can read at 97% or 98% accuracy. What we have for too long failed to realize is the powerful nature of high-success reading activity. It is during high-success reading that students begin to consolidate all the various skills and strategies they are acquiring, and they can focus purely on comprehending what they've read. And it is the sort of reading that brings smiles to students' faces, even those of readers who have been experiencing difficulties.

Once we have the right books in students' hands, we can begin to work on expanding the amount of reading that they do, especially the amount that struggling readers do. Again, we have good evidence that most struggling readers actually read very little, either in school or out. Some of that undoubtedly stems from too many struggling readers being given texts that are too difficult for them. When reading wears students out, they feel like quitting. Beyond that, however, is the fact that our lessons with struggling readers simply have not often required them to read very much (Allington, 1980, 1984). One result of limited reading experiences is the lack of stamina for reading. We can build stamina for reading, and we must, through gradually expanding reading time.

But if we want struggling readers to read more, and we do, then the evidence is clear: We must provide them with easy access to books they want to read as well as to books they can read (Guthrie & Humenick, 2004). I mention this because we have far too many fourth-grade classrooms where there are too few second-grade–level trade books available to read. By too few, I mean under 100 titles. Given that most second-grade trade books can be read in under 20 minutes by second-grade readers, even 100 books won't be a sufficient number for the school year. But 100 second-grade books would be a good start for every fourth-grade classroom.

So let's now assume we have a school where all classroom teachers provide high-quality reading lessons for all students everyday. Every student, including the struggling readers, is now receiving at least 90 minutes of reading instruction on his or her reading level in the general education classroom. Additionally, all students have texts for every subject that cover the grade level material at their reading level. Finally, every struggling reader attends a school where all classrooms have libraries with lots of trade books the struggling reader can and wants to read.

Many of the students who now struggle with reading would largely have their problems solved if the situation just described were available. But some struggling readers, while much better off in these classrooms, still will not accelerate their rate of reading acquisition. That is, there are students who require more expert and more intensive reading instruction than the classroom teacher can provide.

Outside the General Education Classroom

Tier 2

Now we get to what has recently become known as increasingly intensive, tiered instruction. This sort of instruction is at the basis of the U.S. federal legislation that recommends a Response to Intervention (RTI) model. By this I mean that RTI, while situated legislatively in the general education program, also reaches beyond it.

Tier 2 provides an additional layer of reading instruction along with the Tier 1 instruction situated in the general education classroom. Tier 2 is typically conceived as small-group reading lessons provided in addition to the classroom reading lesson. It should be expert reading instruction and could be an extension of the classroom reading lesson. At the very least, the evidence indicates a substantial benefit when Tier 2 lessons are well coordinated with classroom reading lessons (Borman, Wong, Hedges & D'Agostino, 2003).

One might simply move Tier 2 students more quickly through the classroom reading curriculum, perhaps doubling the pace of progress to support catching these struggling readers up to their on-level peers. It might be that the classroom teacher is responsible for teaching even-numbered curriculum units and the reading specialist would teach the odd-numbered units. Or the two teachers could partner up and plan both to teach the same unit but completing each unit in half the time typically taken because reading lessons would substantially expand.

There are other models that could be used, but the key for Tier 2 lessons is their link to the classroom reading instruction. There is no theory or evidence that struggling readers need to be taught a different reading curriculum; there is evidence that when we do offer struggling readers a different curriculum, reading development is slower than if we provide a single coherent reading curriculum for struggling readers regardless of who teaches it. Another model I prefer ties the Tier 1 classroom lessons and the Tier 2 extra lessons together by theme or genre.

Additionally, we could organize the Tier 2 lessons to focus more on developing content, thus supporting not only reading development but also development of social studies or science knowledge. This alternative becomes especially attractive at grade 3 and up since the extra reading lessons sometimes overlap the time period when classroom teachers are providing content area lessons. In such cases, we design the Tier 2 lesson to replace the content area lesson, teaching reading in the context of print materials focused on grade-level content but matched to the student's reading level.

The evidence available suggests that relatively few students continue to struggle when we ensure the quality of classroom reading lessons and provide Tier 2 small-group instruction (Mathes et al., 2005; Vellutino et al., 1996). But a few students still do struggle. It is these students who we provide with the most intensive and expert reading instruction.

Tier 3

This tier offers expert daily tutorial support to those few readers who are still struggling. Again, this tier is in addition to the student continuing to participate in Tiers 1 and 2 reading lessons. That is, if the Tier 1 classroom reading lesson is 90 minutes long and the Tier 2 lesson is 45 minutes long, when we add a 45-minute Tier 3 lesson, the student is participating in reading lessons for 3 hours each school day. The whole point to the tiered approach is increasing both the intensity and the expertness of reading lessons struggling students are offered.

The reading lessons provided in Tier 3 also need to fit coherently with the reading lessons in the other tiers. Again, a guiding principle in RTI is the focus on providing struggling readers a coherent reading instructional environment rather than the sort of fragmented reading instruction that too often characterizes services from Title I programs or special education (Johnston, Allington, & Afflerbach, 1985; McGill-Franzen & Allington, 1990; Vaughn & Linan-Thompson, 2003).

How the RTI Model Differs From Traditional Remediation and Special Education Services

The tiered approach to intervention detailed in the RTI model will provide more and better reading instruction to the students who need it to become achieving readers. This is unlike our traditional intervention programs that have provided a standard amount of intervention services, regardless of the need or of the progress students were making toward becoming grade-level readers. The focus of RTI is typically a brief, intensive, expert reading intervention that succeeds in ameliorating the reading difficulties some children experience. The goal, basically, is to ensure that no struggling readers are created by school systems as a result of simply not providing sufficiently intensive and sufficiently expert instruction.

But for schools to take advantage of what RTI offers may require substantial shifts not just in our behaviors (such as what we spend education funding for) but also, and perhaps more important, in our beliefs. In other words, if we continue to believe that some students can just be expected to be struggling readers, then there will be little reason to work to ensure all students become literate.

Summers and the Reading Gap

Finally, we need to acknowledge the importance of summers in explaining the reading achievement gap that exists between poor and nonpoor students. There have been several research reports focused on this issue, and they concur in the finding that most of the achievement gap observed between poor and wealthier students is attributable largely to what happens during the summer months, months when students are not in school. In the two largest scale studies (Alexander, Entwisle, & Olson, 2007; Hayes & Grether, 1983), roughly 80% of the rich–poor reading achievement gap developed during the summer months, not during the school year. It seems that poor students typically lose about three months of reading achievement during the summers while middle class students typically gain about a month. This is a four-month gap that occurs every summer. Thus, poor students fall about a year behind more financially advantaged students every 2.5 years. Over a K–5 elementary career, then, poor students lose about two years of reading achievement during the summer months.

The basic issue is that students from families that are financially better off are more likely to read during the summer months. These same students are more likely to live in homes where more books are available for them to read and in neighborhoods where it is easier to purchase children's books (Krashen, 2004; Neuman & Celano, 2001). We have good evidence that simply supplying a set of self-selected books to poor students on the final day of school can effectively ameliorate the summer reading loss that currently creates most of the reading achievement gap (McGill-Franzen & Allington, 2008; White & Kim, 2008). Additionally, providing summer books to read produced as much reading growth as did sending these students to summer school (Allington et al., 2010). Educators must be concerned about summer months and provide support such that poor students are just as likely to have access to interesting books during school vacation periods as do middle class students.

This Book of Essential Readings

In an attempt to provide good information on what struggling readers need and how we might go about providing just that, this book presents a collection of articles drawn from *The Reading Teacher* journal. I have selected articles based on the broad view of helping struggling readers. Other titles in the Essential Readings series provide articles on specific areas of reading instruction, and those titles can be used in conjunction with this one to help educators develop the expertise needed to fulfill the promise of RTI and develop a nation of readers.

The first section of this book focuses on assessment, both of readers and of the efforts your school is currently making to address the needs of struggling readers. Both types of assessment are necessary. In fact, the second—assessing the school response—may be more important than the first. Few teachers don't know which students are having difficulty with reading, but in too many schools, no one has ever really asked whether what is being done is sufficient to address the needs of struggling readers.

The second section offers advice for what sorts of planning you might consider in addressing the needs of struggling readers. The articles included here focus on what schools might do differently to better address instructional needs of students having difficulty. These articles address both ambitious plans and smaller efforts to improve reading lessons and their outcomes. Summer reading is also addressed because of the powerful role it plays in creating the reading achievement gap between poor and wealthier students.

The final section focuses on teaching for understanding, if only because that is the primary area of failure among struggling readers. As we learned with the recent large-scale federal Reading First reading program, efforts focused on improving word recognition may improve word recognition, but those efforts do not improve reading achievement if reading comprehension is measured (Gamse, Jacob, Horst, Boulay, & Unlu, 2008). Thus, the articles in the final section address helping struggling readers understand the texts they read. Perhaps because comprehension has only rarely been the focus of programs for struggling readers, there is much ground to be made up in the lessons we design and offer them.

Of course, many more articles could have been included in this book. For those who wish to read further, a list of Additional Recommended Reading concludes this introduction.

In the end, improving what we do is the best path to success for struggling readers. We have enough evidence that virtually all students can be reading at grade level at the end of first grade and beyond. But to make this the reality in every school will require that we do more and do better by those students experiencing difficulty. There is no single answer to the question, What should we do? We know enough to do those things that need to be done. But because students differ, what we need to do differs from students to student. We need to recognize that and begin asking ourselves, What does this student need to be a successful reader? Then we provide that—and a student's future changes.

References

Alexander, K.L., Entwisle, D.R., & Olson, L.S. (2007). Lasting consequences of the summer learning gap. *American Sociological Review, 72*(2), 167–180. doi:10.1177/000312240707200202

Allington, R.L. (1980). Poor readers don't get to read much in reading groups. *Language Arts, 57*(8), 872–877.

Allington, R.L. (1984). Content coverage and contextual reading in reading groups. *Journal of Reading Behavior, 16*(1), 85–96.

Allington, R.L. (2009). *What really matters in Response to Intervention: Research-based designs.* Boston: Allyn & Bacon.

Allington, R.L., McGill-Franzen, A., Camilli, G., Williams, L., Graff, J., Zeig, J.L., et al. (2010). Ameliorating summer reading setback among economically disadvantaged elementary students. Manuscript submitted for publication.

Allington, R.L., & McGill-Franzen, A.M. (1989). School response to reading failure: Chapter 1 and special education students in grades two, four, and eight. *The Elementary School Journal, 89*(5), 529–542. doi:10.1086/461590

Allington, R.L., & Walmsley, S.A. (Eds.). (1995). *No quick fix: Rethinking literacy programs in American elementary schools.* New York: Teachers College Press; Newark, DE: International Reading Association.

Betts, E.A. (1949). Adjusting instruction to individual needs. In Henry, N.B. (Ed.), *The forty-eighth yearbook of the National Society for the Study of Education: Part II, Reading in the elementary school* (pp. 266–283). Chicago: University of Chicago Press.

Borman, G.D., & D'Agostino, J.V. (1996). Title I and student achievement: A meta-analysis of federal evaluation results. *Educational Evaluation and Policy Analysis, 18*(4), 309–326.

Borman, G.D., Wong, K.K., Hedges, L.V., & D'Agostino, J.V. (2003). Coordinating categorical and regular programs:

Effects on Title I students' educational opportunities and outcomes. In G.D. Borman, S.C. Stringfield, & R.E. Slavin (Eds.), *Title I: Compensatory education at the crossroads* (pp. 79–116). Mahwah, NJ: Erlbaum.

Cohen, D.K., & Moffitt, S.L. (2009). *The ordeal of equality: Did federal regulation fix the schools?* Cambridge, MA: Harvard University Press.

Denton, C.A., Vaughn, S., & Fletcher, J.M. (2003). Bringing research-based practice in reading intervention to scale. *Learning Disabilities Research & Practice, 18*(3), 201–211. doi:10.1111/1540-5826.00075

Gamse, B.C., Jacob, R.T., Horst, M., Boulay, B., & Unlu, F. (2008). *Reading First impact study: Final report* (NCEE 2009–4038). Washington, DC: National Center for Education Evaluation and Regional Assistance.

Guthrie, J.T., & Humenick, N.M. (2004). Motivating students to read: Evidence for classroom practices that increase motivation and achievement. In P.D. McCardle & V. Chhabra (Eds.), *The voice of evidence in reading research* (pp. 329–354). Baltimore: Brookes.

Hayes, D.P., & Grether, J. (1983). The school year and vacations: When do students learn? *The Cornell Journal of Social Relations, 17*(1), 56–71.

Johnston, P., Allington, R.L., & Afflerbach, P. (1985). The congruence of classroom and remedial reading instruction. *The Elementary School Journal, 85*(4), 465–478. doi:10.1086/461414

Krashen, S.D. (2004). *The power of reading: Insights from the research* (2nd ed.). Portsmouth, NH: Heinemann.

Mathes, P.G., Denton, C.A., Fletcher, J.M., Anthony, J.L., Francis, D.J., & Schatschneider, C. (2005). The effects of theoretically different instruction and student characteristics on the skills of struggling readers. *Reading Research Quarterly, 40*(2), 148–182. doi:10.1598/RRQ.40.2.2

McGill-Franzen, A. (2006). *Kindergarten literacy: Matching assessment and instruction.* New York: Scholastic.

McGill-Franzen, A., & Allington, R.L. (1990). Comprehension and coherence: Neglected elements of literacy instruction in remedial and resource room services. *Journal of Reading, Writing, and Learning Disabilities, 6*(2), 149–182.

McGill-Franzen, A., & Allington, R.L. (2008). Got books? *Educational Leadership, 65*(7), 20–23.

McGill-Franzen, A., Allington, R.L., Yokoi, L., & Brooks, G. (1999). Putting books in the classroom seems necessary but not sufficient. *The Journal of Educational Research, 93*(2), 67–74. doi:10.1080/0022 0679909597631

Neuman, S.B., & Celano, D. (2001). Access to print in low-income and middle-income communities: An ecological study of four neighborhoods. *Reading Research Quarterly, 36*(1), 8–26. doi:10.1598/RRQ.36.1.1

O'Connor, R.E., Bell, K.M., Harty, K.R., Larkin, L.K., Sackor, S.M., & Zigmond, N. (2002). Teaching reading to poor readers in the intermediate grades: A comparison of text difficulty. *Journal of Educational Psychology, 94*(3), 474–485. doi:10.1037/0022-0663.94.3.474

Phillips, G., & Smith, P. (1997). *A third chance to learn: The development and evaluation of specialized interventions for young children experiencing the greatest difficulty in learning to read.* Wellington: New Zealand Council for Educational Research.

Pianta, R.C., Belsky, J., Houts, R., & Morrison, F., & the National Institute of Child Health and Human Development Early Childcare Research Network. (2007). Opportunities to learn in America's elementary classrooms. *Science, 315*(5820), 1795–1796. doi:10.1126/science.1139719

Scharlach, T.D. (2008). These kids just aren't motivated to read: The influence of preservice teachers' beliefs on their expectations, instruction, and evaluation of struggling readers. *Literacy Research and Instruction, 47*(3), 158–173. doi:10.1080/19388070802062351

Torgesen, J.K. (2004). Lessons learned from research on interventions for students who have difficulty learning to read. In P.D. McCardle & V. Chhabra (Eds.), *The voice of evidence in reading research* (pp. 355–382). Baltimore: Brookes.

Vaughn, S., & Linan-Thompson, S. (2003). What is special about special education for students with learning disabilities? *Exceptional Children, 69*(4), 391–409.

Vellutino, F.R., Scanlon, D.M., Sipay, E.R., Small, S.G., Pratt, A., Chen, R., et al. (1996). Cognitive profiles of difficult-to-remediate and readily remediated poor readers: Early intervention as a vehicle for distinguishing between cognitive and experiential deficits as basic causes of specific reading disability. *Journal of Educational Psychology, 88*(4), 601–638. doi:10.1037/0022-0663.88.4.601

Vellutino, F.R., Scanlon, D.M., Zhang, H., & Schatschneider, C. (2008). Using response to kindergarten and first grade intervention to identify children at-risk for long-term reading difficulties. *Reading and Writing, 21*(4), 437–480. doi:10.1007/s11145-007-9098-2

White, T.G., & Kim, J.S. (2008). Teacher and parent scaffolding of voluntary summer reading. *The Reading Teacher, 62*(2), 116–125. doi:10.1598/RT.62.2.3

Additional Recommended Reading

Bloodgood, J.W., & Pacifici, J.C. (2004). Bringing word study to intermediate classrooms. *The Reading Teacher, 58*(3), 250–263. doi:10.1598/RT.58.3.3

Cunningham, P. (2006). What if they can say the words but don't know what they mean? *The Reading Teacher, 59*(7), 708–711. doi:10.1598/RT.59.7.11

Duffy-Hester, A.M. (1999). Teaching struggling readers in elementary school classrooms: A review of classroom reading programs and principles for instruction. *The Reading Teacher, 52*(5), 480–495. doi:10.1598/RT.52.5.4

Fisher, D., & Frey, N. (2007). Implementing a schoolwide literacy framework: Improving achievement in an

urban elementary school. *The Reading Teacher, 61*(1), 32–43. doi:10.1598/RT.61.1.4
Johnston, P. (2005). Literacy assessment and the future. *The Reading Teacher, 58*(7), 684–686. doi:10.1598/RT.58.7.9
Pinnell, G.S. (2006). Every child a reader: What one teacher can do. *The Reading Teacher, 60*(1), 78–83. doi:10.1598/RT.60.1.9
Scharlach, T.D. (2008). START comprehending: Students and teachers actively reading text. *The Reading Teacher, 62*(1), 20–31. doi:10.1598/RT.62.1.3
Taylor, B.M., Hanson, B.E., Justice-Swanson, K., & Watts, S.M. (1997). Helping struggling readers: Linking small-group intervention with cross-age tutoring. *The Reading Teacher, 51*(3), 196–209. doi:10.1598/RT.51.3.4

Behind Test Scores: What Struggling Readers *Really* Need

Sheila W. Valencia and Marsha Riddle Buly

Every year thousands of U.S. students take standardized tests and state reading tests, and every year thousands fail them. With the implementation of the No Child Left Behind legislation (www.ed.gov/nclb/landing.jhtml), which mandates testing all children from grades 3 to 8 every year, these numbers will grow exponentially, and alarming numbers of schools and students will be targeted for "improvement." Whether you believe this increased focus on testing is good news or bad, if you are an educator, you are undoubtedly concerned about the children who struggle every day with reading and the implications of their test failure.

Although legislators, administrators, parents, and educators have been warned repeatedly not to rely on a single measure to make important instructional decisions (Elmore, 2002; Linn, n.d.; Shepard, 2000), scores from state tests still seem to drive the search for programs and approaches that will help students learn and meet state standards. The popular press, educational publications, teacher workshops, and state and school district policies are filled with attempts to find solutions for poor test performance. For example, some schools have eliminated sustained silent reading in favor of more time for explicit instruction (Edmondson & Shannon, 2002; Riddle Buly & Valencia, 2002), others are buying special programs or mandating specific interventions (Goodnough, 2001; Helfand, 2002), and some states and districts are requiring teachers to have particular instructional emphases (McNeil, 2000; Paterson, 2000; Riddle Buly & Valencia, 2002). Furthermore, it is common to find teachers spending enormous amounts of time preparing students for these high-stakes tests (Olson, 2001), even though a narrow focus on preparing students for specific tests does not translate into real learning (Klein, Hamilton, McCaffrey, & Stecher, 2000; Linn, 2000). But, if we are really going to help students, we need to understand the underlying reasons for their test failure. Simply knowing which children have failed state tests is a bit like knowing that you have a fever when you are feeling ill but having no idea of the cause or cure. A test score, like a fever, is a symptom that demands more specific analysis of the problem. In this case, what is required is a more in-depth analysis of the strengths and needs of students who fail to meet standards and instructional plans that will meet their needs.

In this article, we draw from the results of an empirical study of students who failed a typical fourth-grade state reading assessment (see Riddle Buly & Valencia, 2002, for a full description of the study). Specifically, we describe the patterns of performance that distinguish different groups of students who failed to meet standards. We also provide suggestions for what classroom teachers need to know and how they might help these children succeed.

Study Context

Our research was conducted in a typical northwestern U.S. school district of 18,000 students located adjacent to the largest urban district in the state. At the time of our study, 43% were students

Reprinted from Valencia, S.W., & Buly, M.R. (2004). Behind test scores: What struggling readers *really* need. *The Reading Teacher*, 57(6), 520–531.

of color and 47% received free or reduced-price lunch. Over the past several years, approximately 50% of students had failed the state fourth-grade reading test that, like many other standards-based state assessments, consisted of several extended narrative and expository reading selections accompanied by a combination of multiple-choice and open-ended comprehension questions. For the purposes of this study, during September of fifth grade we randomly selected 108 students who had scored below standard on the state test given at the end of fourth grade. These 108 students constituted approximately 10% of failing students in the district. None of them was receiving supplemental special education or English as a Second Language (ESL) services. We wanted to understand the "garden variety" (Stanovich, 1988) test failure—those students typically found in the regular classroom who are experiencing reading difficulty but have not been identified as needing special services or intensive interventions. Classroom teachers, not reading specialists or special education teachers, are solely responsible for the reading instruction of these children and, ultimately, for their achievement.

Data Collection and Assessment Tools

Our approach was to conduct individual reading assessments, working one on one with the children for approximately two hours over several days to gather information about their reading abilities. We administered a series of assessments that targeted key components of reading ability identified by experts: word identification, meaning (comprehension and vocabulary), and fluency (rate and expression) (Lipson & Wixson, 2003; National Institute of Child Health and Human Development, 2000; Snow, Burns, & Griffin, 1998). Table 1 presents the measures we used and the areas in which each provided information.

To measure word identification, we used two tests from the 1989 Woodcock-Johnson Psycho-Educational Battery–Revised (WJ–R) that assessed students' reading of single and multisyllabic words, both real and pseudowords. We also scored oral reading errors students made on narrative and expository graded passages from the 1995 Qualitative Reading Inventory–II (QRI–II) and from the state test. We calculated total accuracy (percentage of words read correctly) and acceptability (counting only those errors that changed the meaning of the text). Students also responded orally to comprehension questions that accompanied the QRI–II passages, providing a measure of their comprehension that was not confounded by writing ability. To assess receptive vocabulary, we used the 1981 Peabody Picture Vocabulary Test–Revised (PPVT–R), which requires students to listen and point to a picture that corresponds to a word (scores of 85 or higher are judged to be average or above average). As with the comprehension questions, the vocabulary measure does not confound understanding with students' ability to write responses. Finally, in the area of fluency, we assessed rate of reading and expression (Samuels, 2002). We timed the readings of all passages (i.e., QRI–II and state test selections) to get a reading rate and used a 4-point rubric developed for the Oral Reading Study of the fourth-grade National Assessment of Educational Progress (NAEP) (Pinnell, Pikulski, Wixson, Campbell, Gough, & Beatty, 1995) to assess phrasing and expression (1–2 is judged to be nonfluent; 3–4 is judged to be fluent).

Findings

Scores from all the assessments for each student fell into three statistically distinct and educationally familiar categories: word identification (word reading in isolation and context), meaning (comprehension and vocabulary), and fluency (rate and expression). When we examined the average scores for all 108 students in the sample, students appeared to be substantially below grade level in all three areas. However, when we analyzed the data using a cluster analysis (Aldenderfer & Blashfield, 1984), looking for groups of students who had similar patterns across all three factors, we found six distinct

Table 1
Diagnostic Assessments

Assessment	Word identification	Meaning	Fluency
Woodcock-Johnson-Revised			
Letter-word identification	X		
Word attack	X		
Qualitative Reading Inventory-II			
Reading accuracy	X		
Reading acceptability	X		
Rate			X
Expression			X
Comprehension		X	
Peabody Picture Vocabulary Test-Revised			
Vocabulary meaning		X	
State fourth-grade passages			
Reading accuracy	X		
Reading acceptability	X		
Rate			X
Expression			X

profiles of students who failed the test. Most striking is that the majority of students were not weak in all three areas; they were actually strong in some and weak in others. Table 2 indicates the percentage of students in each group and their relative strength (+) or weakness (–) in word identification, meaning, and fluency.

The Profiles

We illuminate each profile by describing a prototypical student from each cluster (see Figure 1) and specific suggested instructional targets for each (all names are pseudonyms). Although the instructional strategies we recommend have not been implemented with these particular children, we base our recommendations on our review of research-based practices (e.g., Allington, 2001; Allington & Johnston, 2001; Lipson & Wixson, 2003; National Institute of Child Health and Human Development, 2000), our interpretation of the profiles, and our experiences teaching struggling readers. We conclude with several general implications for school and classroom instruction.

Cluster 1—Automatic Word Callers

We call these students Automatic Word Callers because they can decode words quickly and accurately, but they fail to read for meaning. The majority of students in this cluster qualify for free or reduced-price lunch, and they are English-language learners who no longer receive special support. Tomas is a typical student in this cluster.

Tomas has excellent word identification skills. He scored at ninth-grade level when reading real words and pseudowords (i.e., phonetically

Table 2
Cluster Analysis

Cluster	Sample percentage	English-language learner percentage	Low socioeconomic status percentage	Word identification	Meaning	Fluency
1–Automatic word callers	18	63	89	++	-	++
2–Struggling word callers	15	56	81	-	-	++
3–Word stumblers	17	16	42	-	+	-
4–Slow comprehenders	24	19	54	+	++	-
5–Slow word callers	17	56	67	+	-	-
6–Disabled readers	9	20	80	--	--	--

regular nonsense words such as *fot*) on the WJ–R tests, and at the independent level for word identification on the QRI–II and state fourth-grade passages. However, when asked about what he read, Tomas had difficulty, placing his comprehension at the second-grade level. Although Tomas's first language is not English, his score of 108 on the PPVT–R suggests that his comprehension difficulties are more complex than individual word meanings. Tomas's "proficient" score on the state writing assessment also suggests that his difficulty is in understanding rather than in writing answers to comprehension questions. This student's rate of reading, which was quite high compared with rates of fourth-grade students on the Oral Reading Study of NAEP (Pinnell et al., 1995) and other research (Harris & Sipay, 1990), suggests that his decoding is automatic and unlikely to be contributing to his comprehension difficulty. His score in expression is also consistent with students who were rated as "fluent" according to the NAEP rubric, although this seems unusual for a student who is demonstrating difficulty with comprehension.

The evidence suggests that Tomas needs additional instruction in comprehension and most likely would benefit from explicit instruction, teacher modeling, and think-alouds of key reading strategies (e.g., summarizing, self-monitoring, creating visual representations, evaluating), using a variety of types of material at the fourth- or fifth-grade level (Block & Pressley, 2002; Duke & Pearson, 2002). His comprehension performance on the QRI–II suggests that his literal comprehension is quite strong but that he has difficulty with more inferential and critical aspects of understanding. Although Tomas has strong scores in the fluency category, both in expression and rate, he may be reading too fast to attend to meaning, especially deeper meaning of the ideas in the text. Tomas's teacher should help him understand that the purpose for reading is to understand and that rate varies depending on the type of text and the purpose for reading. Then, the teacher should suggest that he slow down to focus on meaning. Self-monitoring strategies would also help Tomas check for understanding and encourage him to think about the ideas while he is reading. These and other such strategies

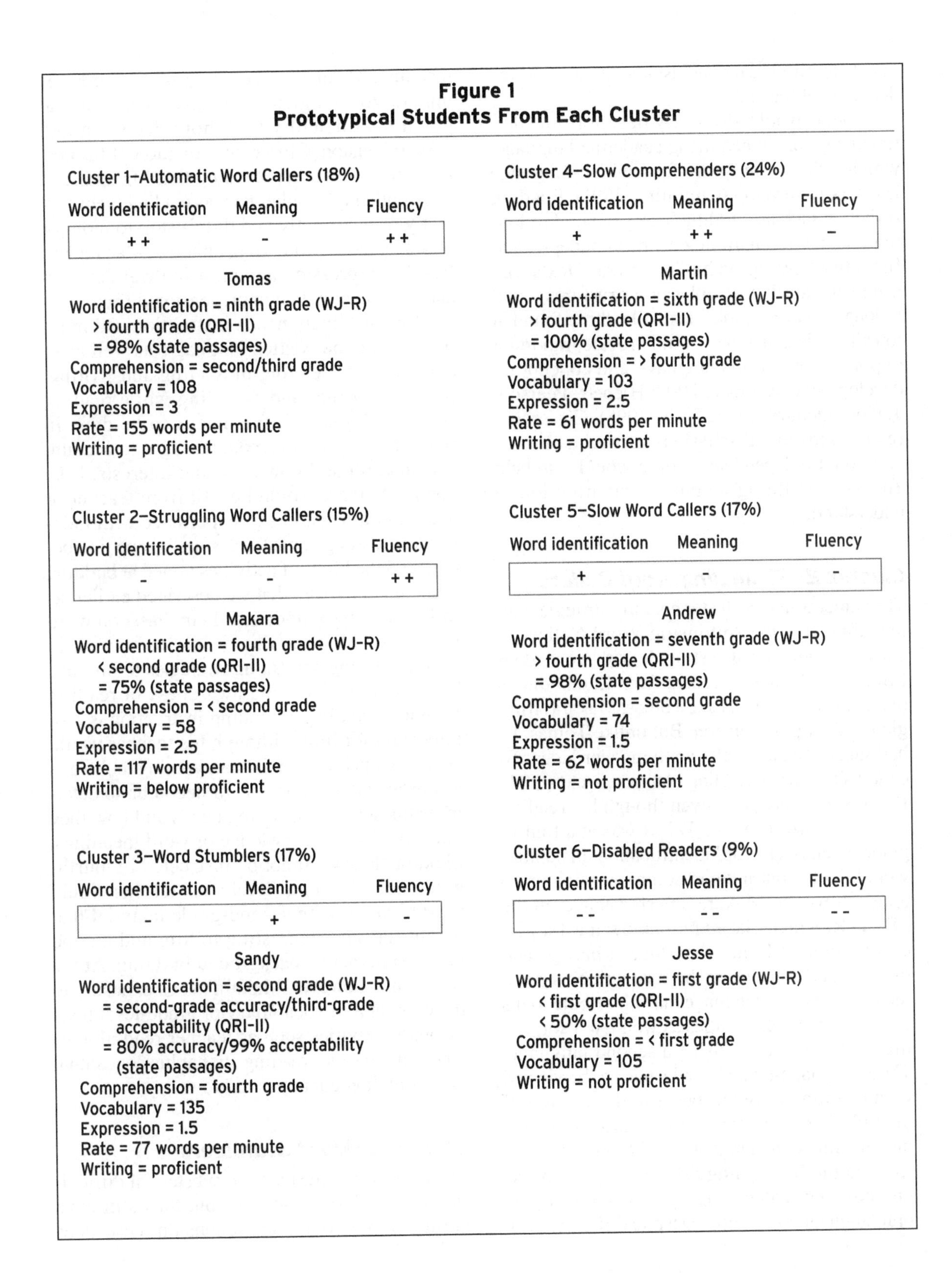

Figure 1
Prototypical Students From Each Cluster

Cluster 1–Automatic Word Callers (18%)

Word identification	Meaning	Fluency
+ +	-	+ +

Tomas

Word identification = ninth grade (WJ-R)
> fourth grade (QRI-II)
= 98% (state passages)
Comprehension = second/third grade
Vocabulary = 108
Expression = 3
Rate = 155 words per minute
Writing = proficient

Cluster 2–Struggling Word Callers (15%)

Word identification	Meaning	Fluency
-	-	+ +

Makara

Word identification = fourth grade (WJ-R)
< second grade (QRI-II)
= 75% (state passages)
Comprehension = < second grade
Vocabulary = 58
Expression = 2.5
Rate = 117 words per minute
Writing = below proficient

Cluster 3–Word Stumblers (17%)

Word identification	Meaning	Fluency
-	+	-

Sandy

Word identification = second grade (WJ-R)
= second-grade accuracy/third-grade acceptability (QRI-II)
= 80% accuracy/99% acceptability (state passages)
Comprehension = fourth grade
Vocabulary = 135
Expression = 1.5
Rate = 77 words per minute
Writing = proficient

Cluster 4–Slow Comprehenders (24%)

Word identification	Meaning	Fluency
+	+ +	–

Martin

Word identification = sixth grade (WJ-R)
> fourth grade (QRI-II)
= 100% (state passages)
Comprehension = > fourth grade
Vocabulary = 103
Expression = 2.5
Rate = 61 words per minute
Writing = proficient

Cluster 5–Slow Word Callers (17%)

Word identification	Meaning	Fluency
+	-	-

Andrew

Word identification = seventh grade (WJ-R)
> fourth grade (QRI-II)
= 98% (state passages)
Comprehension = second grade
Vocabulary = 74
Expression = 1.5
Rate = 62 words per minute
Writing = not proficient

Cluster 6–Disabled Readers (9%)

Word identification	Meaning	Fluency
- -	- -	- -

Jesse

Word identification = first grade (WJ-R)
< first grade (QRI-II)
< 50% (state passages)
Comprehension = < first grade
Vocabulary = 105
Writing = not proficient

may help him learn to adjust his rate to meet the demands of the text.

Tomas would also likely benefit from additional support in acquiring academic language, which takes many years for English-language learners to develop (Cummins, 1991). Reading activities such as building background; developing understanding of new words, concepts, and figurative language in his "to-be-read" texts; and acquiring familiarity with genre structures found in longer, more complex texts like those found at fourth grade and above would provide important opportunities for his language and conceptual development (Antunez, 2002; Hiebert, Pearson, Taylor, Richardson, & Paris, 1998). Classroom read-alouds and discussions as well as lots of additional independent reading would also help Tomas in building language and attention to understanding.

Cluster 2–Struggling Word Callers

The students in this cluster not only struggle with meaning, like the Automatic Word Callers in Cluster 1, but they also struggle with word identification. Makara, a student from Cambodia, is one of these students. Like Tomas, Makara struggled with comprehension. But unlike Tomas, he had substantial difficulty applying word identification skills when reading connected text (QRI–II and state passages), even though his reading of isolated words on the WJ–R was at a fourth-grade level. Such word identification difficulties would likely contribute to comprehension problems. However, Makara's performance on the PPVT–R, which placed him below the 1st percentile compared with other students his age, and his poor performance on the state writing assessment suggest that language may contribute to his comprehension difficulties as well—not surprising for a student acquiring a second language. These language-related results need to be viewed with caution, however, because the version of the PPVT–R available for use in this study may underestimate the language abilities of students from culturally and linguistically diverse backgrounds, and written language takes longer than oral language to develop. Despite difficulty with meaning, Makara read quickly—117 words per minute. At first glance, this may seem unusual given his difficulty with both decoding and comprehension. Closer investigation of his performance, however, revealed that Makara read words quickly whether he was reading them correctly or incorrectly and didn't stop to monitor or self-correct. In addition, although Makara was fast, his expression and phrasing were uneven and consistent with comprehension difficulties.

Makara likely needs instruction and practice in oral and written language, as well as in constructing meaning in reading and writing, self-monitoring, and decoding while reading connected text. All this needs to be done in rich, meaningful contexts, taking into account his background knowledge and interests. Like Tomas, Makara would benefit from teacher or peer read-alouds, lots of experience with independent reading at his level, small-group instruction, and the kinds of activities aimed at building academic language that we described earlier, as well as a more foundational emphasis on word meanings. Makara also needs instruction in self-monitoring and fix-up strategies to improve his comprehension and awareness of reading for understanding. Decoding instruction is also important for him, although his teacher would need to gather more information using tools such as miscue analysis or tests of decoding to determine his specific decoding needs and how they interact with his knowledge of word meanings. Makara clearly cannot be instructed in fourth-grade material; most likely, his teacher would need to begin with second-grade material that is familiar and interesting to him and a good deal of interactive background building. At the same time, however, Makara needs exposure to the content and vocabulary of grade-level texts through activities such as teacher read-alouds, tapes, and partner reading so that his conceptual understanding continues to grow.

Cluster 3–Word Stumblers

Students in this cluster have substantial difficulty with word identification, but they still have surprisingly strong comprehension. How does that happen? Sandy, a native English speaker from a middle class home, is a good example of this type of student. Sandy stumbled on so many words initially that it seemed unlikely that she would comprehend what she had read, yet she did. Her word identification scores were at second-grade level, and she read the state fourth-grade passages at frustration level. However, a clue to her strong comprehension is evident from the difference between her immediate word recognition accuracy score and her acceptability score, which takes into account self-corrections or errors that do not change the meaning. In other words, Sandy was so focused on reading for meaning that she spontaneously self-corrected many of her decoding miscues or substituted words that preserved the meaning. She attempted to read every word in the reading selections, working until she could figure out some part of each word and then using context clues to help her get the entire word. She seemed to over-rely on context because her decoding skills were so weak (Stanovich, 1994). Remarkably, she was eventually able to read the words on the state fourth-grade reading passages at an independent level. But, as we might predict, Sandy's rate was very slow, and her initial attempts to read were choppy and lacked flow—she spent an enormous amount of time self-correcting and rereading. After she finally self-corrected or figured out unknown words, however, Sandy reread phrases with good expression and flow to fit with the meaning. Although Sandy's overall fluency score was low, her primary difficulty does not appear in the area of either rate or expression; rather, her low performance in fluency seems to be a result of her difficulty with decoding.

With such a strong quest for meaning, Sandy was able to comprehend fourth-grade material even when her decoding was at frustration level. No doubt her strong language and vocabulary abilities (i.e., 99th percentile) were assets. As we might predict, Sandy was more than proficient at expressing her ideas when writing about her experiences. She understands that reading and writing should make sense, and she has the self-monitoring strategies, perseverance, and language background to make that happen.

Sandy needs systematic instruction in word identification and opportunities to practice when reading connected text at her reading level. She is clearly beyond the early stages of reading and decoding, but her teacher will need to determine through a more in-depth analysis precisely which decoding skills should be the focus of her instruction. At the same time, Sandy needs supported experiences with texts that will continue to feed and challenge her drive for meaning. For students like Sandy, it is critical not to sacrifice intellectual engagement with text while they are receiving decoding instruction and practice in below-grade-level material. Furthermore, Sandy needs to develop automaticity with word identification, and to do that she would benefit from assisted reading (i.e., reading along with others, monitored reading with a tape, or partner reading) as well as unassisted reading practice (i.e., repeated reading, reading to younger students) with materials at her instructional level (Kuhn & Stahl, 2000).

Cluster 4—Slow Comprehenders

Almost one fourth of the students in this sample were Slow Comprehenders. Like other students in this cluster, Martin is a native English speaker and a relatively strong decoder, scoring above fourth-grade level on all measures of decoding. His comprehension was at the instructional level on the fourth-grade QRI–II selections, and his vocabulary and writing ability were average for his age. On the surface, this information is puzzling because Martin failed the fourth-grade state test.

Insight about Martin's reading performance comes from several sources. First, Martin was within two points of passing the state assessment, so he doesn't seem to have a serious reading problem. Second, although his reading rate is quite slow and this often interferes with comprehension (Adams, 1990), results of the QRI–II suggest that Martin's comprehension is quite strong, in spite of his slow rate. This is most likely because Martin has good word knowledge and understands that reading should make sense, and neither the QRI–II nor the state test has time limits. His strong score in expression confirms that Martin did, indeed, attend to meaning while reading. Third, a close examination of his reading behaviors while reading words from the WJ–R tests, QRI–II, and state reading selections revealed that he had some difficulty reading multisyllabic words; although, with time, he was able to read enough words to score at grade level or above. It appears that Martin has the decoding skills to attack multisyllabic words, but they are not yet automatic.

The outstanding characteristic of Martin's profile is his extremely slow rate combined with his relatively strong word identification abilities and comprehension. Our work with him suggests that, even if Martin were to get the additional two points needed to pass the state test, he would still have a significant problem with rate and some difficulty with automatic decoding of multisyllabic words, both of which could hamper his future reading success. Furthermore, with such a lack of automaticity and a slow rate, it is unlikely that Martin enjoys or spends much time reading. As a result, he is likely to fall further and further behind his peers (Stanovich, 1986), especially as he enters middle school where the amount of reading increases dramatically. Martin needs fluency-building activities such as guided repeated oral reading, partner reading, and Readers Theatre (Allington, 2001; Kuhn & Stahl, 2000; Lipson & Wixson, 2003). Given his word identification and comprehension abilities, he most likely could get that practice using fourth-grade material where he will also encounter multisyllabic words. It is important to find reading material that is interesting to Martin and that, initially, can be completed in a relatively short time. Martin needs to develop stamina as well as fluency, and to do that he will need to spend time reading short and extended texts. In addition, Martin might benefit from instruction and practice in strategies for identifying multisyllabic words so that he is more prepared to deal with them automatically while reading.

Cluster 5—Slow Word Callers

The students in this cluster are similar to Tomas, the Automatic Word Caller in Cluster 1. The difference is that Tomas is an automatic, fluent word caller, whereas the students in this cluster are slow. This group is a fairly even mix of English-language learners and native English speakers who have difficulty in comprehension and fluency. Andrew is an example of such a student. He has well-developed decoding skills, scoring at the seventh-grade level when reading words in isolation and at the independent level when reading connected text. Even with such strong decoding abilities, Andrew had difficulty with comprehension. We had to drop down to the second-grade QRI–II passage for Andrew to score at the instructional level for comprehension, and, even at that level, his retelling was minimal. Andrew's score on the PPVT–R, corresponding to first grade (the 4th percentile for his age), adds to the comprehension picture as well. It suggests that Andrew may be experiencing difficulty with both individual word meanings and text-based understanding when reading paragraphs and longer selections. Like Martin, Andrew's reading rate was substantially below rates expected for fourth-grade students (Harris & Sipay, 1990; Pinnell et al., 1995), averaging 62 words per minute when reading narrative and expository selections. In practical terms, this means he read just one word per second. As we might anticipate from his slow rate and his comprehension difficulty, Andrew did not read with expression or meaningful phrasing.

The relationship between meaning and fluency is unclear in Andrew's case. On the one hand, students who realize they don't understand would be wise to slow down and monitor meaning. On the other hand, Andrew's lack of automaticity and slow rate may interfere with comprehension. To disentangle these factors, his teacher would need to experiment with reading materials about which Andrew has a good deal of background knowledge to eliminate difficulty with individual word meanings and overall comprehension. If his reading rate and expression improve under such conditions, a primary focus for instruction would be meaning. That is, his slow rate of reading and lack of prosody would seem to be a response to lack of understanding rather than contributing to it. In contrast, if Andrew's rate and expression are still low when the material and vocabulary are familiar, instruction should focus on both fluency and meaning. In either case, Andrew would certainly benefit from attention to vocabulary building, both indirect building through extensive independent reading and teacher read-alouds as well as more explicit instruction in word learning strategies and new words he will encounter when reading specific texts (Nagy, 1988; Stahl & Kapinus, 2001).

It is interesting that 50% of the students in this cluster scored at Level 1 on the state test, the lowest level possible. State guidelines characterize these students as lacking prerequisite knowledge and skills that are fundamental for meeting the standard. Given such a definition, a logical assumption would be that these students lack basic, early reading skills such as decoding. However, as the evidence here suggests, we cannot assume that students who score at the lowest level on the test need decoding instruction. Andrew, like others in this cluster, needs instruction in meaning and fluency.

Cluster 6—Disabled Readers

We call this group Disabled Readers because they are experiencing severe difficulty in all three areas—word identification, meaning, and fluency. This is the smallest group (9%), yet, ironically, this is the profile that most likely comes to mind when we think of children who fail state reading tests. This group also includes one of the lowest numbers of second-language learners. The most telling characteristic of students in this cluster, like Jesse, is their very limited word identification abilities. Jesse had few decoding skills beyond initial consonants, basic consonant-vowel-consonant patterns (e.g., *hat*, *box*), and high-frequency sight words. However, his knowledge of word meanings was average, like most of the students in this cluster, which suggests that receptive language was not a major problem and that he does not likely have limited learning ability. With decoding ability at the first-grade level and below, it is not surprising that Jesse's comprehension and fluency were also low. He simply could not read enough words at the first-grade level to get any meaning.

As we might anticipate, the majority of students in this cluster were not proficient in writing and scored at the lowest level, Level 1, on the state fourth-grade reading test. It is important to remember, however, that children who were receiving special education intervention were not included in our sample. So, the children in this cluster, like Jesse, are receiving all of their instruction, or the majority of it (some may be getting supplemental help), from their regular classroom teachers.

Jesse clearly needs intensive, systematic word identification instruction targeted at beginning reading along with access to lots of reading material at first-grade level and below. This will be a challenge for Jesse's fifth-grade teacher. Pedagogically, Jesse needs explicit instruction in basic word identification. Yet few intermediate-grade teachers include this as a part of their instruction, and most do not have an adequate supply of easy materials for instruction or fluency building. In addition, the majority of texts in other subject areas such as social studies and science are written at levels that will be inaccessible to students like Jesse, so alternative materials and strategies will be needed. On the social-emotional front, it will be a challenge to keep Jesse engaged in learning and to provide opportunities for him to succeed in the classroom, even if he is referred for additional reading support. Without that engagement and desire to learn, it is unlikely he will be motivated to put forth the effort it will take for him to make progress. Jesse needs a great deal of support from his regular classroom teacher and from a reading specialist, working together to build a comprehensive instructional program in school and support at home that will help him develop the skill and will to progress.

Conclusions and Implications

Our brief descriptions of the six prototypical children and the instructional focus each one needs is a testimony to individual differences.

As we have heard a thousand times before, and as our data support, one-size instruction will not fit all children. The evidence here clearly demonstrates that students fail state reading tests for a variety of reasons and that, if we are to help these students, we will need to provide appropriate instruction to meet their varying needs. For example, placing all struggling students in a phonics or word identification program would be inappropriate for nearly 58% of the students in this sample who had adequate or strong word identification skills. In a similar manner, an instructional approach that did not address fluency and building reading stamina for longer, more complex text or that did not provide sufficient reading material at a range of levels would miss almost 70% of the students who demonstrated difficulty with fluency. In addition to these important cautions about overgeneralizing students' needs, we believe there are several strategies aimed at assessment, classroom organization and materials, and school structures that could help teachers meet their students' needs.

First and most obvious, teachers need to go beneath the scores on state tests by conducting additional diagnostic assessments that will help them identify students' needs. The data here demonstrate quite clearly that, without more in-depth and individual student assessment, distinctive and instructionally important patterns of students' abilities are masked. We believe that informal reading inventories, oral reading records, and other individually tailored assessments provide useful information about all students. At the same time, we realize that many teachers do not have the time to do complete diagnostic evaluations, such as those we did, with every student. At a minimum, we suggest a kind of layered approach to assessment in which teachers first work diagnostically with students who have demonstrated difficulty on broad measures of reading. Then, they can work with other students as the need arises.

However, we caution that simply administering more and more assessments and recording the scores will miss the point. The value of in-depth classroom assessment comes from teachers having a deep understanding of reading processes and instruction, thinking diagnostically, and using the information on an ongoing basis to inform instruction (Black & Wiliam, 1998; Place, 2002; Shepard, 2000). Requiring teachers to administer grade-level classroom assessments to all their students regardless of individual student needs would not yield useful information or help teachers make effective instructional decisions. For example, administering a fourth-grade reading selection to Jesse, who is reading at first-grade level, would not provide useful information. However, using a fourth- or even fifth-grade selection for Tomas would. Similarly, assessing Jesse's word identification abilities should probably include assessments of basic sound/symbol correspondences or even phonemic awareness, but assessing decoding of multisyllabic words would be more appropriate for Martin. This kind of matching of assessment to students' needs is precisely what we hope would happen when teachers have the knowledge, the assessment tools, and the flexibility to assess and teach children according to their ongoing analysis. Both long-term professional development and time are critical if teachers are to implement the kind of sophisticated classroom assessment that struggling readers need.

Second, the evidence points to the need for multilevel, flexible, small-group instruction (Allington & Johnston, 2001; Cunningham & Allington, 1999; Opitz, 1998). Imagine, if you will, teaching just the six students we have described, who could easily be in the same class. These students not only need support in different aspects of reading, but they also need materials that differ in difficulty, topic, and familiarity. For example, Tomas, Makara, and Andrew all need instruction in comprehension. However, Tomas and Andrew likely can receive that instruction using grade-level material, but Makara would need to use easier material. Both Makara and Andrew need work in vocabulary, whereas Tomas is fairly strong in word meanings. As second-language learners, Tomas and Makara likely need more background building and exposure to topics, concepts, and academic vocabulary as well as the structure of English texts than Andrew, who is a native English speaker.

Furthermore, the teacher likely needs to experiment with having Tomas and Makara slow down when they read to get them to attend to meaning, whereas Andrew needs to increase his fluency through practice in below-grade-level text.

So, although these three students might be able to participate in whole-class instruction in which the teacher models and explicitly teaches comprehension strategies, they clearly need guided practice to apply the strategies to different types and levels of material, and they each need attention to other aspects of reading as well. This means the teacher must have strong classroom management and organizational skills to provide small-group instruction. Furthermore, he or she must have access to a wide range of books and reading materials that are intellectually challenging yet accessible to students reading substantially below grade level. At the same time, these struggling readers need access to grade-level material through a variety of scaffolded experiences (i.e., partner reading, guided reading, read-alouds) so that they are exposed to grade-level ideas, text structures, and vocabulary (Cunningham & Allington, 1999). Some of these students and their teachers would benefit from collaboration with other professionals in their schools, such as speech and language and second-language specialists, who could suggest classroom-based strategies targeted to the students' specific needs.

The six clusters and the three strands within each one (word identification, meaning, fluency) clearly provide more in-depth analysis of students' reading abilities than general test scores. Nevertheless, we caution that there is still more to be learned about individual students in each cluster, beyond what we describe here, that would help teachers plan for instruction. Two examples make this point. The first example comes from Cluster 1, Automatic Word Callers. Tomas had substantial difficulty with comprehension, but his scores on the vocabulary measure suggested that word meanings were likely not a problem for him. However, other students in this cluster, such as Maria, *did* have difficulty with word meanings and would need not only comprehension instruction like Tomas but also many more language-building activities and exposure to oral and written English. The second example that highlights the importance of looking beyond the cluster profile is Andrew, our Slow Word Caller from Cluster 5. Although we know that in-depth assessment revealed that Andrew had difficulty with comprehension and fluency, we argue above that the teacher must do more work with Andrew to determine how much fluency is contributing to comprehension and how much it is a result of Andrew's effort to self-monitor. Our point here is that even the clusters do not tell the entire story.

Finally, from a school or district perspective, we are concerned about the disproportionate number of second-language students who failed the test. In our study, 11% of the students in the school district were identified as second-language learners and were receiving additional instructional support. However, in our sample of students who failed the test, 43% were second-language learners who were *not* receiving additional support. Tomas and Makara are typical of many English-language learners in our schools. Their reading abilities are sufficient, according to school guidelines, to allow them to exit supplemental ESL programs, yet they are failing state tests and struggling in the classroom. In this district, as in others across the state, students exit supplemental programs when they score at the 35th percentile or above on a norm-referenced reading test—hardly sufficient to thrive, or even survive, in a mainstream classroom without additional help. States, school districts, and schools need to rethink the support they offer English-language learners both in terms of providing more sustained instructional support over time and of scaffolding their integration into the regular classroom. In addition, there must be a concerted effort to foster academically and intellectually rigorous learning of subject matter for these students (e.g., science, social studies) while they are developing their English-language abilities. Without such a focus, either in their first language or in English, these students will be denied access to important school learning, fall further behind in other school subjects, and become increasingly disengaged from school and learning (Echevarria, Vogt, & Short, 2000).

Our findings and recommendations may, on one level, seem obvious. Indeed, good teachers have always acknowledged differences among the students in their classes, and they have always tried to meet individual needs. But, in the current environment of high-stakes testing and accountability, it has become more of a challenge to keep an eye on individual children, and more difficult to stay focused on the complex nature of reading performance and reading instruction. This study serves as a reminder of these cornerstones of good teaching. We owe it to our students, their parents, and ourselves to provide struggling readers with the instruction they *really* need.

References

Adams, M.J. (1990). *Beginning to read: Thinking and learning about print.* Cambridge, MA: MIT Press.

Aldenderfer, M., & Blashfield, R. (1984). *Cluster analysis.* Beverly Hills, CA: Sage.

Allington, R.L. (2001). *What really matters for struggling readers.* New York: Longman.

Allington, R.L., & Johnston, P.H. (2001). What do we know about effective fourth-grade teachers and their classrooms? In C.M. Roller (Ed.), *Learning to teach reading: Setting the research agenda* (pp. 150–165). Newark, DE: International Reading Association.

Antunez, B. (2002, Spring). *Implementing reading first with English language learners.* Directions in Language and Education, 15. Retrieved October 15, 2003, from http://www.ncela.gwu.edu/ncbepubs/directions

Black, P., & Wiliam, D. (1998). Assessment and classroom learning. *Assessment in Education, 5*(1), 7–74.

Block, C.C., & Pressley, M. (2002). *Comprehension instruction: Research-based best practices.* New York: Guilford.

Cummins, J. (1991). The development of bilingual proficiency from home to school: A longitudinal study of Portuguese-speaking children. *Journal of Education, 173,* 85–98.

Cunningham, P.M., & Allington, R.L. (1999). *Classrooms that work* (2nd ed.). New York: Longman.

Duke, N.K., & Pearson, P.D. (2002). Effective practices for developing reading comprehension. In A.E. Farstrup & S.J. Samuels (Eds.), *What research has to say about reading instruction* (pp. 9–129). Newark, DE: International Reading Association.

Echevarria, J., Vogt, M.E., & Short, D. (2000). *Making content comprehensible for English language learners: The SIOP model.* Boston: Allyn & Bacon.

Edmondson, J., & Shannon, P. (2002). The will of the people. *The Reading Teacher, 55,* 452–454.

Elmore, R.F. (2002, Spring) Unwarranted intrusion. *Education Next.* Retrieved March 21, 2003, from http://www.educationnext.org

Goodnough, A. (2001, May 23). Teaching by the book, no asides allowed. *The New York Times.* Retrieved March 21, 2003, from http://www.nytimes.com

Harris, A.J., & Sipay, E.R. (1990). *How to increase reading ability* (9th ed.). New York: Longman.

Helfand, D. (2002, July 21). Teens get a second chance at literacy. *Los Angeles Times.* Retrieved March 21, 2003, from http://www.latimes.com

Hiebert, E.H., Pearson, P.D., Taylor, B.M., Richardson, V., & Paris, S.G. (1998). *Every child a reader: Applying reading research to the classroom.* Ann Arbor, MI: Center for the Improvement of Early Reading Achievement, University of Michigan School of Education. Retrieved March 21, 2003, from http://www.ciera.org

Klein, S.P., Hamilton, L.S., McCaffrey, D.F., & Stecher, B.M. (2000). What do test scores in Texas tell us? *Education Policy Analysis Archives, 8*(49). Retrieved March 21, 2003, from http://epaa.asu.edu/epaa/v8n49

Kuhn, M.R., & Stahl, S.A. (2000). *Fluency: A review of developmental and remedial practices* (CIERA Rep. No. 2-008). Ann Arbor, MI: Center for the Improvement of Early Reading Achievement, University of Michigan School of Education. Retrieved March 21, 2003, from http://www.ciera.org

Linn, R.L. (2000). Assessments and accountability. *Educational Researcher, 29*(2), 4–16.

Linn, R.L. (n.d.). Standards-based accountability: Ten suggestions. *CRESST Policy Brief.* 1. Retrieved March 21, 2003, from http://www.cse.ucla.edu

Lipson, M.Y., & Wixson, K.K. (2003). *Assessment and instruction of reading and writing difficulty: An interactive approach* (3rd ed.). Boston: Allyn & Bacon.

McNeil, L.M. (2000). *Contradictions of school reform: Educational costs of standardized testing.* New York: Routledge.

Nagy, W.E. (1988). *Teaching vocabulary to improve reading comprehension.* Urbana, IL: ERIC Clearinghouse on Reading and Communication Skills and the National Council of Teachers of English.

National Institute of Child Health and Human Development. (2000). *Report of the National Reading Panel. Teaching children to read: An evidence-based assessment of the scientific research literature on reading and its implications for reading instruction* (NIH Publication No. 004 769). Washington, DC: U.S. Government Printing Office. Retrieved March 21, 2003, from http://www.nationalreadingpanel.org

Olson, L. (2001). Overboard on testing. *Education Week, 20*(17), 23–30.

Opitz, M.F. (1998). *Flexible grouping in reading.* New York: Scholastic.

Paterson, F.R.A. (2000). The politics of phonics. *Journal of Curriculum and Supervision, 15,* 179–211.

Pinnell, G.S., Pikulski, J.J., Wixson, K.K., Campbell, J.R., Gough, P.B., & Beatty, A.S. (1995). *Listening to children read aloud.* Washington, DC: U.S. Department of Education.

Place, N.A. (2002). Policy in action: The influence of mandated early reading assessment on teachers' thinking and practice. In D.L. Schallert, C.M. Fairbanks, J. Worthy, B. Malock, & J.V. Hoffman (Eds.), *Fiftieth yearbook of the National Reading Conference* (pp. 45–58). Oak Creek, WI: National Reading Conference.

Riddle Buly, M., & Valencia, S.W. (2002). Below the bar: Profiles of students who fail state reading tests. *Educational Evaluation and Policy Analysis, 24,* 219–239.

Samuels, S.J. (2002). Reading fluency: Its development and assessment. In A. Farstrup & S.J. Samuels (Eds.), *What research has to say about reading instruction* (pp. 166–183). Newark, DE: International Reading Association.

Shepard, L.A. (2000). The role of assessment in a learning culture. *Educational Researcher, 29,* 4–14.

Snow, C.E., Burns, M.S., & Griffin, P. (Eds.). (1998). *Preventing reading difficulties in young children.* Washington, DC: National Academy Press.

Stahl, S.A., & Kapinus, B.A. (2001). *Word power: What every educator needs to know about vocabulary.* Washington, DC: National Education Association Professional Library.

Stanovich, K.E. (1986). Matthew effects in reading: Some consequences of individual differences in the acquisition of literacy. *Reading Research Quarterly, 21,* 360–407.

Stanovich, K.E. (1988). Explaining the difference between the dyslexic and garden-variety poor reader: The phonological-core variable-difference model. *Journal of Learning Disabilities, 21,* 590–612.

Stanovich, K.E. (1994). Romance and reality. *The Reading Teacher, 47,* 280–290.

Questions for Reflection

- What do you suppose you would find if you were to conduct a similar study with your struggling readers? What assessments and tools do you have available that you could use in conducting such a study?
- Do you think that different patterns of strengths among students are linked to different patterns in their instruction?

A Critical Analysis of Eight Informal Reading Inventories

Nina L. Nilsson

As a classroom teacher, reading specialist, and university professor, I have always found helpful published summaries or syntheses of professional-related information relevant to my work. In this article, I review the current editions of eight informal reading inventories (IRIs) published since 2002 that are available at the time of this writing [in 2008]. Specifically, I identify key issues surrounding the use of IRIs and examine ways in which the various IRIs reviewed approach them. A goal of this undertaking is to guide teachers, reading specialists, reading coaches, administrators, professionals in higher education, and others charged with the education or professional development of preservice or inservice teachers in their quest to find IRIs best suited to their specific needs. I hope the findings point to new ways in which IRIs can be made even more effective in the near future.

What Are IRIs?

IRIs are individually administered diagnostic assessments designed to evaluate a number of different aspects of students' reading performance. Typically, IRIs consist of graded word lists and passages ranging from preprimer level to middle or high school levels (Paris & Carpenter, 2003). After reading each leveled passage, a student responds orally to follow-up questions assessing comprehension and recall. Using comprehension and word recognition scores for students who read the passages orally, along with additional factors taken into consideration (e.g., prior knowledge, fluency, emotional status, among other possible factors), teachers or other education-related professionals determine students' reading levels. They also use this information to match students with appropriate reading materials, place children in guided reading groups, design instruction to address students' noted strengths and needs, and document reading progress over time. While IRIs serve a variety of purposes, perhaps their greatest value is linked to the important role they play in helping educators to diagnose the gaps in the abilities of readers who struggle the most.

Based on notions implicit in developmental (Chall, 1983; Spear-Swerling & Sternberg, 1996) and interactive models of reading (Rumelhart, 1977; Stanovich, 1980), IRIs provide information about students' reading stages and knowledge sources. For example, by charting and analyzing patterns in oral reading error types, educators identify whether students rely on one cueing system (i.e., graphophonic, syntactic, or semantic cueing system) to the exclusion of the others, as beginning readers typically do, or if they use a balance of strategies, as mature readers at more advanced stages do in their reading development when they encounter challenges while processing text. Supplemented by other measures of literacy-related knowledge and abilities, as needed, IRIs contribute valuable information to the school's instructional literacy program.

Rationale for Selecting IRIs to Evaluate

Given the sweeping, education-related policy changes associated with the No Child Left

Reprinted from Nilsson, N.L. (2008). A critical analysis of eight informal reading inventories. *The Reading Teacher, 61*(7), 526–536.

Behind Act signed into U.S. law in 2002, the IRIs included in this analysis were limited to those published since 2002 because it was felt that they would be more likely to reflect features relevant to the policy changes than IRIs published earlier. For example, federal guidelines specify that the screening, diagnostic, and classroom-based, instructional assessments used by schools receiving Reading First grants to evaluate K–3 student performance must have proven validity and reliability (U.S. Department of Education, 2002)—aspects noted as weak with regard to IRIs published earlier (Kinney & Harry, 1991; Klesius & Homan, 1985; Newcomer, 1985). In addition, specifications in *Guidance for the Reading First Program* (U.S. Department of Education, 2002) require that educators in Reading First schools evaluate students in the five critical areas of reading instruction (i.e., comprehension, vocabulary, fluency, phonemic awareness, and phonics) as defined by the National Reading Panel (NRP; National Institute of Child Health and Human Development [NICHD], 2000) and screen, diagnose, and monitor students' progress over time. Given these federal mandates, it was assumed that IRIs published since 2002 would be more apt to exhibit the technical rigor and breadth in assessment options necessary to help reading professionals achieve these goals.

The names of specific IRI instruments identified were obtained from searches in the professional literature or recommended by professionals in the field of literacy. In all, eight IRIs were identified, examined, and cross-compared with regard to selected features of their most current editions. The following were the IRIs included in this analysis: Analytical Reading Inventory (ARI; Woods & Moe, 2007), Bader Reading and Language Inventory (BRLI; Bader, 2005), Basic Reading Inventory (BRI; Johns, 2005), Classroom Reading Inventory (CRI-SW; Silvaroli & Wheelock, 2004), Comprehensive Reading Inventory (CRI-CFC; Cooter, Flynt, & Cooter, 2007), Informal Reading Inventory (IRI-BR; Burns & Roe, 2007), Qualitative Reading Inventory-4 (QRI-4; Leslie & Caldwell, 2006), and The Critical Reading Inventory (CRI-2; Applegate, Quinn, & Applegate, 2008).

Analyzing the IRIs

In order to cross-compare selected features of the current editions of all eight IRIs, a coding spreadsheet was prepared and used to assist in the systematic collection of data. The categories used were chosen because of their relevance to issues in the professional literature (e.g., length of passages, type of comprehension question scheme used) or to policy and other changes affecting the field today (e.g., assessment options related to the five critical areas of reading, reliability, and validity information).

Interrater Reliability Measures

To ensure the accuracy of the coded data, I enlisted the assistance of a graduate student who independently coded one of the IRIs. Afterward, our data charts were compared and the percentage of agreement was determined with differences resolved by discussion. Following this interrater reliability check, data from the separate coding sheets for each IRI were rearranged and compiled onto additional charts in various ways in order to facilitate comparisons and the detection of patterns among variables of interest.

Results

In all, eight IRIs published since 2002 were analyzed and compared in order to identify the variety of ways in which the instruments approach key issues relevant to their use. Based on the analysis, it is evident that the eight IRIs reviewed range in the assessment components they include and in which critical aspects of reading instruction identified by the NRP (NICHD, 2000) they assess. For example, measures for reading comprehension and vocabulary (i.e., sight word vocabulary) were more common than measures in the other areas. An analysis of the IRI features related to each of the five pillars of reading follows.

Reading Comprehension and Recall

Evidence of Content Validity. According to *Standards for Educational and Psychological Testing* (1999), a fundamental concern in judging assessments is evidence of validity. Assessments should represent clearly the content domain they purport to measure. For example, if the intention is to learn more about a student's ability to read content area textbooks, then it is critical that the text passages used for assessment be structured similarly. Based on their study of eight widely used and cited IRIs, Applegate, Quinn, and Applegate (2002) concluded that there were great variations in the way IRI text passages were structured, including passages with factual content. They observed that biographies and content area text, in some cases, matched up better with the classic definition of a story. In a similar manner, Kinney and Harry (1991) noted little resemblance between the type of text passages included in many IRIs and the text type typically read by students in middle and high school. As researchers have demonstrated through their studies and analyses, narrative and expository texts are structured differently (Mandler & Johnson, 1977; Meyer & Freedle, 1984), and readers of all sorts, including general education students and children with learning disabilities, process contrasting text types in different ways (Dickson, Simmons, & Kame'enui, 1995). Thus, it makes sense that if the goal of assessment is to gain insights on a student's reading of textbooks that are expository, then the text used for the assessment should also be expository. Relative to the IRIs examined for this analysis, text passages varied by genre and length as well as by whether the text included illustrations, photos, maps, graphs, and diagrams. A discussion of the ways in which the various IRIs approach these issues follows.

Passage Genre. With regard to the text types included in the IRIs under review here (aligned with the perspective that reading comprehension varies by text type), five of the eight IRIs provide separate sections, or forms, for narrative and expository passages for all levels, making it easy to evaluate reading comprehension and recall for narrative text apart from expository material (Applegate et al., 2008; Cooter et al., 2007; Johns, 2005; Leslie & Caldwell, 2006; Woods & Moe, 2007). However, caution is advised. Despite the separation of genres, in some of the current IRIs, consistent with Applegate et al.'s (2002) observations, some passages classified as expository are actually more like narrative. For example, in BRI (Johns, 2005), the passage "Have You Played This Game?" contains factual information about the board game Monopoly, but it is written in a narrative style. The passage is placed in the Expository Form LE section; however, the first comprehension question asks, "What is this story about?" Even for passages more expository-like in text structure, at times authors refer to them as "stories" (e.g., "Here is a story about driver's license requirements," Bader, 2005, p. 65; "Tell me about the story you just read," Cooter et al., 2007, p. 275, in reference to the factual passage "Bears"). Of all the IRIs considered, ARI (Woods & Moe, 2007) and QRI-4 (Leslie & Caldwell, 2006) provide expository text passages with features most like text found in science and social studies textbooks. In fact, the authors note most of the passages were drawn from textbooks.

A few of the IRIs appear to take a more holistic approach in their representation of the content domain. For three of the IRIs, the assessment includes a "mix" (Burns & Roe, 2007, p. 227) or "balance" (Bader, 2005, p. 4) of text types with greater emphasis on narratives and no expository passages at lower levels (Bader, 2005; Burns & Roe, 2007; Silvaroli & Wheelock, 2004). In these IRIs, there is no clear separation of narrative and expository text passages.

Passage Length. While the passages generally become longer at the upper levels to align with the more demanding texts read by older students, across inventories passage lengths at the same levels vary; in some cases, within the same inventory, authors offer passages of different lengths as options at the same levels (see Table 1). For example, finding that beginning readers sometimes struggled with the 50-word,

Table 1
IRI Features

IRI	Forms or passage types (grade levels)	Passage word length	Question scheme/retelling rubric focus
Applegate, Quinn, & Applegate (2008)	3 narrative passages (pp-12) 3 expository passages (pp-12)	Varies: 66-844	Questions: Text-based, inferential, and critical response questions Retelling rubrics: A focus on story grammar elements for narrative and macro-/microconcepts for informational text
Bader (2005)	3 forms[a] (pp-8, 9/10, 11/12) Form C (for children) Form C/A (for children, adolescents/adults) Form A (for adults)	Varies: 31-278	Questions: Literal questions and one interpretive question per passage (not included in the total memory score)
Burns & Roe (2007)	4 forms[b] (pp-12)	Varies: 60-195	Questions: Main idea, detail, inference, sequence, cause/effect, vocabulary Retelling rubrics: Two options—a focus on story elements specific to narratives and another rubric option
Cooter, Flynt, & Cooter (2007)	Forms A and B, Spanish, narrative (pp-9) Forms C and D, English, expository (1-9) Form C, Spanish, expository (1-9) Form D, Spanish, expository (10, 11, 12) Form E, English, expository (10, 11, 12) Emergent literacy assessments	Varies: 25-760	Questions: Literal, inferential, and evaluative questions about story grammar elements for narratives and expository grammar elements for expository passages
Johns (2005)	7 forms (not entirely equivalent): Forms A, B: oral reading (pp-8) Form C: oral reading, expository (pp-8) Form D: silent reading (pp-8) Form E: oral reading, expository (pp-8) Form LN: longer narrative (3-12) Form LE: longer expository (3-12) Emergent literacy assessments	Consistent: pp = 25 and 50 Forms A-E = 100 Form LN = 250 words Form LE = 250 words	Questions: Topic, fact (lower level comprehension), evaluation, inference, and vocabulary (higher-level comprehension) questions Retelling rubrics: A variety with a focus on story elements for narratives, major points and supporting details for expository text, and other rubric options
Leslie & Caldwell (2006)	4 narrative, 1 expository (pp) 3 narrative, 2 expository (p-2) 3 narrative, 3 expository (3-5) 3 literature, 2 social studies, 2 science (6) 2 literature, 2 social studies, 2 science (UMS) 1 literature, 1 social studies, 1 science (HS)	Varies: 44-786 (pp-UMS) 354-1,224 (HS, passage sections)	Questions: Explicit and implicit questions that focus on the most important information (e.g., the goal of the protagonist for narratives and the implicit main idea for expository passages and other important information) Retelling rubrics: A focus on the most important information for narratives and main idea/supporting details for expository materials

(continued)

Table 1
IRI Features (continued)

IRI	Forms or passage types (grade levels)	Passage word length	Question scheme/retelling rubric focus
Silvaroli & Wheelock (2004)	3 forms[b] with pre-/posttests for each: Form A, Subskills Format (pp-8) Form B, Reader Response Format (pp-8) Form C, Subskills Format for high school and adult education students (1-8)	Varies: 38-268	Questions (subskills format): Factual, inferential, vocabulary questions Questions (response format): A focus on story grammar elements
Woods & Moe (2007)	3 equivalent narrative forms (pp-9): Form A Form B Form C2 expository forms (1-9): Form S (science) Form SS (social studies)	Varies: 28-352	Questions: Defined by the reader-text relationship: "Retells in Fact" (RIF) "Puts Information Together" (PIT) "Connects Author and Reader" (CAR) "Evaluates and Substantiates" (EAS) Retelling rubrics: A focus on story elements for narratives and expository elements for factual text

Note. pp = preprimer level, p = primer level, UMS = upper middle school, HS = high school

[a]Narrative and expository text passages are distributed across levels as follows: pp-2: narratives only; 3-5: 2 narrative, 1 expository; 6: all expository; 7: 1 narrative, 2 expository; 8: 2 narrative, 1 expository; 9-10: 1 narrative, 2 expository; 11-12: all expository. [b]Forms include narrative and expository text passages that are not explicitly identified by genre.

preprimer passage in earlier editions, Johns (2005) now includes in the ninth edition of BRI a second, shorter passage option of 25 words for each form that offers passages at the preprimer level. In a similar manner, he offers passages of two different lengths at levels 3–12.

Pictures and Graphic Supplements. Noting the benefits and drawbacks of including illustrations and other graphic supplements with the passages, IRI authors vary in their opinions on this matter. To eliminate the possibility of readers' relying on picture clues rather than their understanding of the text, Silvaroli and Wheelock (2004) and Burns and Roe (2007) exclude illustrations entirely. Bader (2005), Cooter et al. (2007), Johns (2005), and Woods and Moe (2007) limit illustrated passages to lower levels only. Providing examiners with options for comparing beginning readers' performance, Applegate et al. (2008) and Leslie and Caldwell (2006) provide passages with and without illustrations or photos. Moreover, Leslie and Caldwell provide a number of assessment choices at levels 5 through high school, allowing for in-depth and varied evaluations of students' abilities to use different types of graphic supplements typically found in science and social studies textbooks, such as diagrams, maps, photos, and pie graphs.

Evidence of Construct Validity. According to *Standards for Educational and Psychological Testing* (1999), a valid test also captures all the important aspects of the construct (i.e., the characteristic or concept that the test is designed to measure), and it also provides evidence that processes irrelevant to the construct do not interfere or distort results. Across IRIs examined, comprehension question frameworks varied in terms of which aspects of narrative or expository text comprehension they centered on, as well as what dimensions, or levels, of comprehension they measured. In addition, across the IRIs reviewed, assorted measures were used to identify extraneous factors potentially affecting comprehension scores. A discussion of the various ways in which each IRI handles these issues follows.

Comprehension/Recall Measures. For most of the IRIs reviewed, question schemes introduced alone or in conjunction with retelling rubrics or scoring guides serve to assess a reader's comprehension or recall in two areas: (1) the reader's grasp of narrative and expository text structure and (2) various dimensions or levels of reading comprehension (e.g., literal and inferential comprehension). All of the IRIs attempt to assess these areas either through their question schemes alone or in combination with a retelling and rubric assessment; however, in some cases, the authors use different terms for the dimensions of comprehension they measure.

For measuring narrative text comprehension and recall, six of the eight IRIs focus their question schemes and retelling rubrics on story elements (e.g., character, setting, problem or goal, resolution; Applegate et al., 2008; Burns & Roe, 2007; Cooter et al., 2007; Johns, 2005; Leslie & Caldwell, 2006; Woods & Moe, 2007) based on story grammar theory. It should be noted that the question schemes of Burns and Roe, Johns, and Woods and Moe are structured differently (see Table 1). Thus, if their question schemes are used to evaluate narrative comprehension independently without a retelling and the associated rubric with story elements criteria, then a student's grasp of narrative text structure will not be evaluated.

In the assessment of expository text comprehension and recall, there is greater variety across IRIs. Four IRIs use question schemes or rubrics based on the levels of importance of information (e.g., macro vs. micro concepts, main ideas vs. details; Applegate et al., 2008; Burns & Roe, 2007; Johns, 2005; Leslie & Caldwell, 2006). Taking a different approach, Woods and Moe (2007) and Cooter et al. (2007) provide checklists and question schemes, respectively, for evaluating student recall of expository elements (e.g., description, collection, causation, problem and solution, comparison). Johns includes a variety of rubric options specific to narrative and expository text passages but also more holistic rubrics that he suggests can be used with retellings of any text type. In addition, in the QRI-4, Leslie and Caldwell provide a think-aloud assessment option useful for capturing information about the strategies readers use while they are in the process of constructing meaning based on the text. To facilitate the use of this assessment option, some of the expository text passages at the sixth, upper middle school, and high school levels are formatted in two different ways that allow for conducting assessments with or without student think-alouds. The authors also provide a coding system for categorizing the think-aloud types based on whether they indicate an understanding or lack of understanding of the text.

It should be noted that Bader (2005) and Silvaroli and Wheelock (2004) use similar criteria for assessing comprehension and recall of narrative versus expository text. For example, in using the BRLI (Bader, 2005) for the assessment of narrative and expository passages, readers are asked to retell the "story" (p. 59), and the idea units recalled are checked off from a list that does not categorize the idea units in any way (e.g., according to story grammar elements in the case of narratives or levels of importance for expository material). In addition, there is a place on the evaluation sheet for checking off whether a student's retelling is organized; however, criteria for making this judgment are lacking. Without a theoretical framework and clearly defined criteria to guide the examiner, it is difficult to determine if the assessment effectively captures the essential qualities of reading comprehension and recall.

The CRI-SW (Silvaroli & Wheelock, 2004) is similar in that there is little distinction in criteria used for judging comprehension or recall of contrasting text types. For example, in the Reader Response Format section of the IRI (the same scoring guide used to evaluate a student's recall of characters, problems, and outcome or solutions for the narrative), "It's My Ball" (p. 136) is provided as a tool for evaluating the factual selection "The World of Dinosaurs" (p. 143). Use of a scoring guide based on story grammar theory seems misplaced as a tool for judging comprehension of expository text.

As noted, in addition to assessing students' understanding of the structural features of narrative and expository text, IRI authors provide measures of various dimensions, or levels, of reading comprehension—most commonly literal and inferential comprehension (Applegate et al., 2008; Bader, 2005; Burns & Roe, 2007; Cooter et al., 2007; Johns, 2005; Leslie & Caldwell, 2006; Silvaroli & Wheelock, 2004; Woods & Moe, 2007). Although the terms for these constructs vary, and there may be subtle differences in meanings across inventories, the dimensions overlap. For example, Leslie and Caldwell refer to explicit and implicit comprehension. Woods and Moe, however, using a reader-text relationship question scheme stemming from Raphael's (1982, 1986) Question-Answer Relationships framework, provide questions measuring fact-based, literal comprehension that call for responses "from the text" as well as questions that measure inferential comprehension or responses "from head to text" (Woods & Moe, 2007, pp. 28–29).

Taking a different approach, Applegate et al. include questions to measure critical response (i.e., a response requiring analysis, reaction, and response to text based on personal experiences and values and usually allowing for more than one possible answer). Cooter et al. (2007) provide questions as measures of evaluative comprehension. Johns's questions measure comprehension dimensions called "lower level" (i.e., assessed by fact questions) and "higher level" (i.e., assessed by topic, evaluation, inference, and vocabulary questions; Johns, 2005, p. 76). It should be noted that Silvaroli and Wheelock include assessment of different levels of comprehension (i.e., inferential vs. factual questions) as part of the question taxonomy in the Subskills Format section of their IRI, but this aspect of comprehension is not assessed by the question scheme in the Reader Response Format.

Despite concerns (Applegate et al., 2002; Duffelmeyer & Duffelmeyer, 1987, 1989; Johns, 2005; Schell & Hanna, 1981), a few of the IRIs reviewed continue to use question taxonomies with main idea, fact and detail, inference, and vocabulary questions, among other question types (Burns & Roe, 2007; Johns, 2005; Silvaroli & Wheelock, 2004). In the past, criticisms targeting these question schemes arose out of concern due to lacking empirical support and confusion over what main idea questions in some of the IRIs actually measured. In the ninth edition of BRI reviewed for this study, citing Schell and Hanna (1981) as his information source, even Johns himself cautions readers, "Lest teachers glibly use the classification scheme suggested, it must be emphasized that these categories of comprehension questions, although widely used, have little or no empirical support" (Johns, 2005, p. 72). For this reason, Johns advises using his own question classification scheme informally and with discretion.

Other scholars in the field of literacy, as well, have suggested that main idea question types included in some IRIs were actually no more than "topic" questions that could be answered in one-word or simple phrase responses rather than full statements of the moral or underlying theme of a story, requiring the integration of selection content (Applegate et al., 2002; Duffelmeyer & Duffelmeyer, 1987, 1989; Schell & Hanna, 1981). As Applegate et al. pointed out, the ramifications of confusions over question types can be serious in that children who are proficient in responding to questions of one sort, such as questions requiring literal recall and low-level inferences that are largely text based, sometimes experience great difficulty in answering questions of other types, such as those that require more critical thinking. The confusion over question types and just what the questions actually measure restricts the usefulness of the assessment data they yield in terms of helping teachers pinpoint and address children's instructional needs.

While IRI-BR (Burns & Roe, 2007) continues to use a question classification system with main idea questions vulnerable to these criticisms, it is evident that Johns (2005) has made changes to address the terminology issue in BRI. Items that he previously called main idea questions are now labeled "topic" questions. Otherwise, his classification system remains similar to that in earlier editions. As a result, some of the confusion over question type is eliminated, but if a teacher relies strictly on Johns's question scheme to assess comprehension, a reader's ability to synthesize the content and come up with the main or "big idea" (Walmsley, 2006) of a passage (an important aspect of reading) will not be evaluated.

Silvaroli and Wheelock (2004) include not only the traditional question scheme from earlier editions of CRI (Silvaroli, 1990), but also the authors have added a whole new question framework that supplements, or serves as another option, to the question scheme of their earlier editions. Those who use the newest edition of CRI-SW have a choice as to whether to administer the passages and follow-up questions that fall into the Subskills Format or an alternative set of questions included in what the authors call the Reader Response Format. Accordingly, the five questions accompanying the passages in the Subskills Format, as in the earlier editions, include factual, inferential, and vocabulary question types. The question types for the retelling portion of the newer Reader Response Format, however, include a prediction question followed by three questions pertaining to the characters (i.e., "Who was the main person in the story?"), the problems (i.e., "What was the problem?"), and the outcomes or solutions (i.e., "How was the problem solved?") of the passage. The authors explain that the rationale for adding the Reader Response Format was to accommodate literacy programs that have shifted from a "subskills instructional emphasis" to a "literacy emphasis" (Silvaroli & Wheelock, 2004, pp. 1–2). They suggest the passages and questions included in each format can be used separately or in some combination, as desired.

Measures of Extraneous Variables. In order to control for extraneous variables that can affect comprehension and recall, some of the IRI authors include measures of prior knowledge (Bader, 2005; Johns, 2005; Leslie & Caldwell, 2006; Silvaroli & Wheelock, 2004; Woods & Moe, 2007), emotional status (Burns & Roe, 2007; Woods & Moe, 2007), and level of engagement (Johns, 2005). Other authors suggest the administrator informally note observations and student comments in related areas (Burns & Roe, 2007).

Form Equivalence/Reliability. Because federal guidelines for Reading First schools require educators to monitor student progress over time (U.S. Department of Education, 2002), it can be valuable to know if the parallel forms within each IRI can be used interchangeably. In order to know how consistent the scores are across forms, it is necessary to obtain the alternate-form reliability coefficient. Generally, a correlation of .85 or higher is desirable, with the maximum a correlation can be at +1.00. It is also necessary to have information about the sample population on which the reliability figure was based in order to generalize to a different student population (Bracey, 2000).

Although the *Standards for Educational and Psychological Testing* (1999) suggests a need to report critical information indicating the degree of generalizability of scores across alternate forms, few of the IRI authors do. Only one IRI (Leslie & Caldwell, 2006) provides data suggesting the forms for determining that reading comprehension levels may be used interchangeably, although the specific IRI edition used for that reliability study is not reported. With respect to the alternate forms of the QRI text passages, Leslie and Caldwell found the reliabilities based on comprehension scores were all above .80, and 75% of the scores were greater than or equal to .90. In addition, the authors examined whether the same instructional level would be determined based on the comprehension scores of each passage and report that 71% to 84% of the time the instructional level was the same on both. The individual reliability levels for each grade-level text from primer level through upper middle school are reported.

In some IRIs, the authors infer that alternate-form reliability levels are acceptable; however, information is lacking to confirm that. For example, based on the similar content that occurs across all three narrative forms in ARI (e.g., all three passages at level 6 are written about famous African American scientists or inventors), Woods and Moe (2007) suggest, "This consistency enables the examiner to change forms when determined necessary" (p. 257); however, because no correlation coefficient indicating degree of equivalence is reported, this inference cannot be made with confidence. With respect to IRI-BR, Burns and Roe (2007) state, "Alternate forms testing revealed that the levels indicated by different forms administered to the same students were consistent" (p. 229); however, without reliability figures reported, the examiner cannot make a judgment about the degree of reliability. Also, without a sample description, even if the forms are equivalent for one sample population, given the possible differences across groups, it may not be possible to generalize those results to another student population.

In addition, in Johns's (2005) ninth edition of BRI, he refers to an alternate-form reliability study (Helgren-Lempesis & Mangrum, 1986) of BRI (Johns, 1981) and two other IRIs, which indicated the Pearson *r* coefficients for BRI were .64 for independent level, .72 for instructional level, and .73 for the frustration level. However, these results pertain to a 1986 study with fourth-grade students who orally read passages from Forms A and B of the second edition of BRI. New reliability information pertaining to all forms in the current edition and for passages at all levels read orally and silently is needed in order to use parallel forms interchangeably without question.

Some of the alternate-form reliability figures reported are lower than is desirable. For example, based on the figures reported by Cooter et al. (2007) for grades 1, 2, and 3 (i.e., .58, .63, and .70), the authors caution that Forms A and B may not be equivalent. The authors also report that due to small sample sizes, they were not able to obtain reliability figures for other grade levels. Of note, CRI-CFC was published in its first edition in 2007.

In some cases, there are not enough data reported for interpreting the degree of reliability. For example, it is not clear just what variables the reliability coefficients (i.e., .80 for oral, elementary; .78 for silent, elementary; .83 for oral, high school and adult; .79 for silent, high school and adult) reported by Bader (2005) apply to, such as word recognition, comprehension, or both.

Vocabulary

Meaning Vocabulary. Although norm-referenced tests typically report scores for vocabulary knowledge both as a separate and combined reading score (Pearson, Hiebert, & Kamil, 2007), none of the IRIs reviewed include enough vocabulary items accompanying the text passages to make this feasible. For example, Burns and Roe (2007), Johns (2005), and Silvaroli and Wheelock (2004) treat vocabulary as an embedded construct contributing to reading comprehension; however, out of five to eight questions, only one or two items are vocabulary related.

Sight Word Vocabulary and Word Recognition Strategies. While Cooter et al. (2007) treat vocabulary as a separate construct with its own set of test items and score in CRI-CFC, this section is more a measure of high-frequency or sight words recognized than meaning vocabulary knowledge. It should be noted that the word list components of the other IRIs reviewed also provide information related more to word recognition than to knowledge of word meanings.

Each of the other inventories takes a different approach to the assessment of sight word recognition, as well as general word identification strategies, by including a series of word lists administered at the beginning of the IRI assessment in order to gain insights on a student's word recognition strategies as well as to determine a reading passage starting point. Across inventories, although the specific sources for the word lists are not always identified (Bader, 2005; Burns & Roe, 2007; Silvaroli & Wheelock, 2004; Woods & Moe, 2007), two of the authors report some or all of the word list words are drawn from the reading passages (Applegate et al., 2008; Leslie & Caldwell, 2006) or various named, high-frequency word lists (e.g., Fry's Instant Words; Applegate et al., 2008; Johns, 2005). With regard to CRI-2 and QRI-4, because some of the words were drawn from the reading passages, evaluators can compare word identification abilities in context versus out of context. These two inventories also allow for making distinctions between words recognized instantly (i.e., sight words) versus words that are decoded when readers are allowed more time.

BRLI (Bader, 2005) includes separate lists of "experiential" words (i.e., words commonly found in instructional materials and on tests), as well as lists of "adult thematic" words (i.e., office-related vocabulary, words related to health and safety, vehicle-related words), which could be useful with English-language learners and adult literacy students. Because students are asked to read each item but to explain the meanings only as needed, this assessment appears to provide more information related to sight word vocabulary and word recognition strategies than meaning vocabulary, similar to the other IRI word lists. Information about the development of these word lists, however, or pilot testing of items is lacking.

Phonemic Awareness

Three of the IRI authors include phonemic awareness assessments (Bader, 2005; Cooter et al., 2007; Johns, 2005) in their manuals. It should be noted that these assessments are not integral parts of the inventories; instead, they are provided as supplements for optional use. Given the fact that there are other instruments available that are more developmental, systematic, and comprehensive for assessing phonemic awareness, these IRI assessment supplements are not recommended for evaluating children's knowledge in this area.

Phonics

As with phonemic awareness, an IRI is not intended to provide a thorough evaluation of a child's phonic knowledge. While the authors of CRI-CFC (Cooter et al., 2007) and BRLI (Bader, 2005) provide supplementary phonics assessments in their manuals, there are other more systematic and comprehensive assessments of this aspect of reading available. For this reason, these supplementary assessments are not recommended for evaluating this pillar of reading.

It should be noted that the miscue analysis and word list components (see the Vocabulary section) featured in most of the IRIs allow the evaluator to gain valuable insights on patterns related to students' word recognition abilities, including insights related to phonics. In addition, miscue analyses of passages read orally provide the advantage of allowing the tester to observe how a child actually applies phonics skills while reading familiar and unknown words in connected text. Because of this powerful function, the miscue analysis portion of an IRI should not be skipped or overlooked.

Fluency

With the exception of CRI-SW (Silvaroli & Wheelock, 2004), each of the IRIs includes some measure of fluency. All but Woods and Moe (2007) suggest, at a minimum, tracking the reading rate, and all but Applegate et al. (2008), who include an oral reading rubric in the manual, provide norms or guidelines in their manuals for interpreting scores. In some of the IRIs, checklists are provided listing additional aspects of fluency to evaluate, such as pitch, stress, intonation, and use of punctuation, among other qualities observed, to check off as applicable. Woods and Moe also include a four-point fluency scoring guide. Given the relevance of fluent reading to reading comprehension (Allington, 1983), these measures provide valuable data for interpreting the results of an IRI assessment and are recommended.

Choosing an IRI

One of the purposes of this article is to cross-compare current IRIs with a goal of providing assistance in selecting one that best fits a teacher's needs. Although each IRI has its strengths and limitations, there are also unique characteristics to consider that may sway someone toward using one instrument or another.

For reading professionals who work with diverse populations and are looking for a diagnostic tool to assess the five critical components of reading instruction, the CRI-CFC, in Spanish and English (Cooter et al., 2007) for regular and special education students, as well as some sections of the BRLI (Bader, 2005), are attractive options. Most likely, those who work with middle and high school students will find the QRI-4 (Leslie & Caldwell, 2006) and ARI (Woods & Moe, 2007) passages and assessment options appealing. The CRI-2 (Applegate et al., 2008) would be a good fit for reading professionals concerned with thoughtful response and higher-level thinking. In addition, the variety of passages and rubrics in BRI (Johns, 2005) and contrasting format options in CRI-SW (Silvaroli & Wheelock, 2004) would provide flexibility for those who work with diverse classrooms that are skills-based and have more of a literacy emphasis. For literature-based literacy programs, the IRI-BR (Burns & Roe, 2007) with its appendix of leveled literature selections is a valuable resource for matching students with appropriate book selections after students' reading levels are determined. In all cases, caution is advised for assessment components lacking technical rigor or for use of alternate forms without proven reliability.

Some of the IRIs had features worth noting because they made the complex manuals and various components easier to navigate and use. Some of these features include the fold-out tabs in CRI-SW (Silvaroli & Wheelock, 2004); indexes (Johns, 2005; Leslie & Caldwell, 2006), which most of the IRIs do not include; and inside-cover quick reference guides (Bader, 2005; Burns & Roe, 2007; Johns, 2005; Woods & Moe, 2007). Some handy resources located conveniently in appendixes include extra passages and rubrics, checklists, and scoring guides (Burns & Roe, 2007; Johns, 2005) and various summary forms (Cooter et al., 2007; Johns, 2005). As a feature of its newest edition, CRI-2 (Applegate et al., 2008) offers a variety of tools on its companion website, including access to Automated Scoring Assistant software to help manage assessment data collected. It should be noted that the theoretical orientation of the evaluator and the technical features (e.g., validity and reliability) of the instruments are fundamental factors to consider in choosing an IRI.

For literacy-related professionals seeking ways to better address the instructional needs of children facing the greatest challenges in their journey to become successful readers, IRIs can serve as valuable diagnostic tools. Perhaps this summary of some key information will provide assistance to others in the selection of IRIs well suited to their particular educational settings and classroom contexts.

References

Allington, R.L. (1983). Fluency: The neglected reading goal. *The Reading Teacher, 36*(6), 556–561.

Applegate, M.D., Quinn, K.B., & Applegate, A.J. (2002). Levels of thinking required by comprehension questions in informal reading inventories. *The Reading Teacher, 56*(2), 174–180.

Applegate, M.D., Quinn, K.B., & Applegate, A.J. (2008). *The critical reading inventory: Assessing students' reading and thinking* (2nd ed.). Upper Saddle River, NJ: Pearson Education.

Bader, L.A. (2005). *Bader reading and language inventory* (5th ed.). Upper Saddle River, NJ: Pearson Education.

Bracey, G.W. (2000). *Thinking about tests and testing: A short primer in "Assessment Literacy".* Washington, DC: American Youth Policy Forum. Retrieved June 14, 2007, from www.aypf.org/publications/braceyrep.pdf

Burns, P.C., & Roe, B.D. (2007). *Informal reading inventory* (7th ed.). Boston: Houghton Mifflin.

Chall, J.S. (1983). *Stages of reading development.* New York: McGraw-Hill.

Cooter, R.B., Jr., Flynt, E.S., & Cooter, K.S. (2007). *Comprehensive reading inventory: Measuring reading development in regular and special education classrooms.* Upper Saddle River, NJ: Pearson Education.

Dickson, S.V., Simmons, D.C., & Kame'enui, E.J. (1995). *Text organization and its relation to reading comprehension: A synthesis of the research* (Rep. No. 17). Eugene, OR: National Center to Improve the Tools of Educators. (ERIC Document Reproduction Service No. ED386864)

Duffelmeyer, F.A., & Duffelmeyer, B.B. (1987). Main idea questions on informal reading inventories. *The Reading Teacher, 41*(2), 162–166.

Duffelmeyer, F.A., & Duffelmeyer, B.B. (1989). Are IRI passages suitable for assessing main idea comprehension? *The Reading Teacher, 42*(6), 358–363.

Helgren-Lempesis, V.A., & Mangrum, C.T., II. (1986). An analysis of alternate-form reliability of three commercially prepared informal reading inventories. *Reading Research Quarterly, 21*(2), 209–215.

Johns, J.L. (1981). *Basic reading inventory* (2nd ed.). Dubuque, IA: Kendall/Hunt.

Johns, J.L. (2005). *Basic reading inventory* (9th ed.). Dubuque, IA: Kendall/Hunt.

Kinney, M.A., & Harry, A.L. (1991). An informal inventory for adolescents that assess the reader, the text, and the task. *Journal of Reading, 34*(8), 643–647.

Klesius, J.P., & Homan, S.P. (1985). A validity and reliability update on the informal reading inventory with suggestions for improvement. *Journal of Learning Disabilities, 18*(2), 71–76.

Leslie, L., & Caldwell, J. (2006). *Qualitative reading inventory-4*. Upper Saddle River, NJ: Pearson Education.

Mandler, J.M., & Johnson, N.S. (1977). Remembrance of things parsed: Story structure and recall. *Cognitive Psychology, 9*(1), 111–151.

Meyer, B.J.F., & Freedle, R.O. (1984). Effects of discourse types on recall. *American Educational Research Journal, 21*(1), 121–143.

National Institute of Child Health and Human Development. (2000). *Report of the National Reading Panel. Teaching children to read: An evidence-based assessment of the scientific research literature on reading and its implications for reading instruction* (NIH Publication No. 00-4769). Washington, DC: U.S. Government Printing Office.

Newcomer, P.L. (1985). A comparison of two published reading inventories. *Remedial and Special Education, 6*(1), 31–36.

Paris, S.G., & Carpenter, R.D. (2003). FAQs about IRIs. *The Reading Teacher, 56*(6), 578–580.

Pearson, P.D., Hiebert, E.H., & Kamil, M.L. (2007). Vocabulary assessment: What we know and what we need to learn. *Reading Research Quarterly, 42*(2), 282–296.

Raphael, T.E. (1982). Question-answering strategies for children. *The Reading Teacher, 36*(2), 186–190.

Raphael, T.E. (1986). Teaching question answer relationships, revisited. *The Reading Teacher, 39*(6), 516–522.

Rumelhart, D. (1977). Toward an interactive model of reading. In S. Dornič (Ed.), *Attention and performance* (Vol. 6, pp. 573–603). Hillsdale, NJ: Erlbaum.

Schell, L.M., & Hanna, G.S. (1981). Can informal reading inventories reveal strengths and weaknesses in comprehension subskills? *The Reading Teacher, 35*(3), 263–268.

Silvaroli, N.J. (1990). *Classroom reading inventory* (6th ed.). Dubuque, IA: William C. Brown.

Silvaroli, N.J., & Wheelock, W.H. (2004). *Classroom reading inventory* (10th ed.). New York: McGraw-Hill.

Spear-Swerling, L., & Sternberg, R.J. (1996). *Off track: When poor readers become "learning disabled."* Boulder, CO: Westview Press.

Standards for educational and psychological testing. (1999). Washington, DC: American Educational Research Association.

Stanovich, K.E. (1980). Toward an interactive-compensatory model of individual differences in the development of reading fluency. *Reading Research Quarterly, 16*(1), 32–71.

U.S. Department of Education. (2002). *Guidance for the Reading First program.* Retrieved June 9, 2007, from www.ed.gov/programs/readingfirst/guidance.pdf

Walmsley, S.A. (2006). Getting the big idea: A neglected goal for reading comprehension. *The Reading Teacher, 60*(3), 281–285.

Woods, M.L., & Moe, A.J. (2007). *Analytical reading inventory* (8th ed.). Columbus, OH: Merrill.

Questions for Reflection

- What sorts of information can you best get from an IRI?
- Along with the descriptions of these eight IRIs, consider the students in your classroom. Which IRI would you elect to use, given the various limitations of each? Why?
- If you or your colleagues are currently using an IRI, do you think it is the one best suited to the students' needs?

Looking Inside Classrooms: Reflecting on the "How" as Well as the "What" in Effective Reading Instruction

Barbara M. Taylor, Debra S. Peterson, P. David Pearson, and Michael C. Rodriguez

We know a great deal about effective elementary teachers of reading (Taylor, Pressley, & Pearson, 2000). From the research of the 1960s and 1970s (Brophy, 1973; Dunkin & Biddle, 1974; Flanders, 1970; Stallings & Kaskowitz, 1974) we learned that effective teachers maintained an academic focus, kept more pupils on task, and provided direct instruction. Effective direct instruction included making learning goals clear, asking students questions to monitor understanding of content or skills covered, and providing feedback to students about their academic progress.

Roehler and Duffy (1984) focused on the cognitive processes used by excellent teachers. More effective teachers use modeling and explanation to teach students strategies for decoding words and understanding texts. Knapp (1995) found that effective teachers stressed higher level thinking skills more than lower level skills. Taylor, Pearson, Clark, and Walpole (2000) found that, compared with their less accomplished peers, more accomplished primary-grade teachers provided more small-group than whole-group instruction, elicited high levels of pupil engagement, preferred coaching over telling in interacting with students, and engaged students in more higher level thinking related to reading.

The National Reading Panel Report (National Institute of Child Health and Human Development, 2000) concluded that instruction in systematic phonics, phonemic awareness, fluency, and comprehension strategies was important in a complete reading program. The panel's conclusions are consistent with the findings of Pressley et al. (2001) regarding the balance that outstanding primary-grade teachers achieve in their classroom reading programs; Pressley et al. found that outstanding teachers taught skills, actively engaged students in a great deal of actual reading and writing, and fostered self-regulation in students' use of strategies.

In short, we have learned different, but complementary, lessons about the teaching practices of outstanding elementary literacy teachers from research on effective teaching. In this article, we discuss a subset of findings from year 1 of a larger national study on school reform in reading (Taylor, Pearson, Peterson, & Rodriguez, 2001) funded by the Center for the Improvement of Early Reading Achievement (CIERA). The purpose of the larger study was to evaluate the impact of all aspects of school reform on student performance. The purposes of the present, more focused analysis are to (a) describe the teacher practices we observed in the classrooms, particularly those that are derived from the research of the last four decades; (b) examine the relationship between teachers' practices and students' growth in reading achievement; and (c) provide vignettes that vividly describe what those practices look like in action.

Reprinted from Taylor, B.M., Peterson, D.S., Pearson, P.D., & Rodriguez, M.C. (2002). Looking inside classrooms: Reflection on the "how" as well as the "what" in effective reading instruction. *The Reading Teacher*, 56(3), 270–279.

Participants and Assessments

Eight high-poverty schools (with 70–95% of the students qualifying for subsidized lunch) were included in the study. Across the schools, 2–68% of the students were nonnative speakers of English, and 67–91% were members of minority groups. The schools represented demographic and geographic diversity—the rural southeast, a large midwestern city, and a large southwestern city. Five of the schools implemented our CIERA School Change Framework, and three were comparison schools. In all schools, two teachers per grade (kindergarten through sixth) were randomly invited to participate in the classroom observations. Within these classrooms, teachers were asked to divide their classes into thirds (high, average, and low) in terms of reading performance, and two children from each third, six per classroom, were randomly selected to be assessed.

The children were given a number of literacy assessments in the fall and spring (depending on grade level and ability level), including the Gates-MacGinitie Reading Tests, 4th ed. (2000; grades 1–6) and assessments of letter names and sounds (Pikulski, 1996; K–1), phonemic awareness (Taylor, 1991; K–1), word dictation (Pikulski, 1996; K–1), concepts of print (Pikulski, 1996; K–1), and fluency (Deno, 1985; 1–6) on passages from the Basic Reading Inventory, 7th ed. (1997).

Documenting Classroom Practices

On three scheduled occasions (fall, winter, and spring) each participating teacher was observed for an hour during reading instruction to document classroom practices in the teaching of reading. The observers were graduate students in literacy or retired elementary teachers, all of whom were trained to use the CIERA Classroom Observation Scheme (Taylor & Pearson, 2000, 2001). The structure of our observation scheme was influenced by the work of Scanlon and Gelzheiser (1992). Each observer was required to meet a criterion (80% agreement with a "standard" coding at each of the seven categories of the coding scheme) in order to have his or her observations included in the study.

The observation system combined qualitative notetaking with a quantitative coding process. The observer took field notes for a five-minute segment, recording a narrative account of what was happening in the classroom, including, where possible and appropriate, what the teacher and children were saying. At the end of the five-minute notetaking segment, the observer first recorded the proportion of children in the classroom who appeared to be on task, that is, doing what they were supposed to be doing. The observer next coded the three or four most salient literacy events (category 4 codes) that occurred during that five-minute episode. Then for each category 4 event, the observer also coded who was providing the instruction (category 1), the grouping pattern in use for that event (category 2), the major literacy activity (category 3), the materials being used (category 5), the teacher interaction styles observed (category 6), and the expected responses of the students (category 7). An example of a five-minute observational segment is provided in Figure 1. (See Table 1 for a list of the codes for all the categories.)

Coding the Observations

On the basis of research on effective teachers of reading, certain aspects of the data from classroom observations were analyzed to investigate the relationship between various classroom instructional practices and students' growth in reading. Except as noted, for a given teacher each of these variables was constructed by summing the number of five-minute segments in which the target practice was observed divided by the total number of observed segments. The numbers resulting from these calculations might be thought of as rates of inclusion of these practices into the teachers' instructional repertoires. The research-based classroom practices analyzed included the following:

- Whole group—the percentage of five-minute segments in which whole-group activities were coded.

Table 1
Codes for Classroom Observations

Category		Code
1. Who	Classroom teacher	c
	Reading specialist	r
	Special education	se
	Other specialist	sp
	Student teacher	st
	Aide	a
	Volunteer	v
	No one	n
	Other	o
	Not applicable	9
2. Grouping	Whole class	w
	Small group	s
	Pairs	p
	Individual	i
	Other	o
	Not applicable	9
3. General focus	Reading	r
	Composition/writing	w
	Spelling	s
	Handwriting	h
	Language	l
	Other	o
	Not applicable	9
4. Specific focus	Reading connected text	r
	Listening to text	l
	Vocabulary	v
	Meaning of text, lower	
	m1 for talk	m1
	m2 for writing	m2
	Meaning of text, higher	
	m3 for talk	m3
	m4 for writing	m4
	Comprehension skill	c
	Comprehension strategy	cs
	Writing	w
	Exchanging ideas/oral production	e/o
	Word Identification	wi

Category		Code
4. Specific focus (*continued*)	Sight words	sw
	Phonics	
	p1 = letter sound	p1
	p2 = letter by letter	p2
	p3 = onset/rime	p3
	p4 = multisyllabic	p4
	Word recognition strategies	wr
	Phonemic awareness	pa
	Letter identification	li
	Spelling	s
	Other	o
	Not applicable	9
5. Material	Textbook, narrative	tn
	Textbook, informtional	ti
	Narrative trade book	n
	Informational trade book	i
	Student writing	w
	Board/chart	b
	Worksheet	s
	Oral presentation	o
	Pictures	p
	Video/film	v
	Computer	c
	Other/not applicable	o/9
6. Teacher interaction	Tell/give info	t
	Modeling	m
	Recitation	r
	Discussion	d
	Coaching/scaffolding	c
	Listening/watching	l
	Reading aloud	ra
	Check work	cw
	Assessment	a
	Other	o
	Not applicable	9

(*continued*)

Table 1
Codes for Classroom Observations (continued)

Category		Code	Category		Code
7. Expected pupil response	Reading	r	7. Expected pupil response (*continued*)	Writing	w
	Reading turn taking	r-tt		Manipulating	m
	Orally responding	or		Other/not applicable	o/9
	Oral turn taking	or-tt		Number of students on task/number of students	
	Listening	l			

- Small group—the percentage of five-minute segments in which small-group activities were coded.
- Word skills—a sum of the number of five-minute segments in which the level 4 activities dealing with word skills were observed, divided by the number of segments in which the level 3 code was designated as reading. An aggregate variable was formed by summing the data from the following practices: (a) word identification work, (b) sight word drill, (c) phonics work, (d) phonemic awareness work, and (e) letter identification work.
- Comprehension skills or strategies—the percentage of five-minute segments in which comprehension skills and strategies were coded divided by the number of category 3 reading segments coded.
- Low-level questioning or writing about text—the percentage of five-minute segments in which the category 4 activities dealing with lower level talking or writing about text were observed, divided by the number of category 3 reading segments coded.
- Higher level questioning or writing about text—the percentage of five-minute segments in which the category 4 activities dealing with higher level talking or writing about text were observed, divided by the number of category 3 reading segments coded. Because word skill work, comprehension skill and strategy work, or questioning or writing about text were almost always coded when the general focus of the lesson was reading, a decision was made to consider the incidence of these three different types of reading activities out of the number of five-minute segments where reading was coded.
- Teacher telling—the percentage of five-minute segments in which the teacher was coded as telling children information.
- Teacher using recitation—the percentage of five-minute segments in which the teacher was coded as engaging children in recitation.
- Teacher coaching—the percentage of five-minute segments in which the teacher was coded as coaching children for independence. Because only telling, recitation, and coaching were coded with regularity, analyses were limited to these three codes from category 6.
- Students actively responding—an aggregate variable: the percentage of responses in which children were coded as engaged in reading, writing, or manipulating out of the total number of student responses coded.
- Students passively responding—an aggregate variable: the percent of responses in which children were coded as engaged in reading turn taking, oral turn taking,

or listening to the teacher out of the total number of student responses coded.

- Because all category 7 codes were frequently coded and because multiple category 7 codes were almost always coded during a five-minute segment, a decision was made to consider the incidence of active (reading, writing, manipulation) and passive (reading turn taking, oral turn taking, and listening) out of all category 7 codes recorded.

To ensure maximum consistency across a large number of observers, one member of the research team read through all of the observations to assess interrater reliability. All disagreements were checked by a second member of the research team, and this second team member agreed with the first member in 97% of the cases. All disagreements between the first and second research team member were resolved by a third research team member.

Descriptive Data From the Classroom Observationsw

The results from the classroom observations are useful data in their own right (see Table 2), quite independent of their relationship to student growth. In a sense, they capture the nature of classroom instruction in schools like those in which we spent the year observing teachers and testing children. These data also provide us with an opportunity to compare what was going on in these "aspiring" schools with the practices we observed two years earlier in our study of low-income, high-performing schools (Taylor et al., 2000) as well as with other research on effective teaching of reading.

Grouping Practices

Across all grades, whole-group instruction was coded more often than small-group instruction. In contrast, a greater occurrence of small-group

Table 2
Incidence of Classroom Factors by Grade

	Mean Percentage of Segments Observed			
	Kindergarten (*n* = 16)	Grade 1 (*n* = 14)	Grades 2-3 (*n* = 31)	Grades 4-6 (*n* = 33)
Whole group[a]	.72 (.28)	.51 (.29)	.59 (.29)	.68 (.27)
Small group[a]	.25 (.28)	.34 (.24)	.36 (.29)	.22 (.25)
Word skills[b]	1.07 (.80)	1.00 (.79)	.26 (.38)	.10 (.24)
Comprehension skills[b]	.05 (.09)	.04 (.09)	.12 (.17)	.24 (.26)
Meaning of text[b]	.40 (.33)	.37 (.15)	.57 (.34).	.57 (.34).
Lower level	.36 (.31)	.34 (.15)	.44 (.26)	.45 (.26)
Higher level	.05 (.08)	.03 (.06)	.13 (.18)	.21 (.29)
Telling[a]	.50 (.22)	.55 (.16)	.51 (.22)	.60 (.25)
Recitation[a]	.58 (.19)	.65 (.20)	.64 (.16)	.56 (.19)
Coaching[a]	.20 (.25)	.25 (.15)	.19 (.15)	.13 (.12)
Active responding[c]	.27 (.13)	.28 (.11)	.29 (.15)	.34 (.14)
Passive responding[c]	.44 (.12)	.49 (.14)	.57 (.16)	.66 (.14)

[a]Percentage of segments coded out of all five-minute segments coded. [b]Percentage of segments coded out of all five-minute reading segments. [c]Percentage of responses coded out of a total number of category 7 responses.

rather than whole-group instruction was found to be a characteristic of the most effective schools in our earlier study of primary-grade reading instruction in schools that were beating the odds (Taylor et al., 2000). These findings from the observations are not exclusive to schools serving high-poverty populations. Similar results have emerged from a case study we conducted in a school where only 30% of the students qualified for subsidized lunch.

Balance Between Word Work and Comprehension Work

Not surprisingly, word-level activities during reading were observed more in grades K–1 than 2–3 or 4–6, and comprehension work was seldom observed in the primary grades. These findings are similar to those in our previous study of primary-grade reading instruction in effective, low-income schools (Taylor et al., 2000), where we found that word-level activities were infrequently observed in grade 3 and that comprehension skill or strategy work was seldom observed in grades 1–3. The findings related to word skill activities also suggest that teachers are focusing on phonics instruction in kindergarten and first grade, a finding compatible with the recommendations of the National Reading Panel Report (National Institute of Child Health and Human Development, 2000), "that phonics instruction taught early proved much more effective than phonics instruction introduced after first grade" (p. 2-85).

Across all grades a relatively small amount of higher level questioning or writing related to stories read was observed. These findings are, unfortunately, all too consistent with the results of our earlier study (Taylor et al., 2000). It is important to note that effective teachers and teachers in more effective schools are more frequently observed asking higher level questions than less effective teachers and teachers in less effective schools (Knapp, 1995; Taylor, Pressley, & Pearson, 2000).

Teachers' Interaction Styles

Telling and recitation were major interaction styles of teachers in all grades; coaching was seldom observed. In our earlier study (Taylor, Pearson, et al., 2000), teacher interaction style varied by level of teacher accomplishment: The least accomplished teachers preferred telling while the most accomplished preferred coaching as their primary interaction style.

Students' Active Versus Passive Involvement

Across all grades, students in the present study were engaged in passive responding more often than in active responding. Passive responding included turn taking during oral reading (e.g., round robin), oral turn taking, or listening to the teacher. Active responding included reading, writing, and manipulating. In contrast, Pressley et al. (2001) found that exemplary first-grade teachers had their students actively engaged in actual reading and writing.

Students' Reading Growth and Teacher Practices

To take a closer look at the relationships between teacher practices during literacy instruction and students' reading and writing growth, we conducted Hierarchical Linear Modeling (HLM) analyses (Bryk & Raudenbush, 1992). The outcome measures for these analyses were reading fluency (as measured by the number of words read correctly on a grade-level passage in one minute) and comprehension (as measured by the comprehension subtest of the Gates-MacGinitie reading tests). Although we were interested in the possible effects of all 11 coded practices, only those practices that were found to be significantly related to students' reading growth are discussed here. The details of these analyses appear in the report of the larger study (Taylor et al., 2001).

Fluency

The HLM analysis for grade 1 revealed that the incidence of students coded as actively responding was positively related to spring fluency scores, after accounting for fall scores. For grades 2–3, the HLM analysis revealed that telling had a significant negative relationship with regard to spring fluency scores (after accounting for fall scores).

Reading Comprehension

Only the classroom-level HLM analysis for grades 4–6 showed significant differences related to reading comprehension. Time spent on higher level questions had a significant positive relationship and telling had a significant negative relationship with regard to spring comprehension scores (after accounting for fall scores).

Emergent Literacy in Kindergarten

For kindergarten, there were fall scores only for the children identified by their teachers as low and average in literacy abilities. The HLM analysis revealed that time spent on word-level activities (positively related) and telling (negatively related) had significant relationships with regard to spring letter-name scores (after accounting for fall scores). The HLM analysis showed that telling was negatively related to spring phonemic awareness scores (after accounting for fall scores). For concepts of print, the HLM analysis revealed that small-group instruction had a significant positive relationship and telling had significant negative relationship with regard to spring scores (after accounting for fall scores). For word dictation, the HLM analysis revealed that telling was negatively related to spring scores (after accounting for fall letter-name scores).

Summary of Classroom Findings and Descriptions of More Helpful and Less Helpful Classroom Practices

The descriptive data of typical effective classrooms indicate that, in general, a shift in certain teaching practices, such as higher level questioning, style of interacting, and encouraging active pupil involvement, may be warranted. The HLM results from the current study further underscore this point. Based on the HLM analyses, reliance on telling as an interaction style was not found to be beneficial to students' reading growth. Several practices were found to be beneficial at particular grade levels: active responding (grade 1), small-group instruction (kindergarten), word skill work (kindergarten), and higher level questions (grades 4–6).

To better explain the findings related to classroom factors, we provide descriptions of teachers who illustrate positive practices. We also provide examples from classrooms in which telling was a common strategy in order to better describe this less helpful practice. These examples were reconstructed from our field notes, and wherever possible, we used direct quotes from teachers and students. All names are pseudonyms.

Kindergarten

Ginger Smith embodied all of the characteristics of an effective kindergarten teacher. She taught reading in groups of six. She emphasized word work: The children made words with plastic letters, practiced sight words in drill and game activities, generated rhyming words, generated words starting with the same sound as a key word such as *sun*, and tried to write the sounds they heard as they wrote in their journals.

Instead of telling children information, Ginger involved her students at every turn. For example, as they listened to the sounds in *fan*, they slid their hand from their shoulder to their elbow, then to their wrist and chorally chimed, /fff-aaa-nnn/. For rhymes, the children came up with the words themselves.

Ginger: What rhymes with boat?

Students: *moat*, *coat*, *boat*, *float*, *troat*, *soat*.

Ginger: That's great. You can make up words.

During making words activities, the children manipulated their own set of letters as Ginger coached:

> Let's do *tub*. Listen to the middle sound. It's not *tab*, it's not *tob*. It's /ttt-uuu-bbb/. You need a letter for /uuu/.

While reading leveled books, students tracked with their fingers as they read independently from their own copies. If they got stuck on a word, Ginger coached by providing hints instead of telling them the word. They frequently read chorally instead of taking turns. While completing a journal entry about their favorite book, children wrote their own sentence(s) while Ginger gave feedback. In another instance, a child needed help with *like*. Ginger enunciated the sounds but allowed the child to generate the letters.

Grade 1

Aaron Brown balanced whole-group and small-group instruction in approximately equal proportions. Instead of relying on telling, Aaron used a recitation framework for discussions, provided coaching through scaffolding techniques, and emphasized students' active involvement in their own learning experiences. As children were rereading familiar stories independently in their small guided reading group, Aaron often listened to individual children. In these settings, as the opportunity arose, he would coach them on a word-recognition strategy as they struggled to decode a word. The following example describes his actions when a child was stuck on *door*.

Aaron: Think of how it begins.

Child: Door.

Aaron: How did you know it was *door*?

Child: The *d* and the *r*.

Aaron: What would be a good strategy to use if you didn't know that word?

Several students: Chunk it, think about what would make sense, skip it.

Later in the lesson as they were reading, they skipped a word, came back to it, and talked about how they had used this particular strategy to figure out the word.

Additional interactions revealed Aaron's commitment to students' active involvement in all of their literacy activities:

1. When a different group couldn't answer a question about how a character had changed, Aaron suggested that they search the book for a clue instead of telling them the answer.
2. As an introduction to a writing activity, Aaron asked students to think of something they enjoyed doing with a family member and share that with a partner.
3. When a student asked about the spelling of a word, instead of spelling it for him, Aaron encouraged the student to think of other ways to find the answer. This elicited a range of independent strategies such as sound it out, look on the word wall, or look in the spelling book. Aaron circulated, checked work, and coached children with spelling and with ideas as they were writing.

In contrast, a first-grade teacher who relied on telling revealed a different pattern of interaction. For example, she generated a morning message for the class rather than asking the students to coconstruct it. Instead of asking students how to spell the words in her sentence, she spelled "Today is a rainy day" and then asked the class to recite what she wrote. When she asked the question, "Why do clouds make rain?" she called on two children who couldn't answer and then answered the question herself instead of coaching children to generate an answer by rephrasing the question or providing further prompts.

In word-level work, she sounded out a word herself and then had the children repeat it, instead of coaching them to sound out the word. After asking the meaning of a word and receiving no immediate answer, she answered herself when she could have had students generate a definition after providing the word in the context of a sentence. As children were writing in their journal, she consistently told her students how to spell a word instead of determining which parts they could spell themselves.

Another telling-oriented first-grade teacher reminded children that they had learned that /ea/ could have the short sound as in *feather*, as opposed to asking them what sounds they had learned for /ea/. When discussing a story on machines, this teacher explained how a shovel worked instead of involving the students in constructing an explanation.

Grades 2-3

Terry Miller was a second-grade teacher who relied on coaching and active responding on the part of the children instead of telling as a teaching style. As children were working on animal reports, Terry circulated and coached:

> How would you spell *nuts*? Say the word slowly.
>
> You need to add some more ideas to this paragraph. Where can you look?
>
> How can a polar bear live in the snow? They have thick fur to keep them warm? Okay, add that idea here.

Virginia Gray, a third-grade teacher, also used very little telling in her teaching. She started her reading lessons with the whole group, listing the lesson objectives on the chalkboard and having children read them aloud. She led them through a quick picture walk, looking at the pictures and making predictions, which she wrote on the chalkboard. Then the children read the story silently, paying attention because they knew they were expected to participate in the small-group discussions that followed. They then formed groups of four in which one student was the leader and one was the recorder. Each group had a list of lower and higher level questions to answer on the story. During this time, Virginia circulated, took notes, and coached as children answered their questions. When the whole group got back together to share their answers, Virginia used coaching techniques to encourage children to elaborate on their ideas.

In contrast, a telling-oriented second-grade teacher missed many opportunities to involve the children. Here is her introduction to a new book:

Teacher: The previous book we read by Ezra Jack Keats, *The Trip* [1978, William Morrow], was a story about a boy who was moving to a new house. Now we'll read a new one, *Peter's Chair* [1998, Puffin]. Keats's books look similar. He is the author and the illustrator. I think the pictures look like wallpaper.

There could have been many ways for the teacher to bring the children into the conversation. As the teacher was reading aloud to the group, she did not stop to ask questions, only to interject a few ideas.

Teacher: He was being sneaky. I couldn't see him hiding, could you?

After reading, the teacher explained the story to the group as opposed to asking them to explain it to her.

Teacher: At the beginning he wanted to keep the chair for himself. That's being selfish.

Grades 4-6

John Merryweather was a sixth-grade teacher who engaged his students in frequent lower and higher level questioning on the stories they read, emphasized small groups for discussing novels, taught comprehension strategies, and did all of this with less telling and more coaching as an interaction style. When reading *The Best Christmas Pageant Ever* (Barbara Robinson, 1982, HarperCollins), John had his students write a prediction in their journal before continuing to read.

John: What do you think Alice is up to? Write your idea in your response journal.

As the class continued to read, John called four of his struggling readers to a table at the back of the room so he could coach them in word recognition. When John returned to the larger group, he asked them to agree or disagree in their response journal with a quote from the book. As the children were writing, he coached an English as a second language child with his answer and then told him he was going to call on him to share that answer with the class. After a few individuals shared their journal responses with the class, the class went to work preparing small-group presentations on questions and vocabulary related to the book to share the next day with the whole class.

In contrast, an intermediate teacher who relied on telling taught reading lessons to the whole class with a great deal of teacher talk, as in the following exchange:

Teacher: What kind of bird is an eaglet?

Without stopping for an answer, he continued,

Teacher: If you put *et* or *ette* at the end of a word it refers to something being small. So an eaglet is a small eagle.

As the teacher read a basal story to the class, he frequently stopped to tell students about information in the story. As he continued to read aloud to the students from their basal, he stopped to explain the story to the class as opposed to asking them to explain it to him.

Teacher: The point of the story is that the father had to accept the fact that he would never have a son and should be happy with his daughter.

The overwhelming sense one gets in examining our observational notes is that some teachers feel so compelled to make sure that key information is discussed that they bring it up themselves, thereby robbing students of opportunities to test their own knowledge and skill acquisition, and themselves of opportunities to evaluate students' growth toward independence. This distinction is rendered all the more important by the consistent relationship we found between an emphasis on telling and lower student achievement at most grade levels.

Figure 1
Sample of Observational Notes

9:38 Small group continues. T is taking running record of child's reading. Others reading familiar books. Next, T coaches boy on sounding out *discovered*. Covers up word parts as he says remaining parts. T: Does that make sense? T: What is another way to say this part [cov with short o]? T passes out new book. T has students share what the word *creature* means. Ss: animals, monsters, dinosaurs, Dr. Frankenstein. 9:42

11/12 OT			wr/t/c/	
(On Task)	C/s/r	r/t/a/r	or(indv)	v/t/r/or-tt
	Levels 123	4567	4567	4567

How Is as Important as What

We believe that the most interesting data from the larger study (Taylor et al., 2001) came from the observational data on classroom reading instruction. A consistent finding of the HLM analyses was that the more a teacher was coded as telling children information, the less the children grew in reading achievement. This finding is compatible with our earlier research which found that less-accomplished teachers engaged in much more telling than highly accomplished teachers (Taylor et al., 2000).

This does not mean that teachers should never tell students information; it would be impossible to teach without doing so. However, excessive amounts of "telling," especially in situations where coaching students to come up with their own responses is possible, may rob children of the opportunity to take responsibility for their own skills and strategies. Telling is indicative of a strong teacher-directed stance, as opposed to a student-support stance toward teaching (e.g., coaching, modeling, and other forms of scaffolding). Our hope is that by receiving feedback on the incidence of telling in one's literacy teaching, teachers may be able to shift somewhat on the continuum of teacher-to-student directedness if their data from the classroom observations suggest that this would be beneficial. This shift, in turn, will ideally lead to enhanced student performance. Over the subsequent years of the current project, as we provide teachers and schools with data on teaching practices tied to students' performance, we plan to investigate the degree to which teaching practices at the classroom and the school level shift toward those practices identified as more effective.

Similarly, students in grade 1 demonstrated more growth in reading fluency the more they were coded as actively, as opposed to passively, responding to reading activities. Instead of listening to the teacher or engaging in reading turn taking or oral turn taking, these students were observed actually reading or writing more often than other students. Similar findings about the large amounts of time students were actually reading and writing were reported by Pressley et al. (2001) in their study of exemplary first-grade teachers.

We did find some evidence for the differential impact of curricular activities across grade levels. Higher level questions emerged as a significant predictor of growth in grades 4–6, while word work emerged most clearly in kindergarten. In light of these findings and those of the National Reading Panel Report (National Institute of Child Health and Human Development, 2000), a gradual shift in emphasis may be warranted. However, this does not mean that comprehension should be delayed until grade 4 or that word work should end in the primary grades, only that some shift in emphasis seems warranted. Clearly more research is needed to help teachers determine the optimum balance between word work and comprehension work for their particular students at any given grade level.

Classroom literacy instruction needs to reflect best practices as identified in the research. In addition to *what* teachers teach, the findings at the classroom level in the current study in corroboration with earlier research suggest that *how* teachers teach is also important to consider when seeking to make changes in reading instruction to improve students' reading achievement. The results of this study show that an overreliance on telling as an interaction mode, indicative of a strong teacher-directed stance, does not appear to be very effective for enhancing students' reading growth. Currently, the improvement of children's reading achievement is a major goal in the United States (Bush, 2001). Schools know that a wealth of information exists to help them move toward this goal, but putting all of the relevant pieces together remains a challenge. Ongoing professional development in which teachers work together within buildings to reflect on their practice is one important piece of the total package that is needed to ensure that "no child is left behind" (Bush, 2001).

To paraphrase, we appear headed on a march toward full literacy that includes all U.S. children in the parade. If we are serious about the metaphor of "leaving no child behind," our data would suggest that we, as professionals, must possess the conviction, the knowledge, and the teaching techniques necessary to ensure that every child in that march is equipped with a "full backpack" of skills, strategies, habits, and dispositions toward literacy.

References

Brophy, J. (1973). Stability of teacher effectiveness. *American Educational Research Journal, 10*, 245–252.

Bryk, A.S., & Raudenbush, S.W. (1992). *Hierarchical linear models.* Newbury Park, CA: Sage.

Bush, G.W. (2001). *No child left behind.* Washington, DC: Office of the President.

Deno, S. (1985). Curriculum-based measurement: The emerging alternative. *Exceptional Children, 52*(2), 199–232.

Dunkin, M., & Biddle, B. (1974). *The study of teaching.* New York: Holt, Rinehart, & Winston.

Flanders, N. (1970). *Analyzing teacher behavior.* Reading, MA: Addison-Wesley.

Knapp, M.S. (1995). *Teaching for meaning in high-poverty classrooms.* New York: Teachers College Press.

National Institute of Child Health and Human Development. (2000). *Report of the National Reading Panel. Teaching children to read: An evidence-based assessment of the scientific research literature on reading and its implications for reading instruction* (NIH Publication No. 00-4769). Washington, DC: U.S. Government Printing Office.

Pikulski, J. (1996). *The emergent literacy survey.* Boston: Houghton Mifflin.

Pressley, M., Wharton-McDonald, R., Allington, R., Block, C.C., Morrow, L., Tracey, D., Baker, K., Brooks, G., Cronin, J., Nelson, E., & Woo, D. (2001). A study of effective first-grade literacy instruction. *Scientific Studies of Reading, 5*, 35–58.

Roehler, L.R., & Duffy, G.G. (1984). Direct explanation of comprehension processes. In G.G. Duffy, L.R. Roehler, & J. Mason (Eds.), *Comprehension instruction: Perspectives and suggestions* (pp. 265–280). New York: Longman.

Scanlon, D.M., & Gelzheiser, L.M. (1992). *Study center observation system.* Unpublished manuscript, University of Albany, State University of New York, Child Research and Study Center, Albany.

Stallings, J., & Kaskowitz, D. (1974). *Follow through classroom observation evaluation 1972–73* (SRI Project URU-7370). Stanford, CA: Stanford Research Institute.

Taylor, B.M. (1991). *A test of phonemic awareness for classroom use.* Minneapolis: University of Minnesota.

Taylor, B.M., & Pearson, P.D. (2000). *The CIERA school change classroom observation scheme.* Minneapolis: University of Minnesota.

Taylor, B.M., & Pearson, P.D. (2001). The CIERA School Change Project: Translating research on effective reading instruction and school reform into practice in high-poverty elementary schools. In C.M. Roller (Ed.), *Learning to teach reading: Setting the research agenda* (pp. 180–189). Newark, DE: International Reading Association.

Taylor, B.M., Pearson, P.D., Clark, K., & Walpole, S. (2000). Effective schools and accomplished teachers: Lessons about primary grade reading instruction in low-income schools. *Elementary School Journal, 101,* 121–166.

Taylor, B.M., Pearson, P.D., Peterson, D., & Rodriguez, M.C. (2001). *Year one of the CIERA school change project: Supporting schools as they implement home-grown reading reform.* Minneapolis: University of Minnesota.

Taylor, B.M., Pressley, M.P., & Pearson, P.D. (2000). *Research-supported characteristics of teachers and schools that promote reading achievement.* Washington, DC: National Education Association, Reading Matters Research Report.

Questions for Reflection

- What is the difference between "telling" and "coaching"? Were you surprised by the finding that more "telling" worked against children becoming readers? Were there other findings that surprised you?
- Ask a colleague to observe your teaching over the course of a few days. Then, meet with him or her to share the observations. How much telling did your colleague observe you doing? Were you aware of the amount of telling you were doing? What impact did that have on the extent to which students were engaged in your classroom?
- Do you do more telling with your struggling learners than with other students in your classroom? What special considerations should you make about your teaching style when you work with struggling readers?

A Whole-Class Support Model for Early Literacy: The Anna Plan

Pamela A. Miles, Kathy W. Stegle, Karen G. Hubbs, William A. Henk, and Marla H. Mallette

The success of an elementary school is measured largely by the literacy levels of its students. For this reason, principals and teachers routinely seek ways to enhance both the *nature* and *delivery* of the reading and writing instruction they provide. This article explains how our primary-level classroom teachers and reading specialists, with the support of our administration in the Anna School District, changed the nature and delivery of our Title I and Reading Recovery support services to significantly increase the reading achievement of our students.

Our whole-class support model has come to be known as the Anna Plan by the many teachers and administrators who visit our school district in Illinois, United States, to observe it in action at Lincoln Elementary School. These educators come to see how we apply the principles of Reading Recovery (Clay, 1979, 1993) and Four Blocks literacy instruction (Cunningham & Hall, 1996) with all of the primary-age students in our school through the distinctive use of our teaching staff.

Although the delivery of the Anna Plan differs uniquely from other successful programs for the prevention of reading problems (see Pikulski, 1994), it shares several essential principles of program success including small-group instruction, an emphasis on first grade, the use of developmentally appropriate texts and repeated readings of them, a focus on word solving and phonemic awareness, consistency between supplementary and classroom reading instruction, a writing component, and ongoing assessment of students' progress.

Success for Our Students

Our reform efforts began in 1996 and have resulted in sweeping changes in the way literacy instruction occurs in our school and in the noteworthy increases in our students' reading abilities. When we began our journey, only 50% of our students met or exceeded the state standards for reading. Not long afterward, nearly 90% of our students consistently met the standards on statewide assessments. Today, although our students come from low socioeconomic status (SES) homes and tend to begin school at very low literacy levels, some 75% of them could be classified as fluent readers by the end of the program in first grade.

As a result of our efforts, we have been recognized by the Illinois State Board of Education as an "elite high poverty/high achieving school," which means that more than 50% of our homes are low income and 60% of our students meet or exceed state standards in reading and math. We are also honored that the Anna Plan (see Table 1) has been adopted or adapted by several other schools in our state and beyond and that we have been recognized nationally as a model site for literacy and early intervention. While we are gratified that our approach has been recognized by the International Reading Association as one of its Exemplary Reading Programs, we care more about the actual literacy success of our students

Reprinted from Miles, P.A., Stegle, K.W., Hubbs, K.G., Henk, W.A., & Mallette, M.H. (2004). A whole-class support model for early literacy: The Anna Plan. *The Reading Teacher*, 58(4), 318–327.

Table 1
The Five-Day Anna Plan at a Glance

Day 1	Day 2	Day 3	Day 4	Day 5
Introduction of new book • Prior knowledge • Book concepts/ language structure • Making predictions and locating unfamiliar words • Strategy instruction • First reading of book • Strategy reinforcement • Review of problem solving and predictions	**Discussion of new book** • Story connections • Comprehension instruction • Language minilesson • Rereading of new book for fluency • Running records	**Word work** (solving words while reading for meaning) • Making Words • Guess the Covered Word • Onsets and rimes • Word-wall work • Practice with white-boards	**Journal writing** • Modeled minilesson • Language experiences • Familiar words • Invented spelling • Linking written and oral language • Author's Chair	**Planning** Team decisions made about the following: • Grouping • Individual progress • Book choices • Word-wall words • Comprehension strategies • Focus of minilessons • Scheduling

and those who have come under its influence. Their accomplishments are why we have been encouraged to share our story with fellow educators, and helping other students is our motivation for writing this article.

In the following sections, we attempt to (a) provide a brief history of our six-year effort, (b) explain each of the seven tenets of the model, (c) describe its research base, (d) detail our five-day plan for instructional delivery, (e) describe how our model has been embraced by two elementary schools in our region, and (f) offer some conclusions about what we believe contributes to the success of whole-class support models for early literacy.

A Brief History

Prior to 1996 our elementary building had one half-time and three full-time reading teachers serving grades 1–7 through a variety of pull-out and instructional programs, including Reading Recovery. While our teachers were pleased with the individualized instruction the program offered, we were intent on finding a way to serve all the primary students in our school because our reading achievement scores were at or below the national average and had been on the decline over several years. The district administration and school board decided to make reading their top priority in the primary grades, and they asked three of us (Pam, Kathy, and Karen), as Title I reading specialists and Reading Recovery teachers, to present a plan of action for reading improvement.

The plan needed to include alternatives to the existing Title I program (Title I is a federally funded program for at-risk students), which until then had consisted of in-class support and Reading Recovery for grade 1, small-group pull-out programs for grades 2 through 5, and in-class support for grades 6 and 7. For this task, we were fortunate to have worked directly within our Title I program and to have received training in, and experience with, Reading Recovery. We had closely observed numerous children's reading behaviors and were pleased that many of our at-risk first graders were becoming independent readers through the program.

As it turned out, the free and reduced-cost lunch count at our school (an index of SES) showed that, in grades kindergarten through second, we would soon qualify for schoolwide designation. This designation would permit Title I funds to be used to serve every student in the primary grades. It also allowed us to implement a preferred-support model based upon seven key tenets. That is, as we originally conceived it, the model for the Anna Plan was required to

- focus on research-based best practices,
- allow for common professional development,
- serve *all* students,
- provide for continuity within and between grade levels,
- permit time each week for collaboration among teachers,
- scaffold each student to work at her or his instructional reading level, and
- maintain a team orientation.

We began the change process with these seven tenets in mind and tried to remain true to them. We spent the remainder of the school year visiting successful programs, attending conferences, reading selected journal articles, and talking with experts about our literacy program. All of these sources contributed to our plan.

Research Base for the Anna Plan

Marie Clay's (1993) Reading Recovery research showed us the importance of explicit reading strategy instruction with at-risk emerging readers. To learn more about strategy instruction, we visited a classroom that used the Arkansas Plan for Early Literacy, a variation of Reading Recovery, which was developed at the University of Arkansas. Here Reading Recovery strategies were taught to small groups of at-risk first graders (Dorn & Allen, 1996) but with an important difference. What made the model innovative was that students whose strategy use needed more scaffolding were given continued help in the first half of second grade. During the second half of the school year, the Arkansas Plan focused on enhancing the reading readiness of at-risk kindergartners instead. This creative use of time became an important part of the Anna Plan.

Our thinking was still not complete, however. At the 1995 National Reading Recovery Conference in Columbus, Ohio, we attended an extremely helpful session that highlighted a team approach for early literacy in one classroom. In this approach, the Title I teacher, aides, and classroom teacher (who was trained in Reading Recovery) assisted small groups of students in guided reading. This example gave us the idea of forming reading teams with our classroom teachers for small-group instruction. By grouping students in each class according to instructional reading levels, we could apply Reading Recovery strategies in reading and writing with every student in our K–2 school.

The National Reading Recovery Conference also exposed us to the philosophy and research base of the Four Blocks literacy instructional model developed by Patricia Cunningham. She introduced us to a balanced approach to literacy lessons in which teachers engage students in meaningful reading and writing activities and model word structure and independent thinking strategies (Cunningham & Allington, 1994, 1998).

Common Professional Development

We knew that shared training for all K–2 teachers on the elements of balanced literacy would help bring about important mutual understandings. For the remainder of the school year, our instructional team (consisting of Pamela, Kathy, and Karen; the entire K–2 faculty; our instructional aides; and our principal) attended literacy workshops. These workshops focused on balanced reading and writing, guided reading, and taking and analyzing running records—all integral aspects of the Anna Plan. Our primary-grades team began to develop a common knowledge base and philosophy for reading instruction, and we would work hard at implementing and maintaining these beliefs through ongoing professional development and teacher dialogue.

Inclusive of All Children

Before the Anna Plan, our at-risk students missed a good deal of regular classroom instruction and related assignments because of their participation in a pull-out program (Allington, 1994). The classroom teachers felt that these students most needed the classroom instruction, and they felt uncomfortable introducing new concepts and skills during these times. They knew that reteaching would be necessary, and because much of it would have to occur during breaks or free time, the students would feel that they were being penalized, especially when they had homework that other students had completed in class.

There was also a stigma attached to pull-out programs that was disturbing to many parents. The Title I program was isolated from the rest of the curriculum, and the isolation frequently prevented transfer from one activity to the other. Not only did the program fail to serve all students in need but also opportunities to exit the program were very limited.

Our first attempt to solve these problems was a push-in program in first grade. Reading Recovery teachers were teamed with classroom teachers, and the model allowed Reading Recovery strategies to be modeled with larger groups of students. However, the daily time spent setting up the classrooms for groups was not productive, and the lack of time for advance planning prevented adequate continuity of instruction.

Continuity Within and Between Grade Levels

Individual teaching philosophies had not been carefully considered prior to the Anna Plan. Teachers were diverse in their philosophies and delivery methods. These differences tended to be based on each teacher's education and experience—whether they were oriented toward whole language, phonics, or a combination of both. The basal program was considered to be the nucleus of our reading curriculum, with instruction dictated by the scope and sequence of the series. This approach lacked consistency because different basals were used in different grades. We recognized that all of our team needed to be "on the same page" in order to determine goals for our school, develop a balanced approach to student-centered instruction, and lessen the confusions that were created for our students within and between grade levels.

Weekly Collaboration and Planning Time

We also knew that common planning time would allow for a clear understanding of our school's shared goals—an important cornerstone of successful reading programs. These shared understandings have been accomplished in the Anna Plan through a creative approach related to the weekly planning time built into our schedule. During this time, one of the Title I reading specialists leads a whole-group activity in the regular classroom, while the classroom teacher discusses student progress and plans with the other two reading specialists.

Scaffolding Children at Their Instructional Reading Levels

The Anna Plan provides daily teaching of students grouped according to their instructional reading levels. Our model for guided reading is based on dynamic grouping in which ability to process text is a determining factor (Cunningham, Hall, & Cunningham, 2000; Fountas & Pinnell, 1996). Change in grouping is expected, and flexible groupings are used for other purposes as appropriate. The students are grouped according to their specific, demonstrated strengths in reading and the related appropriate levels of text difficulty. Books are chosen for each group from a variety of titles on the appropriate level. Within each class, some of the levels overlap, but generally they are not the same for all four groups at any one time.

The process of teaching we use places meaning and language understandings in the foreground with appropriate attention given to words in text. Important skills and strategies are incorporated with our reading lessons by having students apply them directly to texts that lend themselves to this kind of practice. High-frequency words are a consideration, but vocabulary is not artificially controlled. All students read the entire leveled text to themselves and read selections several times to promote fluency and better comprehension. We try to balance our focus on reading for meaning with the use of flexible problem-solving strategies. Evaluation is based on daily observation and weekly running records. This systematic individual assessment indicates whether students' oral reading levels are consistent with their group placement and whether they should progress to the next level.

A Team Orientation

As teachers who had worked with at-risk students, we recognized that inconsistent instruction contributed to their confusion. This awareness prompted us to use a team approach in which classroom teachers, Title I reading specialists, instructional aides, and parents worked as partners. The approach started with the professional development of our staff.

The administrators, teachers, and instructional aides on our team all attended workshops and training sessions together, hearing the same concepts at the same time from the same facilitator. Collaborative planning sessions were scheduled to discuss how and what parts of this new information would be implemented into our curriculum. In addition, parent training sessions were scheduled periodically throughout the school year to model instructional methods. This training helped build relationships and bridge the gap between home and school. With our seven tenets addressed, we began implementing the Anna Plan detailed in Table 1.

The Five-Day Anna Plan

In the Anna Plan, each of the first- and second-grade classrooms is scheduled for its own 25-minute instructional period in a special classroom that has come to be called "The Reading Room." Here the teacher and her students join the three Title I reading specialists for small-group instruction. In the Reading Room, four small groups operate simultaneously, with each one being taught either by the classroom teacher or one of the reading specialists. The four groups are formed within each classroom at the beginning of the school year on the basis of the students' instructional reading levels on the spring testing of the Developmental Reading Assessment.

The Reading Room is divided into work areas by partitions, forming four miniclassrooms. The miniclassrooms are equally furnished with kidney-shaped tables and literacy tools such as magnetic whiteboards, books, word walls, pocket charts, and magnetic letters. An additional area of this room is set up for whole-group modeling with a rug and large whiteboard. Still another space houses the classroom library, which includes multiple copies of leveled Reading Recovery books and beginning chapter books.

Each small group remains with one teacher for two weeks before moving to the next teacher for instruction. The four groups are fluid, with students moving from one group to another as their needs dictate. This rotation allows for each teacher to spend time with students in a small-group setting. It also gives the classroom teacher the opportunity to obtain a sense of all her students' reading and writing strengths and weaknesses before the end of the first grading period and the first parent-teacher conferences.

At the midyear point, we extend our services to the kindergarten classrooms. This expansion is possible because, like the Arkansas Plan, we are able to discontinue our second-grade program at that point because almost all of our students are fluent by then. The instruction provided to our kindergartners centers around readiness levels, concepts about print, and phonological awareness.

Day 1—Introduction to a New Book

On the first day, a new leveled Reading Recovery text (levels 1–20) is introduced to a small group of students all reading at or about the same instructional reading level (e.g., 90%–95% oral reading accuracy as indicated by the weekly running record assessments). Our library of books includes eight copies of each title and represents various genres. The number of titles at any particular level is dependent upon the number of classes served. We typically serve four sections of kindergarten, first grade, and second grade. Multiple copies of the same titles are required when, for instance, first-grade high achievers and lower achieving second graders require books at the same instructional level.

In planning instruction, the teacher selects a book and determines the amount of support necessary to introduce it. This decision will depend upon an assessment of the students' current processing abilities using guidelines described more fully in the section on Day 5 Planning.

When introducing a book, the teacher must be cognizant of the key elements of *before*, *during*, and *after reading*. The teacher's role for *before reading* is to activate the students' prior knowledge about the book, discuss book concepts and language structure, encourage them to predict and locate new or unusual words, instruct them on a particular reading strategy, and give them a purpose for reading. The students' role is to engage in conversation, make personal connections and predictions, raise questions, and notice illustrations and information in the text.

Following the book introduction, the *during reading* phase begins. The teacher distributes a copy of the book to each child in the small group and then listens in to observe the readers' behaviors. Here the teacher is looking for evidence of the reading strategies used, confirming the students' attempts at problem solving, interacting with them when they experience difficulty, and noting individual strengths and weaknesses in reading.

The students' role *during reading* is to softly read aloud the new book at their own pace, check predictions, confirm questions, and self-monitor as they read. This task should not be confused with choral reading or round-robin reading, both of which lack a comprehension dimension. Instead, as the students gain meaning from the text, their attempts at problem solving should include the modeled reading strategy as well as previously learned ones.

When the first reading of the new book is completed, the *after reading* phase gets underway. The teacher and students discuss how they problem solved any "tricky parts" and how their predictions fared. The teacher concludes the daily lesson by praising the students for the strategies they used.

Day 2—Working With the New Book

Day 2 of the Anna Plan is spent on the same new book used on Day 1. This session focuses on reading comprehension and includes a language minilesson, rereading of familiar text, and the taking of running records.

In the first five minutes or so, students discuss or retell the new story. The goal here is to build comprehension skills. The teacher may have the students retell the story without looking at the book, prompting them to include story elements such as character, setting, problem, plot, and resolution. The students are also asked whether their connections to the story are book-to-self, book-to-book, or book-to-world types (Harvey & Goudvis, 2000). At times the teacher may use a graphic organizer to help build comprehension. At other times, the teacher may have the students concentrate on questioning strategies. In effect, the teacher must decide what comprehension strategies will enable a particular group to succeed with a particular book.

In the language minilesson, which takes about two to three minutes, the teacher works on knowledge and skills related to the book that will help the students when reading other new texts. For instance, a sample language minilesson could help them learn how to interpret a punctuation mark, how to make their voices sound when reading words written in italics, or how to use the table of contents.

After the completion of the language minilesson, the new book from Day 1 is handed out to the students to be read again. When the reading is completed, individual reading folders containing familiar books are passed out so the students can practice reading for fluency. At this time the teacher pulls students aside individually to administer a weekly running record.

Running records provide useful measures of how well students read their new books. In the Anna Plan, we use running records to provide important information for planning day-to-day instruction, guiding our decisions about grouping, monitoring their progress, observing strengths and difficulties, and allowing them to move through book levels at different rates while keeping track of individual progress.

Day 3—Word Work

Day 3 of the plan centers on working with words. Here students are taught to be "word solvers," taking words apart while reading for meaning and constructing words while writing to communicate. In both writing and reading, word solvers use a range of skills. The teacher's role on Day 3 is to instruct students on strategies they can use to make connections between letter-sound relationships, visual patterns, and ways to construct meaning. The process of teaching students to become word solvers is always dynamic (Pinnell & Fountas, 1998, 1999). We operate on the principle that word solving is more than mere word learning. It involves the discovery of the rules underlying the construction of the words that make up texts.

In the Anna Plan, teachers must be keen observers of each student's reading and writing behaviors, whether they pertain to word identities or meaning construction. By interpreting these behaviors, they can focus on the individual in order to plan developmentally appropriate word-work lessons for Day 3 (Vygotsky, 1962, as cited in Bear, Invernizzi, Templeton, & Johnston, 2000). These lessons could include activities such as Making Words, Guess the Covered Word, extending word walls, using onsets and rimes, whiteboard practice, and the like (Clay, 1993; Cunningham & Hall, 1996; Cunningham et al., 2000). Through the application of these word-work activities the students develop a foundation for becoming independent readers and writers.

Day 4—Writing

Day 4 of the plan is devoted to student writing. Learning to write letters, words, and sentences helps students make the visual discrimination of detail in print that they will use in reading (Clay & Watson, 1982). During Day 4, the students receive direct instruction, guidance, and support in a learning atmosphere that encourages risk taking. The teacher starts out with a modeled minilesson of a developmentally appropriate skill that the small group of students will need in order to become more independent in their writing.

To enhance writing instruction, each mini-classroom has print-rich environments equipped with word walls and posters for color words and number words. The students write in unlined 8½" × 11" journals that are stapled landscape style. When the journals are opened up for writing, the top page is used for the practice page and the bottom page is used for the "published" page.

The ideas for writing come from the students themselves. They are encouraged to use their own language experience as a springboard to begin writing. The teacher prompts them by saying, "What would you like to tell about today in your writing?" It is important that the response be recorded exactly as the student said it and that it is then read back to the student. Doing anything else will confuse the student about the very things that individual language experience is supposed to be clarifying.

During writing, students are encouraged to pay attention to letter details, phonemes, and the sequence of letters. They are also taught to use familiar words they have learned as a basis for writing unfamiliar words. Invented spelling is acceptable for unknown words. The students reread their written message to themselves to link their oral language to the print form.

The teacher is primarily a facilitator during process writing. He or she monitors the students' work and intervenes when needed to prompt strategies they can use to help themselves when writing. In the last few minutes of Day 4, the teacher has the students share what they have written in the Author's Chair, a special seat that is set aside for the young writers to tell the others in their small group what they have composed.

Day 5—Planning

Day 5 of the Anna Plan is the glue that holds the program together. Time for weekly collaborative planning, which includes conferring, engaging in dialogue about students' progress, and discussing schedules, is vital to implementation of the plan. On this day, one of the three Title I reading specialists goes into a classroom teacher's room for a whole-group activity during the regularly scheduled 25-minute period. This procedure allows each classroom teacher to come to the Reading Room to plan for the following week with the two remaining Title I reading specialists. Planning includes discussions about students' group placements, individual student progress, rotation of groups among the teachers, book level choices, reading and comprehension strategies focus, language minilessons, scheduling for the week, and coordinating word-wall words. All teachers on the team must be consistent in the introduction and study of high-frequency words that will expand the students' word knowledge.

On the weekly planning day, we evaluate possible shifts of individual students within the four small classroom groups. Trends in students' weekly running record evaluations are considered for their group placement. Changes in group placement could be necessary for students making accelerated progress or those who might need a more supportive group in order to assure their continued progress.

On Day 5, the team also decides on upcoming book choices. Factors that we keep in mind when making a book choice for the small groups include concept familiarity, interest and appeal, skill application, students' current ability to use word analysis and prediction, the support provided by illustrations, text length, print clarity, the number of lines of text, word spacing, and the appropriateness of the text layout.

After selecting appropriate texts, we decide on a reading comprehension strategy that needs to be emphasized for each group, and each teacher plans a language minilesson that will help the students read that text and other new texts. A word-work lesson is also selected, and materials are gathered that facilitate this activity. Finally, a modeled writing minilesson is planned that will be used prior to the students' journal writing.

Adaptations of the Anna Plan

Two of the schools in our region that have been influenced by our model are Washington Elementary School and DuQuoin Elementary School. Both of these sites have adapted the Anna Plan to meet their respective needs. One common thread in all of the sites that have modeled themselves after ours is the connection to Reading Recovery, yet both schools built their own distinctive programs.

Small Groups

Washington Elementary School, located in Marion, Illinois, began its implementation in the spring of 1997. The principal at that school first heard about the Anna Plan in connection with the Exemplary Reading Program Award our Lincoln Elementary School had received from the International Reading Association. After spending some time with us at the Southern Illinois Reading Conference, he selected teachers to visit Anna to learn more about the program. He felt that the Anna Plan framework would fill a void in Washington's Title I services because both the pull-out and push-in programs at his school were problematic. After the visit, the teachers reported how impressed they were with what they had observed and worked with the principal to begin establishing their program right away. The version of the Anna Plan used at Washington School became known as Small Groups.

During the first year of the program, only two first-grade classrooms participated. The following year, which became the first full year of implementation, Small Groups took place in all first-grade classrooms. In the second year, the program moved into two second-grade classrooms, and during the third year, kindergarten was added, and full implementation occurred in second grade. Third grade was added during year four, and the fourth and fifth grades were added during year five. Now, in the sixth year, all grades participate in Small Groups with multiple groups running daily.

In order to provide Small Groups to all the students at Washington School, the single Reading Room was expanded to three Reading Rooms. In each Reading Room, one member of the team is always the classroom teacher; however, the other three members vary by grade levels. The three Reading Rooms are run by educators of varying professional degrees and experiences who work together as a team and share the desire to improve literacy services in all grades. In many ways, Small Groups has become the heart of Washington School's overall literacy program.

Team Time

The adaptation of the Anna Plan at DuQuoin Elementary School occurred differently from the way Small Groups developed at Washington Elementary. In DuQuoin, the Reading Recovery teachers first heard about the Anna Plan and asked their principal if they could make a site visit to learn more about it. When the teachers returned, they told the principal that they would like to implement a similar plan at their school. The principal cautioned them that this would be a great deal of work, but the teachers wanted to implement what they had seen, and thus the Anna Plan became the catalyst for what is termed *Team Time* in DuQuoin.

Team Time is actually very similar to the original Anna Plan because the DuQuoin teachers had considerable contact with our school as they developed their program. Team Time has two Reading Rooms. One Reading Room is reserved for first grade where Team Time takes place in the morning and Reading Recovery in the afternoon. The second room provides services for kindergarten and second grade. The teams for each room include two Reading Recovery teachers and one paraprofessional. The Reading Recovery teachers work very closely with the classroom teachers to ensure consistency between classroom instruction and Team Time.

Implications for Teachers and Principals

Beyond the increase in students' reading achievement, the Anna Plan has transformed the atmosphere in our school in exciting ways (see Shrake, 1999). There is a spirit of pride, enthusiasm, and accomplishment that pervades our building. Teachers feel as though they are truly making a difference in students' lives. They are gratified about their professional development, and they are more confident that their literacy instruction has finally "come together." The students themselves are more confident and appreciate the small-group work and increased levels of instructional attention they receive. In fact, all of these statements can be made about the programs at Washington and DuQuoin Elementary schools as well.

We believe that the success of support models like Small Groups and Team Time depends first on the dedication of the teachers and principal and then on how closely the model adheres to the basic tenets of the Anna Plan. Both programs rightly focus on best literacy practices and aim to meet the specific needs of all students in the primary grades, in part through the staff's commitment to professional development. The use of teachers trained in Reading Recovery in the Reading Rooms provides for instructional consistency within and between grade levels and in scaffolding each student to work at her or his instructional reading level. The whole-class support models also maintain a team orientation and place a high value on regularly scheduled collaborations among teachers.

It has been rewarding to watch adaptations of the Anna Plan take hold in school districts within and beyond our state. The many schools that have adapted the plan happily report their success to us. All of them are performing well. For example, Washington and DuQuoin Elementary schools have both been recognized by the state for their stellar literacy programs, and an elementary school in Olney, Illinois, that adapted our model was recently selected for an IRA Exemplary Program Award.

The use of Reading Recovery techniques with small groups is not a novel idea. This practice is now being implemented in many schools nationwide. However, these programs tend to use small groups to provide continued support to current Reading Recovery students (Taylor, Short, Frye, & Shearer, 1992) or to support only those students waiting for Reading Recovery services (see, e.g., MacKenzie, 2001). By contrast, whole-class models like the Anna Plan include *all* students at the grade levels the programs serve.

The Anna Plan provides educators with a unique and fresh approach to reading instruction. It brings together the concepts of team teaching, collaboration, and professional development for teachers as well as the concepts of early intervention, scaffolding, continuity, and balanced literacy for students. As an alternative to pull-out approaches that are reportedly ineffective, the Anna Plan reaffirms the value of small-group instruction in meeting students' literacy needs and targeting their strengths (Allington, 1994; Walp & Walmsley, 1995). In sum, our whole-class literacy model provides a catalyst for rethinking the delivery of high-quality reading instruction and perhaps revitalizing literacy educators. Our hope in sharing our story is that the lives of many more students will be touched by the literacy growth the Anna Plan promises.

References

Allington, R. (1994). What's special about special programs for children who find learning to read difficult? *Journal of Reading Behavior, 26*, 95–115.

Bear, D., Invernizzi, M., Templeton, S., & Johnston, F. (2000). *Words their way: Word study for phonics, vocabulary, and spelling instruction*. Upper Saddle River, NJ: Prentice Hall.

Clay, M.M. (1979). *The early detection of reading difficulties*. Columbus, OH: Heinemann.

Clay, M. (1993). *Reading Recovery: A guidebook for teachers in training*. Portsmouth, NH: Heinemann.

Clay, M.M., & Watson, B. (1982). An in-service programme for Reading Recovery teachers. In M. Clay (Ed.), *Observing young readers* (pp. 22–27). Portsmouth, NH: Heinemann.

Cunningham, P.M., & Allington, R.L. (1994). *Classrooms that work: They can all read and write*. New York: HarperCollins College Publishers.

Cunningham, P.M., & Allington, R.L. (1998). *Classrooms that work: They can all read and write* (2nd ed.). New York: HarperCollins College Publishers.

Cunningham, P.M., & Hall, D.P. (1996). *The Four Blocks: A framework for reading and writing in classrooms that work*. Clemmons, NC: Windward Productions.

Cunningham, P.M., Hall, D.P., & Cunningham, J.W. (2000). *Guided reading: The Four Blocks way*. Greensboro, NC: Carson-Dellosa.

Dorn, L., & Allen, A. (1996). Helping low-achieving first-grade readers: A program combining Reading Recovery tutoring and small-group intervention. *Literacy, Teaching, and Learning*, 2(1), 50–60.

Fountas, I.C., & Pinnell, G.S. (1996). *Guided reading: Good first teaching for all children*. Portsmouth, NH: Heinemann.

Harvey, S., & Goudvis, A. (2000). *Strategies that work*. York, ME: Stenhouse.

MacKenzie, K.K. (2001). Using literacy booster groups to maintain and extend Reading Recovery success in the primary grades. *The Reading Teacher, 55*, 222–234.

Pikulski, J.J. (1994). Preventing reading failure: A review of five effective programs. *The Reading Teacher, 48*, 30–39.

Pinnell, G.S., & Fountas, I.C. (1998). *Word matters*. Portsmouth, NH: Heinemann.

Pinnell, G.S., & Fountas, I.C. (1999). *Voices on word matters*. Portsmouth, NH: Heinemann.

Shrake, L.R. (1999). *Effecting change in an early literacy program: A change agent focus*. Unpublished doctoral dissertation, Southern Illinois University, Carbondale.

Taylor, B.M., Short, R.A., Frye, B.J., & Shearer, B.A. (1992). Classroom teachers prevent reading failure among low-achieving first-grade students. *The Reading Teacher, 45*, 592–597.

Walp, T.P., & Walmsley, S.A. (1995). Scoring well on tests or becoming genuinely literate: Rethinking remediation in a small rural school. In R.L. Allington & S.A. Walmsley (Eds.), *No quick fix: Rethinking literacy programs in America's elementary schools* (pp. 177–196). New York: Teachers College Press.

Questions for Reflection

- Could a variation on the Anna Plan work in your school? Who would you turn to if you wanted to explore the idea of implementing the Anna Plan or an adaptation?
- The Anna Plan and its adaptations Small Groups and Team Time all share a component that involves close, ongoing collaboration among teachers across grade levels and specializations. Consider your colleagues and the staff and volunteer resources you have available. Which approach might work best in your setting? How can you ensure the sort of collaboration required to make this model successful for your school and your students?
- Are you aware of other plans or approaches that work to reduce fragmentation of the school day for struggling readers? How do they compare to the Anna Plan?

A Road Map for Reading Specialists Entering Schools Without Exemplary Reading Programs: Seven Quick Lessons

Alfred W. Tatum

Several years ago, the National Commission on Teaching and America's Future (1996) referred to professional development as the missing link in achieving educational goals in the United States. More recently, U.S. President George W. Bush signed the No Child Left Behind Act (NCLBA) in January 2002. The law was drafted to change the culture of America's schools and improve student achievement across the country to ensure that students of all races, abilities, and ages receive a quality education. It was around the same time that the National Reading Panel (National Institute of Child Health and Human Development, 2000) determined from a small number of studies that inservice professional development produced significantly higher reading achievement. Also, improving the instructional practices of teachers is a major provision of the Reading Excellence Act (REA) of 1998 that targets children who are most in need of additional assistance.

With so much recent attention placed on improving teacher quality and reading achievement in low-performing schools and an emerging focus on using reading specialists to implement professional development experiences and reading programs (International Reading Association, 2000; Snow, Burns, & Griffin, 1998), knowledge about the functions and roles of reading specialists in this capacity is significant. Three recent publications about the roles of reading specialists—*What Do Reading Specialists Do? Results From a National Survey* (Bean, Cassidy, Grumet, Shelton, & Wallis, 2002), *The Role of the Reading Specialist: A Review of Research* (Quatroche, Bean, & Hamilton, 2001), and *Teaching All Children to Read: The Roles of the Reading Specialist: A Position Statement of the International Reading Association* (2000)—indicate that the responsibilities of reading specialists have expanded and are more complex than they were a decade ago. Reading specialists are now responsible for a range of activities that include, but are not limited to, providing instruction to struggling readers. In fact, some reading specialists spend the majority of their time providing professional development aimed at improving the quality of classroom instruction.

Bean, Swan, and Knaub (2003) found that reading specialists in schools with exemplary reading programs were involved in five broad roles: (1) resource to teachers, (2) school and community liaison, (3) coordinator of the reading program, (4) contributor to assessment, and (5) instructor. Although significant, knowledge about the role of reading specialists in schools with exemplary programs is insufficiently robust. However, there is little information about reading specialists entering and performing their roles in schools without exemplary reading programs. This is a major concern because it is highly probable that more reading specialists will be assigned to schools without exemplary reading programs than assigned to schools with them.

Reprinted from Tatum, A.W. (2004). A road map for reading specialists entering schools without exemplary reading programs: Seven quick lessons. *The Reading Teacher, 58*(1), 28–39.

A road map for reading specialists entering schools without exemplary reading programs is warranted. I hope to expand the profile of reading specialists generated by Bean et al. (2003) by sharing seven lessons from my experience as a reading specialist in a school with a chronic pattern of low literacy achievement, a school that initially did not have an exemplary reading program. I bring attention to how a cohesive system of professional development support was framed.

My description of reading specialists moves beyond the existing data in several ways. While most of the current research brings attention to reading specialists working with students in the primary grades, I focus on a reading specialist working with teachers of students in grades 4–8 in an urban school in the United States where more than 95% of the students were eligible for free or reduced-cost lunch. The description considers a broader conceptualization of the role of reading specialists working toward schoolwide reading achievement. It also moves beyond the traditional pull-out model or in-class model when the reading specialist collaborates with the classroom teacher. Focus is placed on the role of the reading specialist as a teacher leader in an environment characterized by a high percentage of students reading below grade level. Finally, I propose a direct link between the support of a reading specialist and improved reading achievement in the school.

The Context of the School

I was a reading specialist at Radnus Elementary (pseudonym), an urban K–8 elementary school with 450 students. All of the students were African American. The school suffered from a pattern of low achievement in both reading and mathematics. Ten years ago, 7% of the students were reading at or above national norms as reflected by data from the Iowa Test of Basic Skills (ITBS). By 1996, the percentage of students reading at or above national norms was 13%. Radnus was one of the lowest performing elementary schools in its large urban school district. At that time the school was placed on academic probation by its district's Office of Accountability.

The school was assigned a probation manager who served as a liaison with the Office of Accountability. A mentor principal joined the faculty, and the school was given external support from an educational organization that worked with staff to improve student achievement. By the 2001–2002 school year and after five years of additional discretionary funding for the external support partner, ITBS test data indicated that 18% of the students were reading at or above national norms. It was at this time that the school's principal sought help from a local university administrator who had extensive experience leading professional development efforts to improve students' reading achievement. To establish a plan of action for supporting the teachers, the university administrator conducted four half days of observation in the school. She observed that a large majority of the teachers relied on test preparation materials to raise students' standardized test scores. In most classrooms reading instruction consisted of filling in blanks in workbook pages, checking the pages by reading aloud orally, and round-robin oral reading.

The university administrator recommended implementing a schoolwide literacy framework that included daily read-alouds, guided reading instruction, independent reading, word study, and writing. This approach was largely derived from research on effective elementary teachers (Allington, 2002; Pressley, 1998; Wharton-McDonald et al., 1997). To move the implementation forward, two certified reading specialists with more than 25 combined years of experience in urban education were hired as part of a University Partnership Team (UPT). The reading specialists were supported by a university grant–funded project and the school's discretionary funds. Although the UPT worked collaboratively on schoolwide issues, I was hired to support eight teachers in grades 4–8 as they implemented the literacy framework, and I functioned primarily as a teacher leader.

After the teachers and I worked together for 19 months they were able to increase schoolwide reading achievement. By the end of school year 2001–2002, 26% of the students were reading at or above national norms, up from 18%. ITBS data indicated gains in the percentage of students reading at or above grade level for all grades 4–8. The largest gains were from the seventh- and eighth-grade students where a more detailed case study of professional development was being conducted. At the beginning of school year 2001–2002, 22% of the seventh-grade students ($n = 28$) and 21% of the eighth-grade students ($n = 33$) were reading at or above national norms. By the end of the school year the percentages increased to 39% and 57%, respectively. ITBS standard scale scores indicated that students in grade 4 were close to achieving national average gains, while students in grades 7 and 8 surpassed national average gains. The gains of the students in grades 5 and 6 were not as large (see Table 1).

Table 1
Gains and Losses Using Iowa Test of Basic Skills Standard Scores

Grade	Average gains[a]
4	12 (14)
5	6 (13)
6	7 (12)[b]
7	25 (11)
8	33 (11)

The scale score was used because it is an equal-unit scale extending from the lowest achievement in kindergarten to the highest achievement in grade 12. Scale scores were developed so that progress can be followed over a period of years. They are used primarily for statistical analysis, such as obtaining and calculating gains.

[a]The number in parentheses is the approximate average growth from one grade to the next in reading in standard score units. [b]Multiple teacher changes

Negotiating a Situational Identity

I entered Radnus Elementary in the middle of school year 2000–2001. The principal introduced me during a staff meeting as an "expert" on reading who was going to get the school off "probation." For two weeks, I engaged in a process Angrosino and Mays de Perez (2000) referred to as "role making" to become familiar with the culture of the school and to determine how best to proceed with the teachers. This role making was critical to the development of my identity as a reading specialist because I did not "step into [a] fixed and fully defined position" (p. 683).

During the first six months, I had access to the teachers' classrooms and their teaching. I observed that the teachers were not implementing some of the recommended teaching practices, continuing instead to inundate students with test preparation materials. I met with teachers individually and in groups. I repeatedly expressed my consternation about their instructional practices during individual conferences and grade-level meetings. There was resistance. I was locked out of one teacher's classroom. Another teacher walked out of the classroom as I was modeling a lesson. The interactions of the first six months were tenuous, causing me to reflect on my ability to move the teachers toward change.

Being close to the students' failures created in me a desire to force teachers to change their instructional practices. Kohn (1999) referred to this as the "arrogance of top-down coercion" when those outside the classroom decide what the people in it are required to do. However, I determined that it was for the best to persuade teachers that the course of instruction I advocated was the one to take. Therefore, I had to find ways to negotiate my identity (Angrosino & Mays de Perez, 2000) with the teachers that would allow them to receive the support I could provide.

Aligning Function as Reading Specialist With School Context

I recorded notes of my efforts over the first six months in a weekly reflection log. My analysis led me to conclude that my support lacked a clear theoretical head. I had focused only on instruction to improve students' reading achievement. The teachers needed more support to implement the literacy framework. I assessed that the following steps were needed to align my role as reading specialist with the school context:

- Provide professional development support that is anatomically complete (see Figure 1).
- Discuss factors that include, but are not limited to, instructional practices that have the potential to improve students' reading achievement.
- Provide teachers with the physical supports and materials for instructing the students.

I expanded my role as reading specialist beyond the initial literacy framework to align my efforts with the needs of the teachers and students at Radnus Elementary. Lyons and Pinnell (2001) suggested the need for literacy programs with a cohesive system (i.e., an arrangement of things so intimately connected that they form a unified whole greater than the sum of their parts). Using the idea of a cohesive system, I examined three bodies of literature as being intimately connected and necessary to frame my role as reading specialist at Radnus Elementary. Understanding of the students' culture and literacy instruction

Figure 1
Anatomy of Professional Development Support

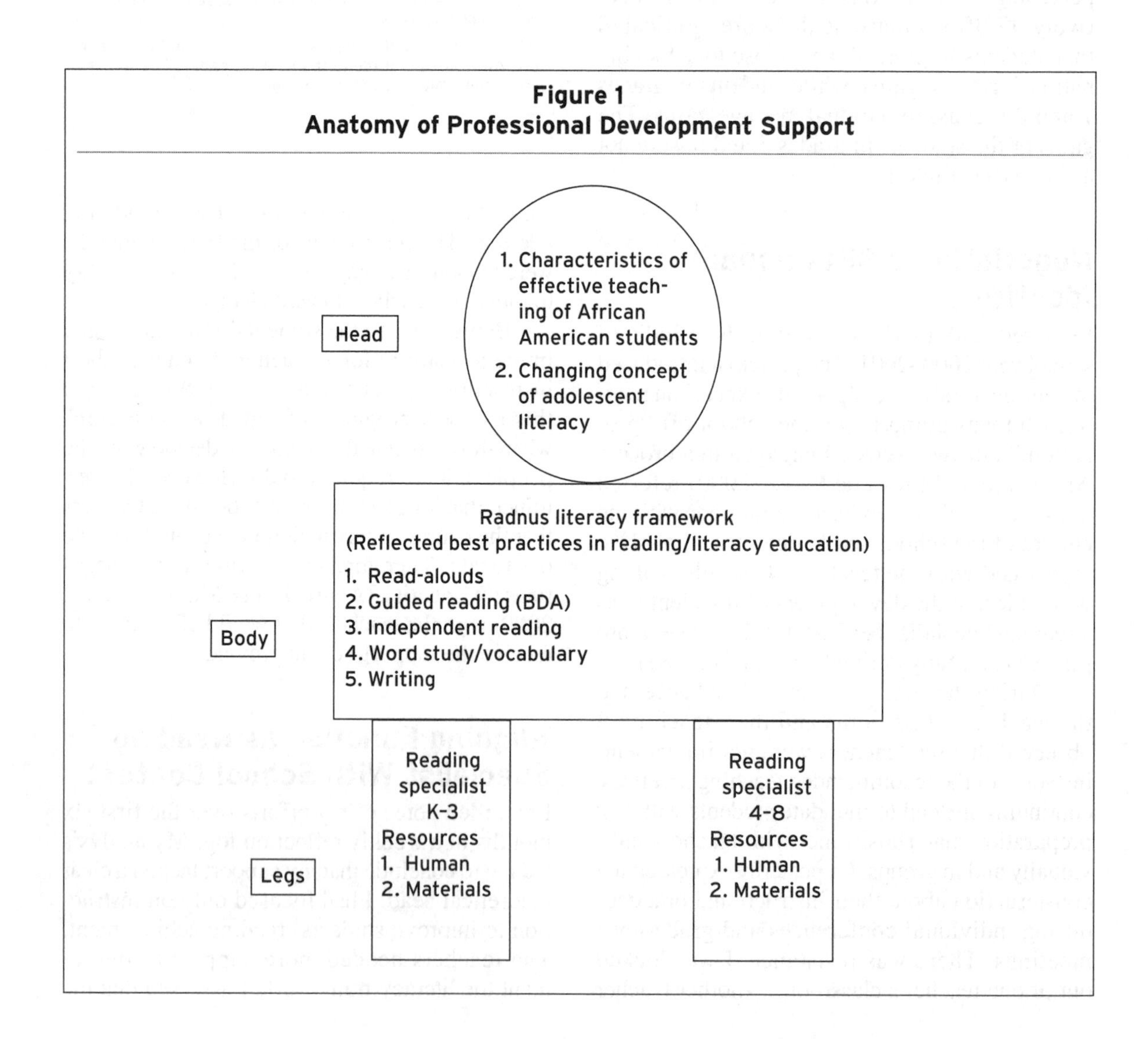

specifically for adolescents were placed at the core of the enhanced supports (see Table 2).

There were several reasons for this broader framing. First, teachers of African American students from impoverished urban communities often have students with a wider array of developmental skills and cultural barriers than do other teachers who are not similarly situated (Louis & Miles, 1990). This problem is exacerbated when teachers responsible for these students have a limited concept of what it means for their students to be literate. A limited concept of pedagogical theories can also interfere with advancing the literacies of African American students. A closer look at the "good teaching" of African American students (Foster, 1993; Irvine, 1991; Ladson-Billings, 1995; Lipman, 1995) has led to a distinctive educational philosophy and pedagogy considered effective for African American students.

Second, with regard to professional development for teachers, what little is invested is too often spent on training aimed at making conventional teachers a little better at what they conventionally do by making them more conscious of what they have been doing all along. There is a need to help teachers think differently about their work and work differently because of what they think (Schlechty, 1990).

Third, the concept of literacy for older children is changing. An emerging concept of literacy for older students moves beyond cognitive approaches confined to in-school literacy materials for teaching students ways to handle text (Moje, Young, Readence, & Moore, 2000). It encompasses complex conceptions of literacy,

Table 2
Three Bodies of Literature

Educating African American students	Teacher professional development	Adolescent literacy
Legitimate African American students' culture and make it a reference for learning.	Establish a strong conceptual basis when implementing the professional development support.	Recognize that the concept of adolescent literacy is changing.
Resist curriculum orientations that stifle or postpone academic growth.	Ground professional development support in teachers' own work and in research that is pertinent to the support.	Work to bridge the gap between adolescents' in-school literacies and out-of-school literacies.
Engage students in authentic discussions where they can analyze their realities in the context of the curriculum and discuss strategies for overcoming academic and societal barriers.	Make continuous learning a valued part of the professional development support.	Recognize that adolescents are developing a sense of self and that they draw on multiple literacies to define that self.
Guide students toward academic success and cultural competence.	Sustain the culture of the professional development support.	Provide explicit strategy instruction.
Address students' cognitive, affective, social, emotional, and developmental needs.	Be context sensitive.	Structure supportive environments.
Require students to meet high academic standards.	Systematically monitor the impact and involve teachers in the evaluation process.	Involve students in the assessment process and develop an assessment plan that pays attention to their cognitive and affective needs.
	Assure available resources and adequate support for teachers when their questions and concerns emerge.	
	Provide support that translates into visible changes in students' academic performance.	

and it is not limited to in-school literacy that is insufficient for a growing population of linguistically, culturally, and socioeconomically diverse students (Greenleaf, Schoenbach, Cziko, & Mueller, 2001; Hull & Schultz, 2002).

Several steps were taken to support the teachers' use of this broader frame. First, I sought ways to help the teachers reconceptualize their literacy instruction to address the needs of their students who were African American, poor, and living in an economically marginalized community. Second, I initiated an assessment profile of the students using multiple methods to identify students' strengths and weaknesses in reading. Third, I offered a core group of strategies to the teachers that they could use to build on students' strengths and address their needs. Fourth, I selected and offered curriculum materials and resources. In the following sections I explain how each goal was addressed.

Helping Teachers Reconceptualize Their Literacy Instruction

The attempt to get the teachers to reconceptualize their literacy instruction beyond their existing beliefs converged on a dialectic between the role of literacy instruction for African Americans historically and the present authority given to standardized tests to control literacy instruction. The reconceptualization focused on several dominant themes for the teachers that included getting them to (a) engage their students with authentic text and in authentic discussions where the students could analyze their realities in the context of the curriculum; (b) use meaningful literacy activities that address students' cognitive and affective domains, taking into account students' cultural characteristics; (c) acknowledge that skill development, increasing test scores, and nurturing students' cultural identity are fundamentally compatible; (d) make African American students' culture a reference for learning; and (e) resist curriculum orientations that stifle or postpone academic growth.

Developing a Comprehensive Assessment Profile

The University Partnership Team and the teachers entered school year 2001–2002 with a limited profile of the students' reading abilities. We were given a school progress report that indicated how well the students performed on the ITBS. There were no other assessments to provide a collection of evidence about students' strengths and weaknesses with reading. The test data were not useful for making instructional decisions. They only indicated that the teachers' practices, primarily aimed at increasing test scores, were marginally effective at best. The University Partnership Team decided that our assessment profile needed to be strengthened.

To ensure that students get the help they need, appropriate assessments should be used to identify the specific strategies and skills the students possess and their response to instructional practices. This is vital to responsive teaching, and even more so for students who struggle with reading. Also, an effective assessment plan is one that is ongoing, involves both informal and formal measures, and extends across several areas of reading. Therefore, there was a need to develop an assessment profile of students' strengths and weaknesses and the instruction they were receiving to respond to their needs.

Several types of assessments were used to identify students' strengths and weaknesses related to reading. The first assessment, completed in October 2001, was a decoding exercise using graded word lists from the Qualitative Reading Inventory–III. This assessment procedure was selected to gather a quick estimate of students' abilities to decode words in isolation. The results indicated that more than 70% of the students at each grade level were able to decode words at their grade level with 90% accuracy or better. However, the results also indicated that less than 70% were able to decode the words automatically (when they were flashed for one second). The results of this assessment were corroborated later with other forms of assessment to determine how students attempted to decode words in context that were unfamiliar to them.

Second, classrooms were observed for two months to identify patterns of literacy behaviors and instructional practices that could be shared with classroom teachers. Oral reading miscues, notes about students' engagement with the text, and students' responses to comprehension questions were recorded. Analysis of this data indicated that there was often a question-answer mismatch when students attempted to answer questions. In many cases, the students could not provide the rationale for their responses—they were passively engaged with the text. Many of the students struggled with the vocabulary in context although the teacher provided a definition.

Observation of the instructional practices revealed that students were not being held individually accountable for comprehension on a daily basis. Word study and vocabulary development were different in each classroom. Individual corrective feedback was sparse. Also, there was a mismatch between the type of questions the students were asked to answer in class and the type of questions generally found on standardized reading assessments.

In November 2001, the teachers were asked to consider the following steps to help gauge the students' needs more effectively: (1) Reduce the number of comprehension questions they had their students respond to during one lesson in hopes of getting students to invest more energy answering fewer questions. This strategy would also increase the time for explicit strategy instruction. (2) Require students to cite text-based evidence in writing for all of their responses to comprehension questions. This requirement would grant opportunities to assess students' responses more fully. (3) Reduce the number of vocabulary terms introduced during one lesson until students understood how to "map" the words.

To help the teachers gauge their students' progress and the usefulness of the recommended changes, the Gates-MacGinitie Reading Test (GMRT) was administered in January 2002 and hand scored to search for information about students' comprehension that might be useful for planning instruction. This gave the teachers a general idea of student reading achievement midway through the school year. The GMRT was selected because it provided teachers with data that extended beyond their classroom assessments. The teachers were asked to monitor and make notes about their students' behavior during the GMRT. They were also encouraged to gather students' reactions to the assessment after it was completed. Quantitative analysis indicated that 29% of the students did not complete the 48-item assessment and 19% of the students did not complete 10 or more of the items. The analysis of the data also indicated that there was no distinguishable difference in students' ability to correctly answer comprehension questions following expository and narrative text. Students had a higher number of incorrect responses on the second half of the assessment (items 25–48). Following a discussion of the results, we decided to continue to provide explicit strategy instruction using narrative and expository text, to nurture reading fluency, and to increase students' reading endurance by providing them with extended time for reading.

Developing an assessment profile that used both formal and informal measures was important because it allowed me to speak to the specific needs of the students and respond to the students' behaviors as they attempted to use the strategies they were taught. Developing an assessment profile this way also allowed the teachers to discuss the assessments with their students and gather information about the aspects of the process with which they had success or difficulty. More important, the ongoing assessment and discussion of the results with the teachers focused the instruction.

Offering a Core Group of Strategies

Fisher (2001) found that the identification of specific instructional strategies that teachers were expected to use was one of the components that led to significant increases in students' reading achievement. Graphic organizers and concept maps for vocabulary development were among the strategies. Using the assessment data, the teachers were asked to rally around a core group of strategies. They were asked to (a) teach students how to decode by analogy, (b) use semantic maps when introducing vocabulary, (c) teach question-and-answer relationships, and (d) use graphic organizers on a regular basis. Each of these approaches or strategies was modeled for the teachers during grade-level meetings and schoolwide staff development sessions.

To assist with the implementation of the strategies, teachers were given blank copies of semantic maps, transparencies of graphic organizers with directions for using them, and sample passages with questions they could use to introduce question-and-answer relationships. This allowed the teachers to focus on the strategies and eased their transition to the recommended approaches. They were also given information about the strategies and made aware of the potential outcomes the strategies would yield. This gave them the opportunity to monitor for observable differences in students' literacy behaviors. The teachers were encouraged throughout the year to continue with the core group of strategies, to engage in discussion about the strategies and students' responses to the instructional approaches, and to adapt the strategies to different curriculum materials.

Selecting and Offering Curriculum Materials and Resources

Having the autonomy to select curriculum materials to support the teachers at Radnus Elementary, I elected to use young adult (YA) literature. Being familiar with specific children's literature—novels written by African American authors and novels with African American characters—I presented the teachers with novels to consider. The goal was to increase students' engagement with the reading materials. It has been suggested that African American adolescents in low-level reading tracks, particularly those who live in poverty, need to read, write about, and discuss literature that is culturally relevant (Ladson-Billings, 1995). Teachers were presented with novels that could be mediated to help the students substantiate their existence. I wanted curriculum materials that would lead the teachers to

- Bridge the in-school and out-of-school literacy of their students,
- Use a culturally informed approach to nurture students' cultural competence,
- Use and discuss rich authentic literature,
- Provide wide opportunities for reading, and
- Rethink their curriculum orientations.

For example, *Slam* (Myers, 1996) was selected for one teacher because its contents provided opportunities to discuss making sound academic decisions and the consequences of inappropriate decisions with an African American teen at the center of the discussions. Other novels (see Figure 2) were selected if they could be mediated in similar ways to address students' adolescent and cultural identities. Most, but not all, of the titles were written by African American authors or had African American characters.

Although the curriculum materials were selected for the teachers and suggestions for using the novels were given, the teachers decided when to use the novels. They also determined the focus of the classroom discussions. I provided the teachers with feedback during postobservation conferences and grade-level meetings about ways to actively engage students in conversations about literature or ways to use literature to teach comprehension strategies. Over the course of the school year, some of the teachers developed rationale for their curriculum choices in relationship to the students' reactions and involvement with the materials. By the end of the school year, the teachers were encouraged to select curriculum materials for the upcoming school year.

Sustaining the Momentum

During my time as reading specialist, the teachers were engaged in several professional development processes to sustain the momentum of the professional development support. Each

Figure 2
Curriculum Materials Selected for Classroom Instruction

African American literature: Voices in tradition. (1998). New York: Holt Rinehart & Winston.
Babbitt, N. (1975). *Tuck everlasting.* Farrar Straus Giroux.
Clements, A. (1996). *Frindle.* New York: Aladdin.
Curtis, C.P. (1995). *The Watsons go to Birmingham–1963.* New York: Bantam Doubleday.
Gregory, D. (1990). *Nigger: An autobiography.* New York: Pocket Books.
Hamilton, V. (1990). *Cousins.* New York: Scholastic.
Johnson, A. (1998). *Heaven.* New York: Aladdin.
Kunjufu, J. (1987). *Lessons from history.* Chicago: African American Images.
Lowry, L. (1989). *Number the stars.* New York: Yearling.
Mead, A. (1998). *Junebug and the Reverend.* New York: Dell Yearling.
Myers, W.D. (1988). *Scorpions.* New York: HarperTrophy.
Myers, W.D. (1993). *Malcolm X: By any means necessary.* New York: Scholastic.
Myers, W.D. (1996). *Slam.* New York: Scholastic.
Naylor, P.R. (2000). *Shiloh.* New York: Aladdin
Neufeld, J. (1999). *Edgar Allan.* New York: Penguin.
Sachar, L. (1998). *Holes.* New York: Yearling.
Woodson, J. (1994). *I hadn't meant to tell you this.* New York: Laurel Leaf.
Wright, R. (1994). *Rites of passage.* New York: HarperTrophy.
Yep, L. (1995). *Hiroshima.* New York: Scholastic.

teacher's classroom was visited an average of three times a month for the entire duration of the designated two-hour reading period to observe implementation of the literacy framework and to plan additional support. The professional development processes included 20-minute postobservation conferences usually held within 48 hours of a class visit, biweekly grade-level meetings, and monthly schoolwide staff development sessions. They were also given professional readings in the form of books, articles from professional journals, and handouts that moved beyond what could be discussed during face-to-face interactions (see Figure 3).

A major facet of sustaining the momentum of the professional development support was gathering teachers' perceptions about the aspects they found most useful for advancing their students' literacies. They found the following aspects useful: (a) a strong conceptual frame of the support provided by the reading specialist, (b) ongoing and specific feedback by the reading specialist, and (c) emphasis placed on culturally informed teaching.

Strong Conceptual Frame

Reading specialists must learn, as I had to learn, that support for teachers can be interrupted when those teachers do not have a strong conceptual grasp of the support provided by the reading specialist when it differs from previous attempts that failed to improve students' reading achievement. A strong conceptual basis in the planning and implementation of support for teachers is a key determinant for its effectiveness (Guskey, 2000; Hess, 1999; Joyce & Showers, 1988; Stallings, 1989). Modeling and remaining consistent helped the teachers at Radnus develop a strong conceptual background for the support provided. Providing information about anticipated changes in students' literacy behaviors reinforced this conceptual framework.

Ongoing and Specific Feedback

Teachers were provided with regular and specific support during postobservation conferences and grade-level meetings. Their concerns were addressed as they surfaced. Providing immediate feedback allowed me to sustain the momentum

Figure 3
Professional Readings

Baker, M. (2002). Reading resistance in middle school: What can be done? *Journal of Adolescent & Adult Literacy, 45,* 364–366.
Colvin, C., & Schlosser, L. (1998). Developing academic confidence to build literacy: What teachers can do. *Journal of Adolescent & Adult Literacy, 41,* 272–281.
Delpit, L. (1988). The silenced dialogue: Power and pedagogy in educating other peoples' children. *Harvard Educational Review, 58,* 280–298.
Foster, M., & Peele, T.B. (1999). Teaching black males: Lessons from the experts. In V. Polite & J. Davis (Eds.), *African American males in school and society: Practices & policies for effective education* (pp. 8–19). New York: Teachers College Press.
Fountas, I., & Pinnell, G.S. (1996). What is guided reading. In I. Fountas & G.S. Pinnell (Eds.), *Guided reading* (pp. 1–10). Portsmouth, NH: Heinemann.
Harvey, S., & Goudvis, A. (2000). Questioning. In S. Harvey & A. Goudvis, *Strategies that work: Teaching comprehension to enhance understanding* (pp. 81–94). York, ME: Stenhouse.
Harvey, S., & Goudvis, A. (2000). Strategy instruction and practice. In S. Harvey & A. Goudvis, *Strategies that work: Teaching comprehension to enhance understanding* (pp. 27–41). York, ME: Stenhouse.
Ivey, G., & Broaddus, K. (2001). "Just plain reading": A survey of what makes students want to read in middle school classrooms. *Reading Research Quarterly, 36,* 350–377.
Ladson-Billings, G. (1992). Reading between the lines and beyond the pages: A culturally relevant approach to literacy teaching. *Theory Into Practice, 31,* 312–320.
Ladson-Billings, G. (1994). *The dreamkeepers: Successful teachers of African American children.* San Francisco: Jossey-Bass.
Moore, D., Bean, T., Birdyshaw, D., & Rycik, J. (1999). Adolescent literacy: A position statement. *Journal of Adolescent & Adult Literacy, 43,* 97–111.
Rosenbaum, C. (2001). A word map for middle school: A tool for effective vocabulary instruction. *Journal of Adolescent & Adult Literacy, 45,* 44–49.
Samway, K.D., & Whang, G. (1996). *Literature study circles in a multicultural classroom.* Portland, ME: Stenhouse.
Tatum, A.W. (2000). Against marginalization and criminal curriculum standards for African American adolescents in low-level tracks: A retrospective of Baldwin's essay. *Journal of Adolescent & Adult Literacy, 43,* 570–572.
Tatum, A.W. (2000). Breaking down barriers that disenfranchise African American adolescents in low level reading tracks. *Journal of Adolescent & Adult Literacy, 44,* 52–63.
Tatum, A.W. (2002). Professional development for teachers of African American adolescents. *Illinois Reading Council Journal, 30,* 42–52.
Tovani, C. (2000). *I read it, but I don't get it.* York, ME: Stenhouse.
Weir, C. (1998). Using embedded questions to jumpstart metacognition in middle school remedial readers. *Journal of Adolescent & Adult Literacy, 41,* 458–467.
Woodson, C.G. (2000). *The mis-education of the Negro.* Chicago: African American Images.

and manage dilemmas related to implementation and continuation of activities. Being welcomed as a support structure for teachers or encountering their resistance can be factors that potentially influence whether the support provided by the reading specialist succeeds or fails to yield desired reading achievement outcomes.

Emphasis on Culturally Informed Teaching

The teachers found the emphasis on providing culturally informed teaching useful for helping them to advance their students' literacies. Culturally informed teaching uses students' culture as a frame of reference to facilitate learning.

Curriculum materials that reflected the students' culture were selected as the primary texts. In some instances, the curriculum materials reflected both the students' African American identities and their adolescent identities. This allowed the teachers to use literature to address concerns specific to their students. The materials also facilitated literature mediations that bridged the gap between the students' in-school and out-of-school literacies.

Learning the Lessons

With increasing demand for highly qualified reading specialists throughout the United States and the need to increase reading achievement in some of the nation's lowest performing schools, many reading specialists will begin their work in schools without exemplary reading programs. There are points of convergence for all reading specialists without regard to the presence of an exemplary reading program. Namely, specialists need to be a resource to teachers, work effectively with allied professionals and parents, have solid knowledge about instructional practices, have familiarity with multiple forms of assessment, provide diagnostic teaching, and be able to work with students. These were the lessons provided to us by reading specialists from schools with exemplary programs (Bean et al., 2003).

However, it is quite plausible that most reading specialists will not be found in such schools. The point of this article is to expand on the lessons provided by Bean et al. (2003) by sharing insights that emerged from my work as a reading specialist in a school that initially did not have an exemplary reading program. I end with seven quick lessons that were illuminated throughout the article.

- Lesson 1: In the absence of exemplary reading programs reading specialists must be able to establish one. The process can be essentially messy and complex and require months to accomplish. Patience is key.
- Lesson 2: A reading specialist who does not enter a fully "fixed" and defined role must be able to negotiate his or her identity.
- Lesson 3: Being reflective is essential for reading specialists. This may lead to rethinking roles and functions and establishing new goals based on self-examination and continual professional development.
- Lesson 4: There may be a need to align the role of the reading specialist with the school context. It will be necessary for many reading specialists to understand cultural and contextual forces that operate inside and outside of the schools in which they work. This might include moving toward an increased understanding of theories of pedagogy and curriculum orientations suitable for the students and teachers at a particular school.
- Lesson 5: Being an effective reading specialist involves establishing measurable goals and planning instructional enhancements. In some cases, theoretical enhancements might be necessary for helping teachers reconceptualize the role of literacy instruction, developing a comprehensive assessment profile to identify students' strengths and weaknesses, offering teachers a core group of instructional strategies to teach students, and selecting appropriate curriculum materials and resources.
- Lesson 6: Reading specialists should be able to sustain the momentum of their efforts to support teachers and students. This may require using various professional development processes and materials.
- Lesson 7: Reading specialists should gather teachers' perceptions about the actions by the reading specialist that they find useful for helping them advance their students' literacies.

Final Thoughts

Being a reading specialist is dynamic and influenced by factors that cannot always be described in advance. A combination of synergistic factors determines how effective one is as a reading specialist. What works successfully in one environment may not be suitable in other environments. However, the emerging knowledge about the roles and functions of reading specialists is critical. The road map for reading specialists entering schools without exemplary reading programs described within this article and the associated lessons are part of the growing knowledge base useful for becoming an effective reading specialist. There are many lessons still to be learned. I hope these lessons will continue to come from reading specialists working across various contexts. Through these lessons, current and future reading specialists—and those who prepare reading specialists—can ask the right questions, make the appropriate decisions, and plan the necessary experiences that will ultimately lead to quality reading instruction and quality reading programs for all children.

References

Allington, R.L. (2002). What I've learned about effective reading instruction from a decade of studying exemplary classroom teachers. *Phi Delta Kappan, 83*, 740–747.

Angrosino, M., & Mays de Perez, K. (2000). Rethinking observation: From method to context. In N. Denzin & Y. Lincoln (Eds.), *Handbook of qualitative research* (2nd ed., pp. 673–702). Thousand Oaks, CA: Sage.

Bean, R., Cassidy, J., Grumet, J., Shelton, D., & Wallis, S. (2002). What do reading specialists do? Results from a national survey. *The Reading Teacher, 55*, 736–744.

Bean, R., Swan, A., & Knaub, R. (2003). Reading specialists in schools with exemplary reading programs: Functional, versatile, and prepared. *The Reading Teacher, 56*, 446–454.

Fisher, D. (2001). "We're moving on up": Creating a schoolwide literacy effort in an urban high school. *Journal of Adolescent & Adult Literacy, 45*, 92–101.

Foster, M. (1993). Educating for competence in community and culture: Exploring the views of exemplary African American teachers. *Urban Education, 27*, 370–394.

Greenleaf, C.L., Schoenbach, R., Cziko, C., & Mueller, F. (2001). Apprenticing adolescent readers to academic literacy. *Harvard Educational Review, 71*, 79–129.

Guskey, T. (2000). *Evaluating professional development.* Thousand Oaks, CA: Corwin Press.

Hess, F. (1999). *Spinning wheels: The politics of urban school reform.* Washington, DC: Brookings Institution Press.

Hull, G., & Schultz, K. (2002). *School's out! Bridging out-of-school literacies with classroom practice.* New York: Teachers College Press.

International Reading Association. (2000). *Teaching all children to read: The role of the reading specialist.* Newark, DE: Author.

Irvine, J. (1991). *Black students and school failure: Policies, practices, and prescriptions.* Westport, CT: Praeger.

Joyce, B., & Showers, B. (1988). *Student achievement through staff development.* New York: Longman.

Kohn, A. (1999). *The schools our children deserve: Moving beyond traditional classrooms and tougher standards.* Boston: Houghton Mifflin.

Ladson-Billings, G. (1995). Toward a theory of culturally relevant pedagogy. *American Education Research Journal, 32*, 465–491.

Lipman, P. (1995). "Bringing out the best in them": The contribution of culturally relevant teachers in educational reform. *Theory Into Practice, 34*, 202–208.

Louis, K., & Miles, M. (1990). *Improving the urban high school: What works and why.* New York: Teachers College Press.

Lyons, C., & Pinnell, G. (2001). *Systems for change in literacy education: A guide to professional development.* Portsmouth, NH: Heinemann.

Moje, E., Young, J., Readence, J., & Moore, D. (2000). Reinventing adolescent literacy for new times: Perennial and millennial issues. *Journal of Adolescent & Adult Literacy, 43*, 400–410.

Myers, W.D. (1996). *Slam.* New York: Scholastic.

National Commission on Teaching and America's Future. (1996). *What matters most: Teaching for America's future.* New York: Author.

National Institute of Child Health and Human Development. (2000). *Report of the National Reading Panel: Teaching children to read: An evidence-based assessment of the scientific literature on reading and its implications for reading instruction* (NIH Publication No. 00-4769). Washington, DC: U.S. Government Printing Office.

Pressley, M. (1998). *Reading instruction that works: The case for balanced teaching.* New York: Guilford.

Quatroche, D., Bean, R., & Hamilton, R. (2001). The role of reading specialists: A review of research. *The Reading Teacher, 55*, 282–294.

Schlechty, P. (1990). *Schools for the 21st century.* San Francisco: Jossey-Bass.

Snow, C., Burns, M.S., & Griffin, P. (Eds.). (1998). *Preventing reading difficulties in young children.* Washington, DC: National Academy Press.

Stallings, J.A. (1989, March). *School achievement effects and staff development: What are some critical factors?* Paper presented at the annual meeting of the American Educational Research Association, San Francisco, CA.

Wharton-McDonald, R., Pressley, M., Rankin, J., Mistretta, J., Yokoi, L., & Ettenberger, S. (1997). Effective primary grades literacy instruction = balanced literacy instruction. *The Reading Teacher, 50*, 518–521.

Questions for Reflection

- Do you have a reading specialist or literacy coach working in your school? Do you think he or she would agree with Tatum about the seven principles?
- The author describes some of the hostility he experienced when he first began working at Radnus Elementary. For what reasons can such hostility exist? What should both specialists/coaches and classroom teachers keep in mind when they work together in order to establish effective collaboration?
- Tatum says that reading specialists must be reflective. What do you think he means by that?

How to Maintain School Reading Success: Five Recommendations From a Struggling Male Reader

Shawyn Jenkins

In 2006, the Maryland State Task Force on the Education of African American Males (Maryland State Department of Education, 2006) acknowledged "that, at every level, there's been a fundamental failure on behalf of our African American male students and a persistent bias against them" (p. 10). Many go to the extent of describing the underachievement of boys as a crisis (Aratani, 2007). To rectify this situation, the Task Force put forth a number of teacher recommendations. Yet, most committees charged with addressing underachievement are overwhelmingly comprised of educators, policymakers, and parents. Consequently, their recommendations rarely privilege the voices of the students being served. Therefore, in an effort to increase the achievement of male readers, this article provides five teacher recommendations from the perspective of Derek (pseudonym), a sixth grader and struggling reader.

First, who is Derek? In October 2005, I began to tutor Derek, a then 9-year-old African American male third grader. He is a soft-spoken, well-dressed, only child of divorced professionals and has attended the same multicultural elementary/middle school since third grade. His family lives in an east coast inner city where he enjoys weekly league bowling, video games, text messaging, surfing on his laptop, and completing local art programs. Although he frequently travels to beaches, ski resorts, and cultural outings with his mother and is repeatedly described as amiable by teachers, he has always experienced difficulty with school literacy.

In kindergarten, Derek received therapy for speech delays. Later, he repeated the first grade (because of low reading achievement) and by October 2005, his third-grade teacher had already referred him to the Institutional Support Team, requested special education testing, and implied that he would repeat the third grade. It was at this time that I became involved to provide weekly tutorial sessions and advocate on the family's behalf. As the result of a lot of hard work, Derek successfully completed third, fourth, and fifth grades (he is currently completing sixth grade). However, he continues to experience difficulty retaining new vocabulary and successfully completing subsequent reading comprehension questions (Jenkins, 2007).

Derek yawns at the mere thought of completing language arts homework and describes school book reading as boring. During a December 2006 tutorial session, for instance, when asked to describe his in-class language arts activity completed earlier that day, Derek explained:

Derek: We're reading this story about climbing some hills and mountains...I don't know....

Shawyn: You don't remember anything else about the story? Who is the main character?

Derek: I...think this guy. I can't remember.

Reprinted from Jenkins, S. (2009). How to maintain school reading success: Five recommendations from a struggling male reader. *The Reading Teacher, 63*(2), 159–162

Shawyn: Can you remember anything else, did something funny happen?

Derek: When Demetrius fell out the chair, that was funny.

Shawyn: No, funny in the story.

Derek: No, nothing funny about the hill. Really, I can't remember the story. It is kinda long and boring. I start thinking about things when they [classmates] are reading. [December 4, 2006]

Because he is uninterested in school reading and largely unfamiliar with the vocabulary used, Derek's reading rate is below grade level and he often guesses on comprehension questions to quickly finish an assignment. Nonetheless, during our weekly tutorial sessions he openly evaluates his literacy instruction, discusses ongoing academic challenges, and shares his school successes. After reviewing field notes of our tutorial sessions, I selected five of Derek's most often recommended suggestions and compiled them into the following list in an effort to help teachers examine their instruction from the perspective of a struggling reader.

Recommendation 1: Teamwork Helps My Dream Work

Above all else, Derek's suggestions reveal the importance of teachers, after-school staff, reading specialists, tutors, students, and parents working together as a team, rather a *united front*, to reinforce home and school literacy practices. For example, some may have seen the cell phone commercials in which the customer with a weak, disjointed network has poor performance and the customer with the large, united network has superior performance; Derek's reading success happens the same way. Working in isolation, Derek's teachers and parents would be ineffective and disjointed. However, by working together (parents, tutor, teacher, and school staff) as the strongest influences in Derek's life, we are able to help him to remain on grade level to a greater extent than we can in isolation.

During Derek's most successful school years, we have made connections with his classroom teachers at the beginning of the year to do the following:

- Discuss Derek's strengths and weaknesses
- Share home and tutorial literacy routines
- Collect school vocabulary words and assigned stories

Then, we maintain monthly contact through face-to-face meetings, e-mails, or phone calls. Although teamwork undergirds Derek's success; realistically, creating and maintaining our team remains one of the greatest difficulties we face each school year.

Establishing and maintaining communication among busy classroom teachers, school staff, professionals, and overworked parents is challenging. However, we have been able to form effective teams when teachers, parents, and the student do the following:

- Select knowledgeable, trustworthy team members
- Converse on a regular basis (monthly at a minimum)
- Stay focused on each team member working to improve upon an identified area of need

Recommendation 2: Build on My Past Successes

Sadly, it seems that once the previously described team has been formed, bonds have been made, and trust has been built among team members, the school year ends. Then, a new school year begins with another classroom teacher who, according to Derek, often "doesn't even talk to the old teacher to use the same stuff that worked." Consequently, Derek suggests that struggling readers need flexible teachers who are willing to continue using the instructional adaptations, collaborations, and programs that have been successful in previous school years. To build upon the past successes, schools can do the following:

- Allow students to loop, or remain with effective classroom teachers for two or more years
- Design after-school programs to individualize activities and routines to specifically address students' areas of need and loop effective after-school teachers with their students for two or more years
- Assign teachers to classes by late May or early June; therefore, parents (and team members) can conference with the new teacher and begin building their team before the new school year begins

Recommendation 3: Connect Book Reading to My World

Although Derek finds many of the assigned books in his Language Arts classes "boring," he has a wide range of interests and experiences that teachers can use when selecting books and subsequent school literacy activities. This can be accomplished by using Derek's interests (computers and technology), passions (art), extracurricular activities (bowling), home life (as an African American, inner city preteen), personal histories (as the only male child), and local or world events (the Presidential inauguration) as points of comparison during discussion or activity completion and as a basis for book selection. According to Derek, "It makes more sense to do this project than just reading the book."

Researcher Alfred Tatum (2006) affirmed this recommendation by explaining the importance of using what he terms *enabling* texts with African American males, "An enabling text is one that moves beyond a sole cognitive focus—such as skill and strategy development—to include a social, cultural, political, spiritual and economic focus" (p. 47). The use of enabling texts allows students such as Derek the opportunity to "analyze their realities in the context of the curriculum and discuss strategies for overcoming academic and societal barriers" (p. 48), thus providing the engagement with school literacy that Derek currently lacks.

Recommendation 4: Allow Me to Help Select Books, Topics, and Activities

According to William Brozo, author of *To Be a Boy, To Be a Reader* (Brozo, 2002), teachers frequently "say over and over again that the students who are the hardest to motivate [and] who are most often in special education are boys" (International Reading Association, 2006). To increase his motivation, Derek suggests teachers allow him to help select books, topics, and activities. By providing him with regular opportunities to choose the books he is required to read and the activities he has to complete, Derek can begin to develop the sense of ownership of his literacy learning needed for reading success and strengthen the level of trust between student and teacher.

Recommendation 5: Provide Me With a Variety of Texts on a Single Topic

Derek often explains that if he had more time to read a given text he would perform better on the final test. Therefore, in order for him to fully comprehend and retain important textual information, he suggests that teachers spend more time reading and discussing texts. Here are a few ways in which teachers can increase exposure to a given text and topic:

- *Read a variety of texts on a single unit or topic.* To facilitate comprehension, read and analyze a variety of trade books on a single topic, across disciplines and subject areas. For example, when Derek was assigned to read *The Diary of Anne Frank*, he could have also been assigned to read related speeches, plays, memoirs, websites, picture books, newspaper accounts, magazine articles, or book reviews while examining related art exhibits, song lyrics, photographs, or movies. Exposure to these texts across subject areas (such as social studies, science, math, art, music, and computer skills) will provide him with the in-depth understanding he needs to successfully retain textual information.

- *Link book reading to interdisciplinary, practical projects.* To foster a lifelong love of reading, students must be exposed to the wide array of literacies that exist beyond completing academic tasks, such as researching histories, writing postcards, sending e-mails, following arts and crafts directions, building models, creating to-do lists, reading maps, and cooking using recipes.
- *Connect book reading to technology.* Derek and his friends enjoy using the latest technology such as e-mails, websites, avatars, podcasts, blogs, social networking sites, and text messaging. Collier (2008) referred to the 21st-century skills that today's students need to be successful "as the C's of change" (p. 6). These skills include "producing information using multimodal tools (audio and video as well as text); publishing what you've created; and networking with others online" (p. 6). Teaching these skills using the technology enjoyed by Derek and his friends serves as an avenue to fill the chasm which exists between home and school literacies.

Final Recommendations

The debate continues as to whether the underachievement of boys has reached crisis levels. However, Derek's recommendations reveal that educators' daily instructional decisions determine the extent to which struggling male readers will be able to make the connections needed to create and maintain school literacy success. Furthermore, Derek's experiences remind us that struggling readers need teachers who are committed to reaching out to parents, adapting their instruction, partnering with colleagues, and using innovative instructional approaches to decrease failure for struggling readers. Finally, to be more effective educators of 21st-century skills, we must begin to truly listen to the voices of the students we serve.

References

Aratani, L. (2007, May 17). Finding ways to better school African American boys: Group proposes mentors, single-sex classrooms. *Washington Post*, T03.

Brozo, W.G. (2002). *To be a boy, to be a reader.* Newark, DE: International Reading Association.

Collier, L. (2008). The "C's of change": Students—and teachers—learn 21st century skills. *The Council Chronicle*, *18*(2), 6–9.

International Reading Association. (2006). Boys and books. *Reading Today*, *24*(1), 1.

Jenkins, S. (2007, November). *To help an African American struggling male reader: You need collaboration.* Poster presentation at the annual meeting of the National Council of Teachers of English Conference, New York.

Maryland State Department of Education. (2006). *Task force on the education of Maryland's African-American males.* Baltimore: Author.

Tatum, A. (2006). Engaging African American males in reading. *Educational Leadership*, *63*(5), 44–49.

Questions for Reflection

- Do you notice that more boys than girls in your class struggle with reading? Are there differences in the types of challenges boys and girls experience? How can you differentiate your teaching to reach both girls and boys with the most appropriate support?
- One of Derek's suggestions is to allow continuity of staff from year to year. What do you think of the idea of one teacher staying with a group of students for more than a single grade level? Could this be a successful approach in your school or district? How would you make it happen?

Building Schoolwide Capacity for Preventing Reading Failure

Jane Moore and Vickie Whitfield

From the first moment we meet our students we begin assessing their needs. We listen to their responses to our questions for depth of understanding. We watch as students interact with one another for developing social skills. We administer screening instruments to determine students' strengths. We evaluate their responses and value their individual learning styles. We gather the data that will allow us to get a big picture of each and every child.

Then we prepare for the work. We create supportive and engaging environments for optimal learning. We model the strategies that will lead to success. We allow all students time to think and talk about how the new strategy is working. We watch for indicators of progress. We carefully base our instruction on group and individual needs. We give struggling learners time to develop new strategies through meaningful activities. We administer diagnostic assessments that will reveal in-depth information about students' strengths and weaknesses. We create instructional groups that are flexible and temporary based on needs or interests. We feel a sense of urgency to provide for each student so that he or she can learn. And through it all we understand that all students can and will learn but at different rates and in different ways. We also understand that it is up to us to intervene when they are not making the mark.

Intervening With Prevention in Mind

It is our responsibility to establish a prevention model for all students rather than a wait-and-see failure model. Response to Intervention (RTI) is an approach outlined for those students who need intensive and specific intervention to determine the extent needed for progress. Increasingly more layers, or tiers, of instruction are recommended as a means of identifying students with reading and learning difficulties (Vaughn & Klingner, 2007). The first level of instruction is provided by the general education classroom through a teacher who uses data-based decisions to inform instruction. The model reminds us that all students need to be ensured of good instruction in a core reading program by a trained teacher. A second layer of instruction increasing the intensity of key reading components may then be provided by a highly trained teacher in addition to instruction in the core reading program. The third layer of instruction, if needed, should be highly research-based and systematically and explicitly delivered in addition to the instruction in the first two layers. At each level the student should receive an additional 30 minutes of instruction sessions 4–5 times per week. Each tier of instruction requires a teacher to carefully monitor the progress of the instruction for each student.

RTI is not just for those students receiving special services. It is a process for any student who shows signs of falling significantly behind his or her peers. It will help identify struggling learners who have a chance of becoming proficient with proper and timely intervention.

Lack of success at any of the levels requires that we attend to students' needs by delivering more frequent, longer, and intensive interventions. It may require that students at the third

Reprinted from Moore, J., & Whitfield, V. (2009). Building schoolwide capacity for preventing reading failure. *The Reading Teacher, 62*(7), 622–624.

level receive one-on-one instruction. The general education teacher is the primary provider of initial intervention instruction. As intensity increases, other professionals can deliver interventions in which they have been trained. This may include reading teachers, special education teachers, and instructional assistants. This team approach gives the safety net that cradles all students, moving them toward success.

Monitoring for Success

Progress monitoring is a critical component of the RTI model because it provides immediate feedback as to how well the student is responding to the teaching. With timely feedback, the teacher has the opportunity to change direction or increase the intensity of instruction. The key to progress monitoring is that it is done frequently, at least once every 1–2 weeks, and measures incremental steps of success. By analyzing these incremental measures, adjustments can be easily and quickly made to the instruction. It is here that sometimes even the best educators appreciate a reminder of where we can go for resources to meet the needs of our readers.

Reutzel and Cooter (2008) and Strickland (2005) offer If–Then thinking models in relation to the student and the assessment data. This method offers a guide to your reading instruction:

> **If** you have identified specific learning needs in reading for a student(s), **then** which reading skills and strategies are appropriate to offer the student(s) next in your classroom instruction? (Reutzel & Cooter, 2008, p. 360)

As literacy leaders in our schools, we can use the resources in the tables provided by Reutzel and Cooter (2008) and Strickland (2005) and add to the list another dimension that details the targeted areas' supplemental programs and progress monitoring resources that are available in our buildings. Keeping a document like this (see Table 1 for a sample If–Then chart) updated as resources are purchased and implemented can be a valuable resource saving the time needed to inform instruction.

Literacy leaders may choose to begin the process by guiding teachers to list important literacy skills assessed by the screening, diagnostic, and outcome assessments used to monitor reading progress. This will require teachers to dig deep into the assessments and study what is actually being assessed. Teachers then can group the skills into larger categories and start building their charts. Also required by the teachers will be an in-depth look at what programs the school or district uses for interventions. Digging deep into these programs may reveal holes in interventions or programs to which the teachers have access. This will inspire further research into what programs may be available and an allocation of resources to provide for it.

Building Capacity

An excellent by-product of this activity is the sharing of resources, thereby providing all teachers with a ready list of strategies to refer to when planning for whole- or small-group differentiated instruction. The easy exchange of ideas and expertise sharing will allow for a structure that will permit staff members to rely on each other. The more personalized the list becomes for your building or district, the more likely it will be a tool that can provide for a prevention model that supports the instruction for all students. Other questions that could be explored are as follows:

- What instructional adjustments were made based on the data?
- What considerations for small-group, Tier 1 instruction did the data provide?
- Did the data indicate a need for intervention?
- If so, what program will best fit the instructional need of the student?
- Who will deliver the program?
- Does additional training need to be provided to deliver the program?
- How long should the program be delivered?
- Where are the programs housed or delivered in the building?
- How is the program progress monitored?

Table 1
A Sample If-Then Chart for Reading Fluency

IF a child has this learning need...	THEN try using a strategy like...	Resources for this strategy	Programs we have that provide for this need	Progress monitoring assessments could be...[a]
Reading rate	Model fluent reading	Quality picture books	Read Naturally	Timed reading rates
	Shared reading	Big Books		TPRI progress monitoring
	Repeated readings	Books on tape		Records of oral reading
	Buddy reading	*Buddy Reading: Cross-Age Tutoring in a Multicultural School* (Samway, Whang, & Pippett, 1995)		Developmental Reading Assessment 2
	Computer reading		Imagination Station (istation.com)	
	Readers Theatre	www.Margiepalatini.com www.aaronshep.com/rt	Leveled Reader's Theater by Benchmark	
	Multiple strategies	*Building Fluency: Lessons and Strategies for Reading Success* (Blevins, 2002) *Good-Bye Round Robin: Twenty-Five Effective Oral Reading Strategies* (Opitz & Rasinski, 1998) *The Fluent Reader: Oral Reading Strategies for Building Word Recognition, Fluency, and Comprehension* (Rasinski, 2003)		
	Reading television captions			
Reading accuracy	Oral recitation	Poetry, passage, or verse memorization	Poetry Power ESL by Modern Curriculum Press	
	Assisted reading	Books on tape	Read Naturally Imagination Station (istation.com)	
	Guided oral reading	Instructional level reading materials		
Quality and prosody	Repeated readings	Books on tape		Rubrics
	Choral reading			
	Guided oral reading	Instructional level reading materials		

[a]Reading rate progress monitoring assessments also apply to Reading accuracy.

- Who will do the progress monitoring?
- Based on progress-monitoring data, what adjustments need to be made?
- Has the student been in a core or tiered program long enough to expect progress to be made?

Once these questions and their answers are explored, literacy leaders and teachers can plan a better streamlined delivery of instruction and intervention meant to meet the needs of all students.

References

Blevins, W. (2002). *Building fluency: Lessons and strategies for reading success.* New York: Scholastic Professional.

Opitz, M.F., & Rasinski, T.V. (1998). *Good-bye round robin: 25 effective oral reading strategies.* Portsmouth, NH: Heinemann.

Rasinski, T.V. (2003). *The fluent reader: Oral reading strategies for building word recognition, fluency, and comprehension.* New York: Scholastic.

Reutzel, D.R., & Cooter, R. (2008). *Teaching children to read: The teacher makes the difference.* Upper Saddle River, NJ: Pearson.

Samway, K.D., Whang, G., & Pippett, M. (1995). *Buddy reading: Cross-age tutoring in a multicultural school.* Portsmouth, NH: Heinemann.

Strickland, K. (2005). *What's after assessment? Follow-up instructions for phonics, fluency, and comprehension.* Portsmouth, NH: Heinemann.

Vaughn, S., & Klingner, J. (2007). Overview of the three-tier model of reading intervention. In D. Haager, J. Klingner, & S. Vaughn (Eds.), *Evidence-based reading practices for response to intervention* (pp. 3–9). Baltimore: Paul H. Brookes.

Questions for Reflection

- What happens when you use If–Then statements in describing your RTI plan? Do the students who most need expert reading instruction receive it?
- Are you aware of other possible models for RTI, other than the "tiered" approach described in this article? What are the advantages and disadvantages of each approach?

Reading Intervention Models: Challenges of Classroom Support and Separated Instruction

Melissa M. Woodward and Carolyn Talbert-Johnson

In a recent literacy workshop for elementary educators, the researchers noted common concerns among classroom teachers and reading specialists when the presenter asked participants to identify factors that affect the quality of literacy instruction. There was silence for several seconds before several teachers responded in unison, "Time." The management of time in the classroom for language development activities, as well as how to differentiate instruction for the needs of readers at all levels, seemed to be of utmost concern for this group of teachers. The reality is that regardless of the quality of any program or teacher, there will always be students who need supplementary instruction designed to meet their specific needs.

Fortunately, education is not an isolated endeavor. Although some decisions regarding resources and reading programs are mandated by administrators or district leaders, the classroom teacher has the responsibility to make sure that the instructional needs of all students are met. This is a daunting task, as students are at varying skill levels in each subject area. For example, in a typical third-grade class, most students are able to comprehend grade-level material independently, while another group of students in the class may be reading one or more levels behind, and another group may need to be challenged because they can understand material three years ahead of the rest of the class. Valencia and Buly (2004) asserted that it is the teacher's responsibility to ensure that the individualized needs of struggling readers are addressed; however, classroom teachers are not expected to meet these needs alone. Research supports that some students will need expert, intensive intervention for sustained periods of time—possibly throughout their entire school careers—if they are to attain and maintain on-level reading proficiencies (Allington, 2004). Many schools provide some form of intervention support for at-risk students, including daily sessions with reading specialists through separated intervention or within the regular classroom.

Reading specialists have the responsibility of providing level-specific reading services to struggling readers. Bean (2004) suggested that reading specialists in today's schools are taking on additional roles. For example, many reading specialists are in an excellent position to assume the role of reading coach and mentor to classroom teachers in schools with many struggling readers. The goal of this article is to provide the advantages and disadvantages of separated instruction versus classroom support models as seen by teachers and researchers. We first provide the roles and responsibilities of reading specialists, determine the impact of the No Child Left Behind Act, identify possible models, and share feedback from teachers currently in classrooms.

Roles of an Elementary Reading Specialist

Reading specialists can play a critical role in the professional development of teachers (Dole,

Reprinted from Woodward, M.M., & Talbert-Johnson, C. (2009). Reading intervention models: Challenges of classroom support and separated instruction. *The Reading Teacher, 63*(3), 190–200.

2004), as they have extensive knowledge about the reading process and about high-quality reading instruction. It is evident that they have an important role to play in school leadership and instructional intervention in many schools (Bean, Cassidy, Grumet, Shelton, & Wallis, 2002; Quatroche, Bean, & Hamilton, 2001). It is not surprising that reading specialists have taken on the responsibility of providing quality instruction for all students. In the 1940s, reading specialists were referred to as "remedial" reading teachers and most recently as Title I reading teachers; however, reading specialists in today's schools have assumed additional roles (Bean, 2004). The International Reading Association expects reading specialists to be highly qualified literacy professionals who have prior experience as classroom teachers. Reading specialists are often responsible for supporting, supplementing, and extending quality classroom teaching. They also communicate effectively with key stakeholders (e.g., parents).

A reading specialist may be available in some schools to provide intervention for the groups that are developmentally reading below grade level, but how is this resource being used? Is it possible for classroom teachers to effectively use reading specialists to support instruction for all students in a class? What are the benefits of separated instruction for specific groups of students? Although most classrooms would benefit in some way from additional literacy support, the deciding factor for which students or which classrooms are assigned to a reading specialist often is determined by test results. It is not surprising that instructional groups change because of achievement test results; however, other reading performance factors are usually considered by the classroom teacher and reading specialist.

The Impact of No Child Left Behind on Reading Intervention

Every year thousands of students take standardized tests and state reading tests, and every year thousands of students fail them (Valencia & Buly, 2004). With the implementation of No Child Left Behind (NCLB), which mandates testing all children from grades 3 to 8 every year, these numbers will grow exponentially, and, unfortunately, alarming numbers of schools and students will be labeled as in need of improvement. The key provisions of NCLB include performance expectations in reading. Each state "must set annual targets that will lead to the goal of all students reaching proficiency in reading and mathematics by 2013–14" (U.S. Department of Education, 2006, p. 12). In the meantime, districts are expected to determine where improvement is needed in comprehensive instruction to address the five target areas identified by the National Reading Panel (National Institute of Child Health and Human Development, 2000): comprehension, fluency, vocabulary, phonemic awareness, and phonics.

According to recent reports from the Title I executive summary (U.S. Department of Education, 2006), there are concerns regarding intervention-based reading programs implemented in schools because there is little known about the effectiveness of these reading programs for struggling readers. As students are assessed by the state, and in the schools by teachers or reading specialists, there may be students identified who need additional intervention to overcome achievement gaps. Under the Response to Intervention process, to which many schools are now making the transition, "students who continue to struggle despite receiving initial intervention instruction will require more intense, targeted interventions" from reading specialists (Mesmer & Mesmer, 2008, p. 283). These students frequently continue to fall further behind because they do not possess the requisite skills to achieve (Dole, 2004).

To address this concern, schools are struggling to find solutions for improved performance in reading. For example, some schools have eliminated sustained silent reading in favor of more time for explicit instruction (Edmondson & Shannon, 2002), while other districts are buying special programs or mandating specific interventions. It is common to find teachers spending enormous amounts of time preparing students for these high-stakes tests (Olson, 2001).

The U.S. Department of Education (2006) identified at least 10 characteristics of effective reading intervention, including the following: small group size of three to six students who share the same reading difficulties, daily intervention for at least 30 minutes, intervention that addresses all five essential components of reading instruction, instruction that is explicit and direct but engaging and fast paced, feedback for students when errors are made, and many opportunities for students to respond to questions. Most important, intervention decisions are data driven. Therefore, ongoing assessment data determine the intensity and duration of the reading intervention, which is based on degree of reading risk. Although there are resources available to choose effective programs, there continues to be debate regarding how interventions should be implemented. There are proponents who believe that interventions should evolve in the classroom, with a reading specialist available to support all students during literacy instruction. The alternative would be to allow small groups of students to leave the classroom to work with a reading specialist for a block of time each day.

Approaches to Reading Intervention

Separated Intervention

There are several reasons why schools may prefer to implement separated (pull-out) reading intervention programs. First, they may want to target a specific group of students who may benefit from the individualized attention and quiet setting associated with this approach. Bean (2004) asserted that this approach may be beneficial when instruction is provided by a highly qualified teacher and instruction is tailored to address the individualized needs of students. Second, some reading intervention programs are designed for individualized instruction away from the classroom. Examples include Reading Recovery and Success for All (Allington, 2001). In addition, students receiving small-group, separated instruction may develop an increase in reading confidence by practicing specific skills and reading aloud with peers who share similar literacy development levels (Bean, 2004).

Unfortunately, separated instruction has been associated with a negative connotation since the 1930s and 1940s when students were sorted into ability groups and assigned to special reading teachers who would use instructionism-based approaches designed to drill until mastery is achieved (Bean, 2004; Johnson, 2004; Primeaux, 2000). According to Primeaux (2000), reading specialists are now trained to apply constructivist approaches that use students' current skill level as a starting point, requiring an ongoing cycle of authentic assessment, planning, and guided instruction using appropriate texts.

Additional concerns regarding separated instruction include the fact that children who experience reading difficulties are frequently separated from (pulled out of) their classrooms for level-specific reading instruction (Bean, 2004). Another concern is that separated instruction tends to lack integration with the regular classroom, which may result in a lack of communication between the teachers and reading specialists (Bean, 2004).

Classroom Support

Highly qualified teachers are needed to intervene effectively on the literacy skills of struggling readers (Dole, 2004). High-quality reading instruction is essential in every primary-grade classroom in schools with many struggling readers. This high-quality instruction is expected to minimize the number of students who will need intervention or supplementary instruction and will also minimize the number of students recommended for special education services.

One approach for involving reading specialists in the classroom is referred to as student-focused coaching, which is based on encouraging collaborative problem solving between classroom teachers and reading specialists to address an identified problem, such as a student's lack of progress in acquiring a specific academic skill (Hasbrouck & Denton, 2007). In this model, the grade-level teaching teams and reading specialists plan and collect data together to learn from observing student responses to interventions and instructional strategies developed collaboratively with teachers. Additional benefits of in-class reading intervention include less stigma and less negative attention for students who formerly left the classroom for reading services and the ability to maximize instructional time efficiently (Bean, 2004; Ziolkowska, 2007).

A school in Illinois implemented a similar collaboration-based program and improved student test scores on statewide tests using a building-wide support model named after the Anna School District. The Anna Plan [see Chapter 4 in this volume] involved taking strategies that were previously used only in Reading Recovery and Title I pull-out interventions and adapting strategies for use in primary-grade classrooms with flexible, daily guided reading groups:

> In the reading room, four small groups operate simultaneously, with each one being taught either by the classroom teacher or one of the reading specialists.... The four groups are fluid with students moving from one group to another as their needs dictate. (Miles, Stegle, Hubbs, Henk, & Mallette, 2004, p. 322)

In addition, students are assigned to groups based on Developmental Reading Assessment (DRA) levels, and leveled texts are used for instruction using an established reading plan for day 1 through day 5, including introduction of the text, comprehension minilessons, working with words, writing, and collaborative planning among reading specialists and teachers while another teacher conducts whole-group literacy activities.

The inclusion of reading specialists in the classroom presents special challenges, which may include conflicting philosophies and teaching styles. Overcrowded classrooms may also be a problem, as it limits areas needed for additional instruction. The dynamics of performing in a regular classroom may be too challenging and distracting for some students who have attention difficulties. In addition, collaborative planning, as described in the Anna Plan, between the classroom teacher and reading specialist may be limited.

Teacher Perspectives

In response to expectations for data-driven instructional decisions and accountability, school districts are looking for ways to use best practices to improve student achievement. The setting for this study was a suburban district in a Midwestern state with an enrollment of more than 10,000 students in grades K–12. Elementary students are identified for participation in the school reading intervention program using a matrix that looks at students' performance in the classroom based on teacher observations, scores from diagnostic or standardized tests, and DRA levels. Students who did not pass the third-grade achievement test in the fall or spring are also selected. Current policies require a parent or guardian to sign a permission form prior to beginning intervention with a specialist. A majority of reading specialists schedule selected students to meet daily in a small-group setting away from the regular classroom for 30 minutes of supplemental literacy instruction.

Methodology

Participants

The researchers designed and distributed a survey comprised of short answers and scaled responses to given statements (see Figure 1). A voluntary and anonymous sample of 50 classroom teachers was selected to allow for two teachers from each grade level at each of the five elementary buildings to provide feedback. Additional surveys were given to 14 elementary reading specialists in the district. Out of 64 total surveys distributed through the school mail system, 47 were completed and returned, producing a 73% response rate. A majority of the respondents were veteran classroom teachers or reading specialists, with 70% reporting they have taught for at least six years. Of these respondents, 26% have more than 21 years of experience teaching.

Figure 1
Reading Intervention Survey

Current position: ______________________ Grade levels (circle one): K 1 2 3 4 other

School building: ______________________

Total years of teaching experience: 1 2-5 6-10 11-20 21+

1. Classroom teachers only: How many below-average and/or at-risk readers are in your class this year?

 ________ out of ________ total students (for example: 5 out of 23)

 Reading specialists only: How many students do you work with at each grade level?

 K ________ 1st ________ 2nd ________ 3rd ________ 4th ________

2. At this time, which method do you prefer for your below-average and/or at-risk readers?
 - ❑ Inclusion with a reading specialist in the classroom.
 - ❑ Separated instruction (pull-out) or small-group intervention with a reading specialist.
 - ❑ A combination of both approaches.
3. Is your preferred method currently used in your setting? q Yes q No
4. When you think of pull-out reading instruction, list two positive and two negative aspects of this form.

 Positive: ________ ________ Negative: ________ ________

5. When you think of inclusion for reading instruction, list two positive and two negative aspects of this form.

 Positive: ________ ________ Negative: ________ ________

6. Please indicate whether you strongly agree (SA), agree (A), feel undecided (U), disagree (D), or strongly disagree (SD) with these statements:

Statement					
Students who are pulled out of the classroom miss instruction and/or time to work on assignments.	SA	A	U	D	SD
Reading lessons taught in intervention should match the ones that are being taught in the classroom.	SA	A	U	D	SD
Reading specialists and classroom teachers communicate effectively regarding the readers they work with.	SA	A	U	D	SD
The same students qualify for reading service year after year.	SA	A	U	D	SD
Parents often have concerns about allowing students to participate in intervention programs.	SA	A	U	D	SD
More state or federal funding of intervention programs will help at-risk readers.	SA	A	U	D	SD
30 minutes a day is enough time for students to work with a reading specialist.	SA	A	U	D	SD

7. Please list additional comments or questions you may have regarding this topic:

The survey asked participants to respond to prompts including the following: (a) the number of below-average readers a teacher or reading specialist worked with, (b) an indication of reading intervention preferences, (c) an evaluation of whether the preferred intervention was used, (d) identification of at least two positive and two negative aspects of separated instruction versus classroom support, and (e) key issues regarding the separated versus classroom support interventions and student needs. A Likert 5-point scale from strongly agree to strongly disagree was used. Participants were also asked to list additional questions or comments.

Analysis of Results

According to the responses provided by the 12 reading specialists, the number of students a full-time reading specialist works with each day may range from 47 to 82, depending on the needs of the building, the number of reading specialists, and the number of classrooms serviced. The average number of students in a classroom was 25, and the number of below-average or at-risk readers in each classroom ranged from 2 to 10, as reported by the classroom teachers. A majority of classroom teachers, or 57%, would prefer to have a combination of classroom support and separated instruction interventions; however, only half of these teachers currently have the option. A majority of the reading specialists, or 58%, would also prefer a combination of intervention models.

Relevant to student outcomes, the classroom teachers and reading specialists both agreed that 30 minutes a day is not enough time for students to work with a reading specialist, although this is the amount of time allotted in most classroom schedules for reading intervention. This is important because it gives insight to quality of instruction and the efficiency of the services provided. The teachers and reading specialists indicated that collaborative endeavors benefit all students, as having another adult in the classroom can assist student performance in reading.

Open-ended responses from the survey were coded and sorted according to the nature of the positive and negative aspects stated by classroom teachers and reading specialists. In regard to separated instruction, classroom teachers' responses for listing two positive aspects included small-group benefits, individualized attention, benefits of reading specialist instruction, impact on instruction for students remaining in the classroom, ability grouping, quietness, and daily reading consistency (see Table 1). However, negative aspects of separated instruction listed by classroom teachers included limited communication between the "regular" teacher and reading specialist, concerns related to scheduling and classroom routines, impact on student socialization as a result of peer labeling, and limited time for intervention students to read with the classroom teacher.

The positive and negative aspects listed by reading specialists regarding separated instruction were similar; however, reading specialists also noted attention to specific needs and materials available as positive aspects, as well as concerns for students as they travel to and from the classroom to the reading room (see Table 2). In addressing the positive factors of separated intervention, classroom teachers and reading specialists most frequently cited the benefits of individualized attention in a small-group setting, followed by a quieter or less distracting work area, and increased participation and opportunities for students to feel successful. The negative factors of separated intervention included the fact that students miss whole-group classroom instruction or activities with peers, the difficulties with scheduling, and the stigma associated with being labeled as a "reader" and leaving the classroom.

The comments by classroom teachers and reading specialists regarding the advantages and disadvantages of in-classroom support (see Tables 3 and 4) were focused on three areas: differentiating instruction, the physical learning environment, and potential for student improvement. Classroom teachers and reading specialists listed the following benefits of classroom support: (a) the opportunity for flexible grouping and peer reading models, (b) increased collaboration and communication between the reading

Table 1
Classroom Teachers' Survey Comments Regarding Separated Instruction

Positive aspects listed	Negative aspects listed
• *Small-group benefits*: Instruction without distractions from the class; taking time and not worrying about keeping up with other groups; students get small-group instruction and this allows them to feel comfortable to read; they are not as distracted by other stimuli in the classroom • *Individualized attention*: One-to-one ratio; ability to focus on students' individual needs • *Reading specialist instruction*: More chance to actively participate; better opportunity for interaction in a small-group setting; students get a preview or reinforcement of what is being done in class; pinpoint strategies needed for improvement; they work with a specialist and get fabulous support and instruction; extra time spent on concepts; reading teacher is specialized; reports of how students progress; direct instruction • *Classroom benefits*: Allows the regular education teacher to do more difficult large-group lessons; smaller class size • *Ability grouping*: Homogeneous group moves at same speed; reading level improved; leveled groups • *Quietness*: Quiet environment for students; less noise—easier to concentrate • *Daily reading sessions*: Regular schedule; chance to meet more times/on a daily basis; more classes can be served	• *Limited communication*: Communication between regular education teacher and reading teacher limited; sometimes we might not be at the same level because of time crunches and we do not see each other; overlapping titles of books • *Scheduling and accessibility*: Scheduling can be difficult; higher readers miss out on an opportunity to meet with a reading specialist to challenge them; time lapse in between traveling from room to room; not all at risk get serviced • *Socialization*: Removed from peers; other children want a turn to leave; being labeled as a "reader" by other students; some don't like being pulled out; self-esteem issues; child starts to realize they go to reading for a reason • *Classroom schedules and routines*: Watching what to teach so kids don't have to catch up; missing whole-group instruction; missing class work; with 20–25% of the class gone, I don't introduce new material while they are gone • *Limited reading with classroom teacher*: Difficult for classroom teacher to take reading grade for that 30 minutes; I see less of them to monitor progress

specialist and classroom teacher, and (c) having the reading specialists available in the classroom as a resource for the classroom teacher as well as readers at all ability levels. The drawbacks to in-classroom support instruction cited by teachers and reading specialists included the following: (a) an increased number of distractions by noise and space limitations, (b) inadequate planning time or a general lack of interest in collaboration, and (c) fewer opportunities for providing one-on-one instruction or remediation. The varied responses may possibly be attributed to the teaching styles, needs of students, or dynamics of the classroom.

As noted in Table 5, the scaled responses to the position statements were similar between classroom teachers and reading specialists, with the exception of the first statement. More than half of the classroom teachers agreed or strongly agreed that students who receive separated intervention miss classroom instruction or time to work on assignments, while more than half of the reading specialists disagreed or strongly disagreed with this statement.

Although the classroom teachers and reading specialists are aware of the positive and negative aspects of each form of intervention, the teachers are always willing to seek a variety

Table 2
Reading Specialists' Survey Comments Regarding Separated Instruction

Positive aspects listed	Negative aspects listed
• *Attention to specific needs*: Give more attention to group; learn the child's specific needs better and can address them • *Less distractions*: At-risk readers are often more distractible—focus can be better • *More time learning*: No lost time changing classes; less waste of time • *Materials available*: Materials are easily accessible, which means more flexibility with materials on hand for impromptu lessons or something a reader needs • *Control*: I control the structure and behavioral expectations; more space if classroom teacher's room is small or poorly managed • *Instructional benefits*: Students receive a double dose of reading instruction; intense instruction geared at small group; reading specialist can plan own lessons for at-risk readers; very distracted students and very low-performing students can use alternative approaches • *Quietness*: Quiet atmosphere; quiet working environment • *Active participation*: They can feel successful; students more willing to open up in reading discussions; small group allows students more opportunity to ask questions and participate	• *Professional interaction limited*: No opportunity for modeling for the classroom teacher by the reading specialist; lack of communication between specialist and classroom teacher • *Limited number of students benefit*: No positive peer role models for readers; working with less students; limited, not flexible, grouping • *Transition time*: Travel time equals less work time; kids lose time in traveling to the reading room • *Potential for problems*: Materials forgotten in classroom; students moving in/out of the building without supervision (modular classrooms outside); some students tend to act out in front of a small peer group • *Student confidence*: Older students sometimes feel labeled or embarrassed; pulled away from classmates; some kids feel singled out • *Scheduling whole-group instruction*: Classroom teacher is limited to what can be done while the students are out; miss assignment work time and sometimes instruction

of options and implement practices that will benefit the needs of all students. Teachers and reading specialists are visiting other reading programs or going to professional development events together to identify effective strategies that will benefit struggling readers. For instance, in one building, the principal redesigned building schedules to allow for uninterrupted blocks of literacy instruction, using the reading specialists as guided reading group models in the classroom. In another building at the third- and fourth-grade levels, classroom teachers are rotating students for specialist intervention based on need by using flexible grouping rather than keeping a static group from September to June. All buildings have implemented some form of before- or after-school intervention program, allowing for specialized instruction to prepare students for achievement tests or to provide skill reinforcement as needed.

Conclusions and Recommendations for Further Study

As educators, we constantly encounter students who struggle with reading. These students frequently fail standardized tests, and typically their needs cannot be met by the standard school curriculum. These struggling readers are instructionally needy. It is imperative that schools examine how reading instruction is implemented at each grade level. This may include having a reading specialist available

Table 3
Reading Specialists' Survey Comments Regarding In-Class Intervention

Positive aspects listed	Negative aspects listed
• *Collaboration and communication*: More time to collaborate with the classroom teacher by using a minute here or there; modeling for the classroom teacher by the reading specialist; teacher support • *More students work with reading specialist*: Affects entire classroom and teacher; more students are influenced; flexible grouping is more efficient; all students know reading specialist and grouping can be flexible based on skill being taught; allows peers with stronger abilities to be role models • *Reading specialist participation*: Classroom teacher and reading specialist are on the same page; connection to class work; hearing other lesson(s) being taught; work on same skills, topics, etc. as classroom teacher; gives reading teacher perspective on how at-risk readers are doing compared to peers • *Students stay in the classroom*: Student never leaves classroom; less travel time equals more instruction time; no student travel time lost	• *Potential for distractions*: Students distracted by other activities; at-risk students may not be as focused; confusion–loud–too many things going on in the classroom • *Instructional changes*: Students don't get double dose of reading instruction; can miss specific needs of a student that small pull-out group may reveal; loss of intensive instruction needed by struggling readers; not enough remediation skill work; less 1:1 time with specialist; still servicing the same number of kids • *Time*: Lose teaching time traveling from room to room and trading materials; being stopped in the hall by other teachers; need time to plan with teacher; not enough time in our reading service slots to do inclusion properly; students move much quicker than teachers! • *Limited space and materials*: Baggie book baskets not accessible; some teachers don't like to share their classroom; materials and space not readily available for reading teacher; some classrooms lack physical space for another group to be going on • *Teacher and specialist differences*: Some teaching styles don't match; classroom teacher and reading specialist may disagree on noise level/classroom management; teacher is not always ready to collaborate

at each grade level in each building, including one who works primarily with at-risk kindergarten students as a form of early intervention. A survey comment from a kindergarten teacher said, "Sometimes early intervention helps some children not need reading [intervention] in first and second grade," while another kindergarten teacher lamented that her students "do not receive enough intervention time because it is prioritized by fourth grade on down," because of the emphasis on statewide testing in the third and fourth grades.

Before trying a new approach to reading intervention in the classroom, it is important for a teacher or instructional team to reflect on responses to the following questions:

- What is the data telling us about our current methods? Are students who are receiving intervention services making progress as measured by formative and summative assessments?
- Can I make changes to my instructional routine to allow for more blocks of time for guided reading, and will a reading specialist be available to model effective guided reading lessons and strategies?
- As a grade level, or as a school, what are the best practices that we are currently using for effective reading instruction? Do we need to revisit these approaches or provide training for new staff members?

Table 4
Classroom Teachers' Survey Comments Regarding In-Class Intervention

Positive aspects listed	Negative aspects listed
• *Instructional consistency*: I can expand my teaching when necessary and not have to stop when they leave and come back to it when students return; can cover same skills at the same time; do what the rest of the class is doing; don't miss any instruction; follows my plans; aligning with your curriculum/current units is easier • *Mixed-ability groups*: Higher-level readers can be role models; more opportunities for small-group discussion • *Collaboration and mentoring*: Having another adult in the classroom who can help anyone or help me with guided reading groups would be great; extra expertise in the classroom; communication would be better between specialist and teacher • *Instructional support for all readers*: Students can still be working on same types of activities but differentiated instruction is better with two teachers available; able to help other students as well as those identified; gives higher readers a chance to work with reading intervention teacher to enhance and challenge • *Socialization*: Stay with peers; kids don't feel isolated; harder to identify the readers because they are being helped within the confines of the regular classroom; self-esteem	• *More distractions and less space*: Not enough room or table space for all groups to work; some lessons would not lend themselves to needing extra help from the (reading) teacher; if there are too many students in a classroom, it is nice to separate at times for noise level and distractions that happen just because of the amount of kids in one area at the same time; students have to ignore two different voices for independent work; interruptions • *Less small-group instruction*: Hard to work on specific needed skills with some lessons; distractions of classroom activities and environment; larger setting; perhaps they might miss out on more 1:1 instruction • *Different levels and needs*: Various levels; may feel bad because they don't know what other kids know; more obvious to other students that reading lab children are struggling; those not needing intervention taking time from those needing intervention • *Scheduling*: Needs to be scheduled during same time each day; scheduling will probably still be challenging; common planning?

- How often am I communicating with the reading specialist who works with my students? Does the reading specialist have additional resources that could be used to differentiate instruction for reading at all levels in my classroom?

By analyzing the feedback of district colleagues and sampling available research in the area of reading intervention, it is true that teachers can indeed teach children to read (Lose, 2007). There were no conclusive statements regarding the most effective model based on the feedback from the district's teachers and reading specialists; however, it is vital that a combination of effective separated and supportive instructional strategies be employed to address the unique learning needs of all students.

It is important to note that the results of the survey are a reflection of each teacher's perceptions, shaped by years of experience and professionalism regarding how to deliver instruction appropriate to the differentiated literacy skills of each child. Determining which reading intervention approach is best depends on the needs of students, the facilities and qualified personnel available, and the willingness of classroom teachers and reading specialists to collaborate to maximize quality instructional time and resources to improve student achievement.

Table 5
Classroom Teacher (CT) and Reading Specialist (RS) Statement Responses

	Strongly agree	Agree	Undecided	Disagree	Strongly disagree
Pulled-out students miss classroom instruction and/or time to work on assignments.	CT 20% RS 8%	CT 40% RS 8%	CT 17% RS 8%	CT 20% RS 58%	CT 3% RS 18%
Intervention reading lessons should match the lessons taught in the classroom.	CT 14% RS 16%	CT 34% RS 25%	CT 14% RS 16%	CT 29% RS 25%	CT 9% RS 18%
Reading specialists and classroom teachers communicate effectively.	CT 51% RS 42%	CT 31% RS 50%	CT 12% RS 0%	CT 3% RS 8%	CT 3% RS 0%
The same students qualify for reading service every year.	CT 9% RS 0%	CT 29% RS 34%	CT 9% RS 16%	CT 37% RS 50%	CT 16% RS 0%
Parents have concerns about intervention programs.	CT 9% RS 16%	CT 29% RS 16%	CT 9% RS 8%	CT 37% RS 42%	CT 16% RS 18%
More funding is needed for reading intervention programs.	CT 40% RS 50%	CT 40% RS 25%	CT 17% RS 25%	CT 0% RS 0%	CT 3% RS 0%
30 minutes a day is enough time for students to work with a reading specialist.	CT 20% RS 8%	CT 23% RS 16%	CT 26% RS 26%	CT 26% RS 42%	CT 5% RS 8%

References

Allington, R.L. (2001). *What really matters for struggling readers: Designing research-based programs.* New York: Addison Wesley.

Allington, R.L. (2004). Setting the record straight. *Educational Leadership, 61*(6), 22–25.

Bean, R.M. (2004). *The reading specialist: Leadership for the classroom, school, and community.* New York: Guilford.

Bean, R.M., Cassidy, J., Grumet, J.E., Shelton, D.S., & Wallis, S.R. (2002). What do reading specialists do? Results from a national survey. *The Reading Teacher, 55*(8), 736–744.

Dole, J.A. (2004). The changing role of the reading specialist in school reform. *The Reading Teacher, 57*(5), 462–471.

Edmondson, J., & Shannon, P. (2002). The will of the people. *The Reading Teacher, 55*(5), 452–454.

Hasbrouck, J., & Denton, C.A. (2007). Student-focused coaching: A model for reading coaches. *The Reading Teacher, 60*(7), 690–693.

Johnson, G.M. (2004). Constructivist remediation: Correction in context. *International Journal of Special Education, 19*(1), 72–88.

Lose, M. (2007). A child's response to intervention requires a responsive teacher of reading. *The Reading Teacher, 61*(3), 276–279.

Mesmer, E.M., & Mesmer, H.A.E. (2008). Response to Intervention (RTI): What teachers of reading need to know. *The Reading Teacher, 62*(4), 280–290.

Miles, P.A., Stegle, K.W., Hubbs, K.G., Henk, W.A., & Mallette, M.H. (2004). A whole-class support model for early literacy: The Anna Plan. *The Reading Teacher, 58*(4), 318–327.

National Institute of Child Health and Human Development. (2000). *Report of the National Reading Panel. Teaching children to read: An evidence-based assessment of the scientific research literature on reading and its implications for reading instruction* (NIH Publication No. 00-4769). Washington, DC: U.S. Government Printing Office.

Olson, L. (2001). Overboard on testing. *Education Week, 20*(17), 23–30.

Primeaux, J. (2000). Shifting perspectives on struggling readers. *Language Arts, 77*(6), 537–542.

Quatroche, D.J., Bean, R.M., & Hamilton, R.L. (2001). The role of the reading specialist: A review of research. *The Reading Teacher, 55*(3), 282–294.

U.S. Department of Education. (2006). *National assessment of Title I interim report: Executive summary.* Washington, DC: Institute of Education Sciences.

Valencia, S.W., & Buly, M.R. (2004). Behind test scores: What struggling readers really need. *The Reading Teacher, 57*(6), 520–531.

Ziolkowska, R. (2007). Early intervention for students with reading and writing difficulties. *Reading Improvement, 44*(2), 76–86.

Questions for Reflection

- Do you agree with the authors that collaborative planning between classroom teachers and reading specialists in order to assist struggling readers is often difficult to achieve and limited in many schools? What is one way you feel this issue could be better addressed in your school?
- The authors note that pullout reading instruction has a number of potential disadvantages. If you were to gather the same data the authors did, do you think teachers in your school or district would respond in similar ways regarding pullout programs? If pullout programs are in place in your school, what alternatives might be considered? What would be the advantages and disadvantages for students? For teachers?

Crossing Boundaries and Initiating Conversations About RTI: Understanding and Applying Differentiated Classroom Instruction

Doris Walker-Dalhouse, Victoria J. Risko, Cathy Esworthy, Ellen Grasley, Gina Kaisler, Dona McIlvain, and Mary Stephan

The reauthorized Individuals with Disabilities Education Improvement Act (IDEA, 2004) in the United States enables early identification of students experiencing academic problems, most often in reading, and a multi-tier instructional plan before evaluating students for specific learning disabilities. This legislation allows for models of Response to Intervention (RTI) as a method for identifying students who will profit from differentiated and appropriate instruction in the classroom. It is expected that differentiated instruction will reduce the overrepresentation of culturally and linguistically diverse students in special education placements or students experiencing difficulties because of inadequate instruction instead of a learning disability. Most states, including Tennessee and Wisconsin, are currently developing RTI models.

As coauthors of this column, we represent different areas of reading instructional practice: classroom teachers, reading specialists who teach children and provide district- and schoolwide professional development, and teacher educators.

We examine across geographical (Wisconsin and Tennessee) and school boundaries (urban and suburban) the current practices of teachers who are initiating RTI instruction and related research. We address three goals for RTI instruction, goals that were also addressed by the International Reading Association's (IRA) Commission on RTI (2009): providing systematic assessment of student performance, differentiated instruction, and high-quality professional development.

Systematic Assessment to Inform Differentiated Instruction

Although no specific assessments are required by the IDEA legislation, some states or school districts use a screening instrument to identify students' reading abilities and needs. Often this screening tool is narrowly conceived, measuring a small set of skills (e.g., letter sounds, rapid letter naming, oral reading fluency), limiting its usefulness for databased instructional planning. A comprehensive assessment is needed for identifying most appropriate instruction.

Some states are choosing one assessment tool for three purposes: screening, instructional planning, and progress monitoring. The certified RTI model in Minnesota uses the *Observation Survey of Literacy Achievement* (Clay, 2002) for all three purposes; thus, time is well spent collecting data with one instrument on multiple aspects

Walker-Dalhouse, D., Risko, V.J., Esworthy, C., Grasley, E., Kaisler, G., McIlvain, D., & Stephan, M. (2009). Crossing boundaries and initiating conversations about RTI: Understanding and applying differentiated classroom instruction. *The Reading Teacher, 63*(1), 84–87.

of children's literacy development (Reading Recovery Council of North America, 2009). The Wisconsin school represented here uses the *Classroom Assessment Based on Standards* to provide feedback on student performance and to identify struggling readers. Additional assessment measures vary according to grade level. The K–3 teachers use the *On-The-Mark Assessment Kit* (Wright Group, 2008) to measure word study skills, sight word fluency, and comprehension. Teachers add running records to monitor student progress as well as informal observations of students during small-group instruction. Our fifth-grade teacher in Wisconsin uses reading inventories and describes herself as a "real numbers person" who collects multiple forms of data to plan for small-group instruction.

The reading specialists and classroom teachers in the Tennessee school district administer several assessments that go beyond a screening instrument that focuses primarily on fluency and phonics. Similar to the Wisconsin fifth-grade teacher, these additional measures include individual reading inventories that assess oral reading and silent reading, word identification skills and strategies, vocabulary, and comprehension, including literal and deep understandings of texts. In both states, assessments are formative and aligned with state and local standards. Assessment tools that are multidimensional and ongoing, and that go beyond tests of single skills areas are most optimal for meeting RTI goals (McIntosh, Graves, & Gersten, 2007).

Providing Differentiated and Appropriate Instruction

Intense and differentiated instruction that is data based and appropriately implemented can mediate reading problems (O'Connor & Simic, 2002). Many states adopting RTI use three tiers of intervention (Berkeley, Bender, Peaster, & Saunders, 2009), with differentiated instruction for all students in the classroom initiated in Tier 1 based on assessments of students' current levels of performance. Additional, intensive, and systematic instruction is provided at Tiers 2 and 3, if reading problems persist.

In the Wisconsin and Tennessee schools of the coauthors, differentiated instruction has long been an important part of classroom literacy instruction. Teachers are implementing differentiated instruction through guided reading or reading and writing workshop formats with texts chosen to match students' abilities and skill needs and increase the amount of daily reading (Allington, 2001). Minilessons during whole-class instruction target skills and strategies that are then practiced with teacher guidance in small groups with leveled texts. Analysis of applications or reteaching occurs during individual conferences or additional small-group work. This instruction mirrors procedures described as highly effective by McIntosh et al. (2007) after examining teaching for Tiers 1 and 2 of RTI. Important within their study was the consistency and predictability of these instructional routines.

In the Wisconsin classrooms, reading materials are chosen to correspond to both instructional levels and content themes; thus, shared reading events and literacy instruction provide access to vocabulary and content for students who may not be reading these higher level texts during guided reading. Literacy workstations (Diller, 2005) are also used to reinforce core skills and to differentiate classroom work, while homework is differentiated by student needs, recorded on labels, and placed in homework notebooks.

In the Wisconsin and Tennessee schools, students select materials on the basis of their interests, recommended in differentiating instruction (Tobin, 2008), for independent reading, partner reading, and peer group discussions. Instruction focuses on multiple skills including both comprehension (e.g., use of strategies) and word study (e.g., use of keywords and rimes from the Integrated Strategies Approach; Allen, 1998). Instruction is evidence based (IRA, 2002), aligned with state and district standards, systematic, and focused on specific areas of instructional needs. The long-term goal is teachers assuming responsibility for adjusting instruction according to students' specific needs rather than following a predetermined skill sequence that may not match students' development. This form of teacher responsiveness requires careful guidance and expertise (McIntosh et al., 2007) but, optimally, provides timely mediation of problems when they occur.

Providing High-Quality Professional Development

Professional development is essential when implementing any systemic change. For RTI, in particular, communication and shared decision making is essential (Haager & Mahdavi, 2007). Classroom teachers need sustained support in their efforts to monitor student progress and determine effectiveness of instruction, in determining how to use daily observational data to identify modifications that may be required (Richards, Pavri, Golez, Canges, & Murphy, 2007), and determining how to address time management, especially in upper grades where departmental organizations can constrain instructional schedules and limit opportunities for individualizing instruction.

One professional development approach, applied by the Tennessee reading specialists, provides for coplanning by reading specialists and classroom teachers, demonstrations of implementation of planned instruction, and gradual release of teaching responsibility to the classroom teacher with feedback and additional cycles of coteaching (Literacy Collaborative, 2009). Observations and coaching by reading specialists are also recommended as follow-up options for supporting teachers and ensuring that the intervention principles are being implemented (Haager & Mahdavi, 2007).

Ongoing professional development is needed with attention to instruction, materials, and assessments that are especially appropriate for students with cultural and linguistic differences (Drame & Xu, 2008). A problem-solving model that emphasizes one-to-one professional development and facilitation by a designated case manager, preferably a reading specialist, is recommended to teach teachers more effective classroom intervention strategies. For example, the problem-solving, team-driven approach (Gravois & Rosenfield, 2006), which employs instructional consultation teams, was found to be effective in reducing the number of African American, special education referrals and is proposed as one way to help teachers differentiate instruction based on sociocultural factors. Traditional inservice professional development programs that are unresponsive to these factors will not help teachers gain the knowledge and skills needed to provide high-quality instruction for all students, especially culturally and linguistically diverse students (Xu & Drame, 2008).

In conclusion, RTI holds great promise for students experiencing reading difficulties for its emphasis on prevention rather than failure.

References

Allen, L. (1998). An integrated strategies approach: Making word identification instruction work for beginning readers. *The Reading Teacher, 52*(3), 254–268.

Allington, R.L. (2001). *What really matters for struggling readers: Designing research-based programs.* White Plains, NY:Longman/Pearson.

Berkeley, S., Bender, W.N., Peaster, L.G., & Saunders, L. (2009). Implementation of response to intervention: A snapshot of progress. *Journal of Learning Disabilities, 42*(1), 85–95.

Clay, M. (2002). *An observation survey of early literacy achievement.* Plymouth, NH:Heinemann.

Diller, D. (2005). *Practice with purpose: Literacy work stations for grades 3–6.* Portland, ME: Stenhouse.

Drame, E.R., & Xu, Y. (2008). Examining sociocultural factors in response to intervention models. *Childhood Education, 85*(1), 26–32.

Gravois, T.A., & Rosenfield, S.A. (2006). Impact of instructional consultation teams on the disproportionate referral and placement of minority students in special education. *Remedial and Special Education, 27*(1), 42–52.

Haager, D., & Mahdavi, J. (2007). Teacher roles in implementing interventions. In D. Haager, J. Klingner, & S. Vaughn (Eds.), *Evidence-based reading practices for response to intervention* (pp. 245–264). Baltimore: Paul H. Brookes.

Individuals with Disabilities Education Improvement Act of 2004, Pub.L.108-466.

International Reading Association. (2002). *What is evidence-based reading instruction?* (Position statement). Newark, DE: Author. Retrieved March 29, 2009, from www.reading.org/Libraries/Position_Statements_and_Resolutions/ps1055_evidence_based.sflb.ashx

International Reading Association Commission on RTI. (2009). *Working draft of guiding principles.* Retrieved March 29, 2009, from www.reading.org/General/Publications/ReadingToday/RTY-0902-rti.aspx

Literacy Collaborative. (2009). *Research of program effectiveness.* Retrieved March 30, 2009, from www.literacycollaborative.org/research/findings/

McIntosh, A.S., Graves, A., & Gersten, R. (2007). The effects of response to intervention on literacy development in multiple-language settings. *Learning Disability Quarterly, 30*(3), 197–212.

O'Connor, E.A., & Simic, O. (2002). The effect of Reading Recovery on special education referrals and placements. *Psychology in the Schools, 39*(6), 635–646.

Reading Recovery Council of North America. (2009). *Reading Recovery and IDEA legislation: Early Intervening Service (EIS) and Response to Intervention (RTI).* Retrieved March 29, 2009, from www.readingrecovery.org/pdf/reading_recovery/SPED_Brief-07.pdf

Richards, C., Pavri, S., Golez, F., Canges, R., & Murphy, J. (2007). Response to intervention: Building the capacity of teachers to serve students with learning difficulties. *Issues in Teacher Education, 16*(2), 55–64.

Tobin, R. (2008). Conundrums in the differentiated literacy classroom. *Reading Improvement, 45*(4), 159–169.

Wright Group. (2008). *On-the-mark assessment kit.* Desoto, TX: Wright/Pearson.

Xu, Y., & Drame, E. (2008). Culturally appropriate context: Unlocking the potential of response to intervention for English language learners. *Early Childhood Education Journal, 35*(4), 305–311.

Questions for Reflection

- The assessments used in the schools described differ in many ways from those used in many RTI projects. What are the advantages of using the assessments mentioned in the article?
- The authors note that it is the long-term responsibility of teachers to provide differentiated reading instruction based on student need rather than on a predetermined set of skills and strategies. Is this the framework your RTI plan uses?

Response to Intervention (RTI): What Teachers of Reading Need to Know

Eric M. Mesmer and Heidi Anne E. Mesmer

In the most recent "What's hot, what's not for 2008?" *Reading Today* survey, 75% of prominent literacy researchers believed that Response to Intervention (RTI) was "very hot" and the same percentage believed that it should be "hot" (Cassidy & Cassidy, 2008). RTI is a new approach to identifying students with specific learning disabilities and represents a major change in special education law, the Individuals With Disabilities Act (IDEA). This change shifts the emphasis of the identification process toward providing support and intervention to struggling students early and is similarly reflected in the Reading First provisions of No Child Left Behind, which calls for proven methods of instruction to reduce the incidence of reading difficulties. RTI will alter the work of reading teachers because more than 80% of students identified for special education struggle with literacy (Lyon, 1995), and the law names "reading teachers" as qualified participants in the RTI process because of the International Reading Association's (IRA, 2007) lobbying efforts. However, RTI has only recently attracted the attention of the reading community (Bell, 2007), despite having roots in approaches such as prereferral intervention (Flugum & Reschly, 1994; Fuchs, Fuchs, & Bahr, 1990), curriculum-based measurement (Shinn, 1989), and Reading Recovery (Clay, 1987; Lyons & Beaver, 1995).

RTI in Theory

Background and Rationale

RTI was developed because of the many problems with the discrepancy model for identifying students with learning disabilities (e.g., Francis et al., 2005; O'Malley, Francis, Foorman, Fletcher, & Swank, 2002; Stanovich, 2005; Vellutino, Scanlon, & Lyon, 2000; Walmsley & Allington, 2007). In 1977, a learning disability was defined as "a severe discrepancy between achievement and intellectual ability" (U.S. Department of Education, 1977, p. G1082). In practice, this involves schools administering IQ tests and achievement tests and then examining scores for discrepancies between intellect and achievement to identify a learning disability (see Table 1). The discrepancy model has drawn four major criticisms. First, it requires that a learning problem becomes considerably acute in terms of an IQ/achievement discrepancy before a learner can receive additional support, a problem called "waiting to fail" (Vaughn & Fuchs, 2003, p. 139). Second, establishing a discrepancy is not necessary to improve outcomes for struggling readers, as students both with and without a discrepancy are qualitatively the same in their literacy instructional needs (Fuchs, Mock, Morgan, & Young, 2003; Vellutino et al., 2000). Third, the IQ/achievement discrepancy has shifted focus away from understanding the impact of other possible factors, such as opportunities to learn (Walmsley & Allington, 2007). These factors need to be considered prior to determining that a learning disability exists. Fourth, under the discrepancy model, many districts and states have seen skyrocketing percentages of students identified as learning disabled, particularly minorities (IRA, 2007; Walmsley & Allington, 2007).

Reprinted from Mesmer, E.M., & Mesmer, H.A.E. (2008). Response to Intervention (RTI): What teachers of reading need to know. *The Reading Teacher, 62*(4), 280–290.

Table 1
Definitions of RTI Terms

Term	Definition
Discrepancy model	The standard for identifying students with learning disabilities based on the 1977 federal regulations. This process required that a significant difference be documented between a student's ability (IQ) and achievement in order for a learning disability to be identified. RTI models respond to the many problems identified with the discrepancy model.
Intervention	Targeted instruction provided in addition to the regular classroom program that addresses a student's documented instructional needs; instruction that intends to prevent students who are struggling from falling farther behind their peers and intends to improve their future educational trajectory.
Level data	Information that reflects how students are performing in comparison to peers at a specific point in time.
Slope data	Information that reflects how a student is learning across time in comparison to his or her previous learning. These data capture rate of learning and can also be called growth rates. Slopes that are steeper show more growth over a smaller period of time than slopes that are flatter. Slope data are obtained by repeatedly measuring student performance in a particular area. They are displayed using a line graph.
Student progress monitoring	An assessment technique required by RTI regulations. Teachers administer quick assessments (1–5 minutes) frequently (weekly) to gauge the improvement of a student. The assessments provide information about the student's rate of learning and the effectiveness of a particular intervention (National Center on Student Progress Monitoring, 2007).
Literacy screening	The process of assessing the most basic and predictive literacy skills for all students in a school. The goal of screenings is to select learners whose reading achievement is significantly below standards. Literacy screenings are intended to identify students who require additional help so that further slippage and literacy failure can be prevented.

The Law

In 2004, IDEA, Public Law 108-446, introduced RTI language (U.S. Department of Education, 2006). In Table 2, the section entitled "Specific learning disabilities" (§ 300.307) asserts that states cannot be required to use the discrepancy model for identifying learning disabilities but may "permit the use of a process based on the child's response to scientific, research-based intervention." This is RTI, a process measuring whether a learner's academic performance improves when provided with well-defined, scientifically based interventions. In an RTI model, the "tests" of whether students possess learning disabilities are not standardized measures but students' measured responses to interventions. Within RTI, student potential (IQ) is replaced by a goal that allows for the evaluation of a performance relative to a defined academic standard (e.g., performance of other students in the class or grade level). Students responding quickly and significantly to interventions are less likely to possess a disability than students responding more slowly or not at all. However, data showing a student's response to an intervention serves as only one source of information for determining whether a learning disability is present. Learning disabilities cannot be diagnosed when appropriate instruction, socioeconomic status, culture,

Table 2
Additional Procedures for Identifying Children With Specific Learning Disabilities

IDEA terminology	IDEA definition
§ 300.307 Specific learning disabilities.	A State must adopt, consistent with 34 CFR 300.309, criteria for determining whether a child has a specific learning disability as defined in 34 CFR 300.8(c)(10). In addition, the criteria adopted by the State: • Must not require the use of a severe discrepancy between intellectual ability and achievement for determining whether a child has a specific learning disability, as defined in 34 CFR 300.8(c)(10); • Must permit the use of a process based on the child's response to scientific, research-based intervention; and • May permit the use of other alternative research-based procedures for determining whether a child has a specific learning disability, as defined in 34 CFR 300.8(c)(10). A public agency must use the State criteria adopted pursuant to 34 CFR 300.307(a) in determining whether a child has a specific learning disability. [34 CFR 300.307] [20 U.S.C. 1221e-3; 1401(30); 1414(b)(6)]
§ 300.309 Determining the existence of a specific learning disability.	The group described in 34 CFR 300.306 may determine that a child has a specific learning disability, as defined in 34 CFR 300.8(c)(10), if: • The child does not achieve adequately for the child's age or to meet State-approved grade-level standards in one or more of the following areas, when provided with learning experiences and instruction appropriate for the child's age or State-approved grade-level standards: • Oral expression. • Listening comprehension. • Written expression. • Basic reading skills. • Reading fluency skills. • Reading comprehension. • Mathematics calculation. • Mathematics problem solving. • The child does not make sufficient progress to meet age or State-approved grade-level standards in one or more of the areas identified in 34 CFR 300.309(a)(1) when using a process based on the child's response to scientific, research-based intervention; or the child exhibits a pattern of strengths and weaknesses in performance, achievement, or both, relative to age, State-approved grade-level standards, or intellectual development, that is determined by the group to be relevant to the identification of a specific learning disability, using appropriate assessments, consistent with 34 CFR 300.304 and 300.305; and the group determines that its findings under 34 CFR 300.309(a)(1) and (2) are not primarily the result of: • A visual, hearing, or motor disability; • Mental retardation; • Emotional disturbance; • Cultural factors; • Environmental or economic disadvantage; or • Limited English proficiency. To ensure that underachievement in a child suspected of having a specific learning disability is not due to lack of appropriate instruction in reading or math, the group must consider, as part of the evaluation described in 34 CFR 300.304 through 300.306: • Data that demonstrate that prior to, or as a part of, the referral process, the child was provided appropriate instruction in regular education settings, delivered by qualified personnel; and • Data-based documentation of repeated assessments of achievement at reasonable intervals, reflecting formal assessment of student progress during instruction, which was provided to the child's parents.

Note. From U.S. Department of Education. (2006). *Assistance to states for the education of children with disabilities and preschool grants for children with disabilites* (Federal register 34 CFR Parts 300 and 301). Washington, DC: Author.

sensory issues, emotional issues, or English as a second language may be of concern.

In the section entitled "Determining the existence of a specific learning disability" (§300.309), the law states that a learning disability may be present when a student's performance is not adequate to meet grade-level standards when provided with appropriate instruction and research-based interventions. The term *appropriate* refers to instruction in the classroom that matches a student's skill level. The descriptors *scientific* or *research-based* indicate that interventions should be based on practices that have produced verifiable results through research studies.

RTI Processes

The processes undergirding RTI have been used for evaluating the success of schoolwide supports, individualized interventions, and special education (O'Connor, Fulmer, Harty, & Bell, 2005; Powell-Smith & Ball, 2002; Taylor-Greene et al., 1997). However, in this article we focus on RTI as an initial referral and identification process for students suspected of having learning disabilities.

Step 1

Universal literacy practices are established. Prevention begins with universal literacy screenings to identify students who could be at risk (see Table 3). Any state receiving Reading First monies has identified a literacy screening in grades K–3. All students are screened on basic literacy skills approximately three times per year. Typically, student performance is compared with minimal benchmark scores and students not meeting benchmarks receive help.

Step 2

Scientifically valid interventions are implemented. When students do not meet benchmarks, they need additional instruction. Within most RTI models, interventions are first delivered to a small group and are intended to assist students in developing skills that will allow them to improve their reading skills.

Step 3

Progress of students receiving intervention instruction is monitored. RTI requires that progress-monitoring data are continuously collected as students receive interventions. Progress-monitoring assessments should address the skills that are being targeted for intervention and should indicate if the intervention is changing the student's reading. Also, the assessments should be administered repeatedly (weekly or biweekly) without introducing test-wise bias, which occurs when the results of an assessment reflect the testtaker's acquired knowledge about a test rather than true performance. In addition, the assessments should be sufficiently sensitive to small changes in the student's reading

Table 3
Examples of Literacy Screening Assessments

Screener	Authors
Dynamic Indicators of Basic Early Literacy Skills (DIBELS)	Good & Kaminski, 2002
Phonological Awareness Literacy Screening (PALS)	Invernizzi, Juel, Swank, & Meier, 2005
Texas Primary Reading Inventory (TPRI)	Texas Education Agency & University of Texas System, 2006
Illinois Snapshots of Early Literacy (ISEL)	Illinois State Board of Education, 2004

performance (i.e., those that might occur within a few days) because if students are showing growth on the more sensitive, microlevel progress-monitoring measures, they will also be showing growth in the more comprehensive measures (Deno, Mirkin, & Chiang, 1982; Fuchs & Deno, 1981; Riedel, 2007). Finally, progress-monitoring measures must be reliable, valid, and brief (National Center on Student Progress Monitoring, 2007). For a list of tools for progress monitoring, see the National Center on Student Progress Monitoring website at [www.rti4success.org/chart/progressMonitoring/progressmonitoringtoolschart.htm].

Step 4

Individualize interventions for students who continue to struggle. Students who continue to struggle despite receiving initial intervention instruction will require more intense, targeted interventions. These interventions may require additional assessments to clarify the nature of the difficulty. The data generated from these additional assessments should be used collaboratively by teachers, reading specialists, school psychologists, and parents to develop more intensive intervention strategies. Upon implementation, the student's progress continues to be monitored.

Step 5

A decision-making process to determine eligibility for special education services occurs when necessary. In the last step, a team of school-based professionals and the student's parents review all data to determine whether the student is eligible for special education services. Special services may be indicated when the student has not responded to interventions that have been well implemented for a sufficient period of time. If the team suspects that the student's lack of response may be explained by some other factor (i.e., not explained by a learning disability), then it should request additional assessment of the student's social, behavioral, emotional, intellectual, and adaptive functioning.

RTI in Real Life: Making a Difference for Mark

To illustrate RTI processes, we use a vignette (with pseudonyms) based on our experiences in schools. This vignette shows how a team including Donisha, a reading teacher, Julie, a special educator, Carol, a second-grade teacher, and Sandra, a school psychologist, worked collaboratively (and sometimes painstakingly) within an RTI model to assist a student named Mark.

Step 1: Universal Literacy Practices Are Established

In September, Mark was administered the Phonological Awareness and Literacy Screening (PALS; Invernizzi, Juel, Swank, & Meier, 2005), an assessment that begins with two screening measures, the first-grade word list, given in the fall of grade 2, and a spelling assessment. From these measures, an entry benchmark score is formed. If the benchmark score does not meet the grade-level minimum, then additional diagnostics are administered (preprimer and primer lists, letter naming, letter sounds, concept of word, blending, and sound-to-letter). Students also read passages through which accuracy, reading rate, phrasing (a 3-point subjective scale), and comprehension scores are collected.

In the fall, Mark received a benchmark score of 22 (7/20 on the first-grade word list) and 15/20 on the spelling assessment. An expected benchmark score of 35, based on 15 words on the first-grade list, and 20 spelling feature points is expected for the beginning of second grade. Mark read instructionally at the primer level (1.1) with moderate phrasing and expression and answered five-sixths of the questions correctly. He read the 120 words in the primer story in 4 minutes and 20 seconds, a rate of about 28 words correct per minute (WCPM) and 20 words below the 50th percentile for second graders in the fall (Parker, Hasbrouck, & Tindal, 1992). When diagnostic assessments were administered, data showed that Mark had mastered alphabetic skills, such as phonemic awareness and letters. Carol described her initial analysis: "Mark seemed to have the basic building blocks for reading but needed more practice at his level." Initially, Mark received small-group classroom instruction, including reading daily in on-level materials and working with Carol on comprehension and decoding. In September, October, and November, Carol took running records on the books that Mark and the other students had been reading. Although the accuracy and book levels of other students were steadily increasing, Mark's accuracy was averaging 90% in less difficult books. Carol explained, "I felt like Mark needed more help, and we needed to act because I was concerned that he would continue to fall behind."

Step 2: Scientifically Valid Interventions Are Implemented

RTI requires that instructional interventions be scientifically valid, public, implemented with integrity, and systematically evaluated. Julie, who had recently attended the district's RTI workshop, explained that "The who, what, when, where, and how of interventions must be clear." The content of the intervention should be designated, the teacher responsible for implementing it identified, and the assessments determined. Often different team members plan, implement, or assess the intervention based on availability and expertise. For this reason, educators must collaborate and share information.

The team discussed Mark's needs and designed an intervention. Based upon its review of the data, the team determined that accurate, fluent reading in connected text seemed to be the problem. Mark could easily understand books above his reading level, but his progress was being impeded by word recognition. The group decided that an intervention increasing the amount of reading practice for Mark would build up his reading level. The designed intervention comprised the following components: modeling of fluent reading, repeated readings, error correction, comprehension questions, and self-monitoring. They decided that Donisha would implement the intervention with three other students in the classroom in 20-minute sessions, three times per week. In addition, Carol continued to work with Mark in the classroom during small-group instruction. Specifically, she had Mark read from the same materials used by Donisha to further increase practice opportunities, and she set a daily goal for Mark on comprehension questions. Mark checked his answers each day and provided the results to his teacher at the end of the reading block.

Step 3: Progress of Students Receiving Intervention Instruction Is Monitored

As the intervention was implemented, Sandra tracked Mark's accuracy and fluency in reading passages at the primer and second-grade levels, because the goal was to understand Mark's progress toward grade-level norms. She used a PDA device loaded with passages at different levels. As Mark read these passages weekly, Sandra kept track of his accuracy (percentage of words correct) and reading rate (WCPM). Figure 1 shows Mark's accuracy and Figure 2 shows his reading rate before and after implementing the intervention for six weeks. Mark demonstrated some gains in accuracy and fluency, but his progress was not increasing at a rate that would allow him to meet established second-grade goals.

As we have described RTI to this point, it sounds smooth and trouble free. But it was anything but that for the professionals involved. Donisha's first reaction to RTI was strong:

> At first, I felt like this group was shrinking reading down to something very simplistic. I had to advocate for comprehension questions to be included in the intervention. Even though Mark's comprehension was fine, we did not want him to believe that comprehension didn't matter. We also clarified that interventions are *additive* and by nature narrower because their power lies in solving specific problems. The comprehensive reading program is broad and multifaceted, and it keeps going on while a child is receiving an intervention. So Carol wasn't going to stop guided reading or doing the rest of her program.

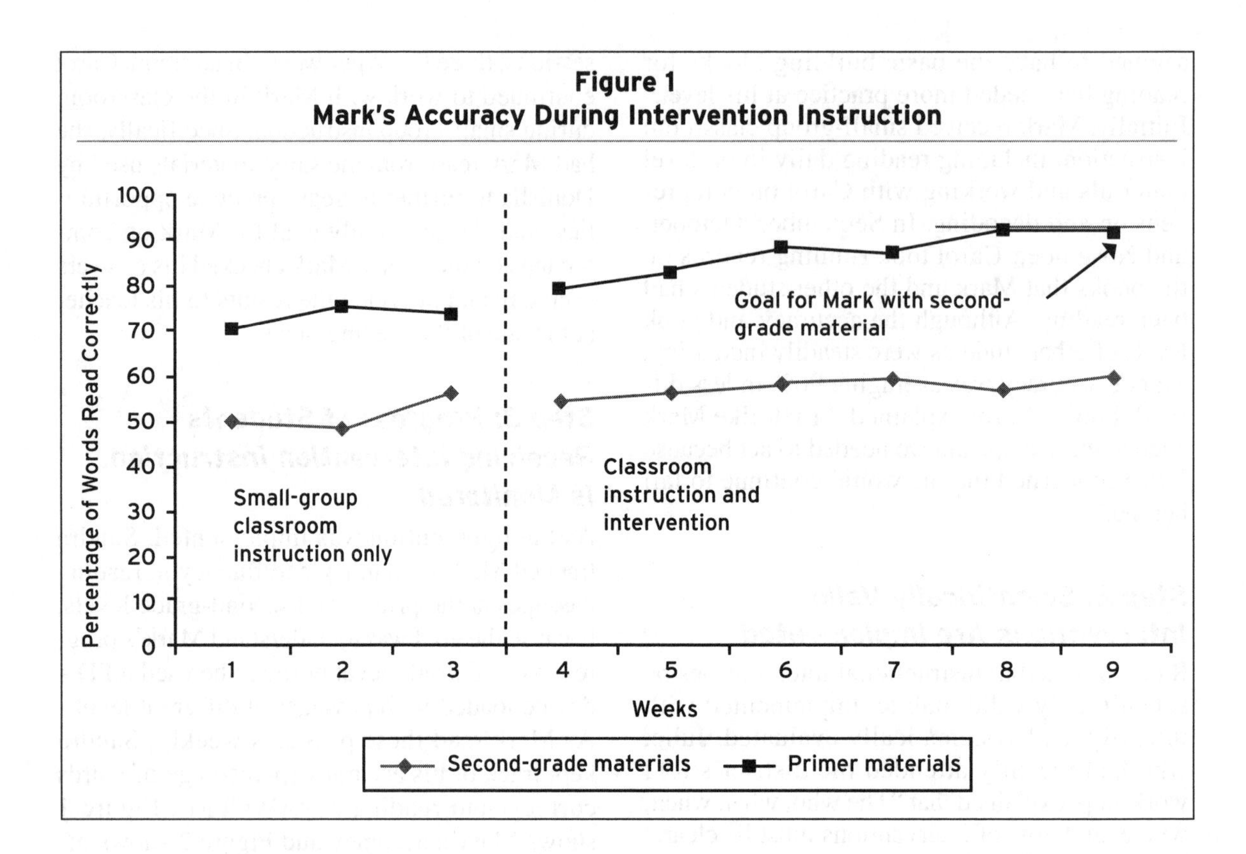

We liken the intervention and the reading program to a balanced diet. The intervention is like an extra serving of milk, but it doesn't replace meat, fruits, or vegetables.

Donisha was also concerned that the intervention would be scripted. Scripts are directions to teachers that are read verbatim during instruction. Interventions are specific and systematic, but nothing in the law requires them to be scripted.

Carol also had concerns. "I was not used to people asking me specific questions about exactly what I was doing, and how often, and what my results were. At first, it felt invasive and suspicious." Given the frequency with which blame is placed on classroom teachers, Carol's reaction was understandable. However, the team members pointed out that the instruction was working well for almost all of the other students and acknowledged the time limitations and demands placed on Carol as a classroom teacher. Although she had felt it in the past, Carol did not feel as though fingers were being pointed at her. Sandra had faced equal frustration before:

> I come in because a teacher has a concern and when I start asking questions, I get tight responses and defensiveness. It's like asking questions is stepping on toes. I can't help others further understand the problem or contribute to a useful intervention if we can't talk nitty-gritty. Once I had a teacher tell me, "You're not a teacher. You won't be able to help." While I am not a teacher, I can contribute to the development of interventions, and I have particular skill in measuring effects.

In addition to reviewing Mark's progress during the six weeks of intervention instruction, Mark's mid-year PALS scores were evaluated by the team. He was independent at the primer (1.1) level and barely instructional at the first-grade level with 14 errors and a reading rate of 42 WCPM. Despite his increase in instructional

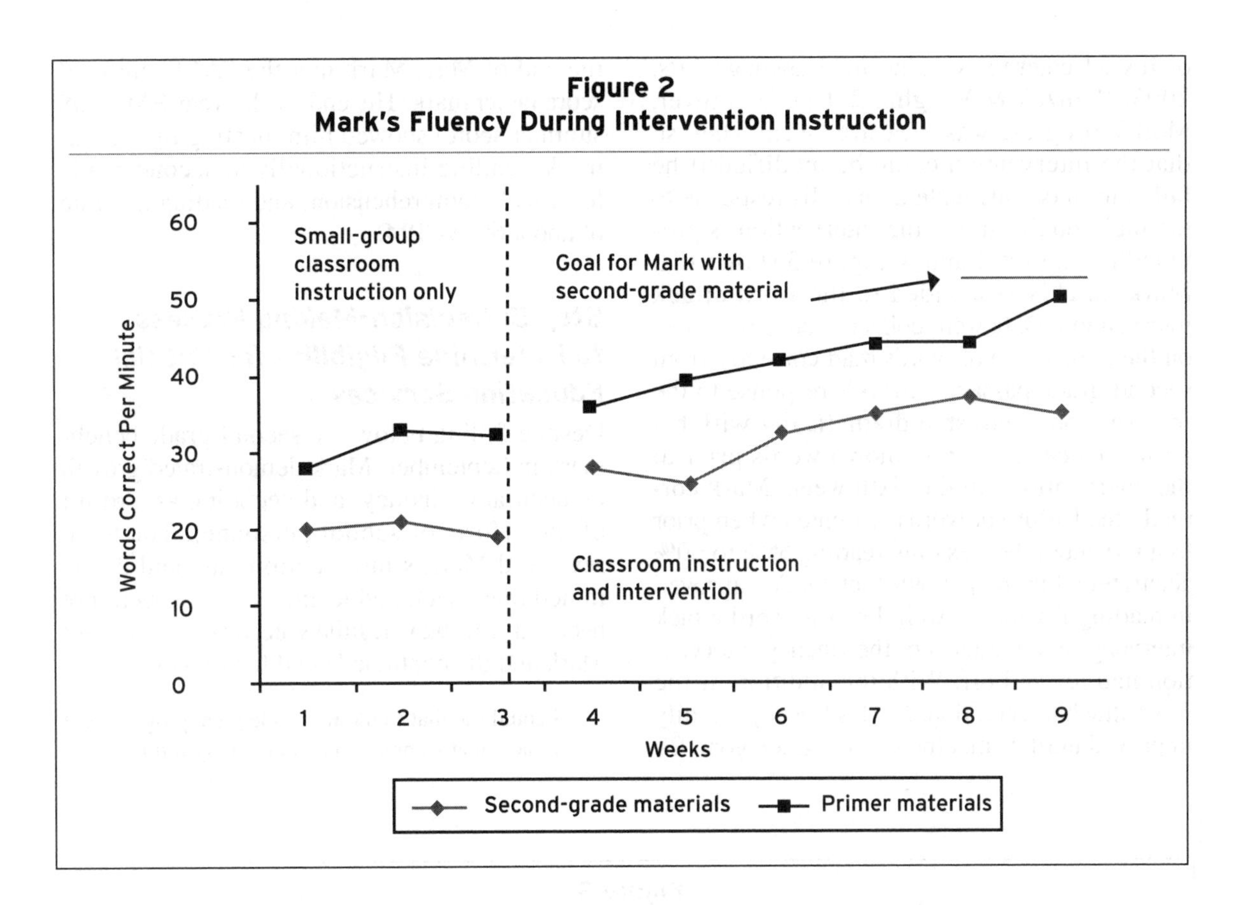

level and fluency, the team remained concerned about the lack of reduction in the number of errors that Mark was making. The team decided that these errors would ultimately become detrimental to Mark's fluency and comprehension, particularly as text increased in difficulty. The team determined that individualized intervention was warranted.

Step 4: Individualize Interventions for Students Who Continue to Struggle

Because they had no measure of decoding, the team decided to assess Mark using the Word Attack Test from the Woodcock Reading Mastery Test. Results from this assessment revealed that Mark was having difficulty decoding words with more than one syllable or those that contained difficult vowel patterns. This resulted in reduced accuracy and fluency. The team enhanced the intervention by adding practice with problem words. Mark practiced incorrectly read words, received instruction in how to analyze word parts, extended analytic skills to similar words, and practiced through word sorts. Following word sorts, Mark read each word within a sentence. Donisha implemented this individualized intervention for 10 minutes each day following the reading practice intervention (discussed earlier in the article).

Mark's reading accuracy and fluency continued to be monitored weekly by Sandra. The team determined that the intervention would be implemented for a minimum of 6 weeks, as this time frame would correspond with the end of the school year. However, the team recognized that interventions in early literacy often need to run longer, between 10 and 20 weeks, depending on factors such as the needs of the student and the intensity of the intervention (University of Texas Center for Reading and Language Arts, 2003; Wanzek & Vaughn, 2008). Moreover, Mark's progress was measured each week so that the intervention could be modified if he failed to make adequate gains. His response to the individualized reading intervention is provided in Figures 3 and 4. Figure 3 shows that Mark quickly responded to the word attack intervention. Data were collected once per week on the percentage of words read correctly from second-grade passages. Mark's response to the intervention contrasted dramatically with his performance reading unknown words prior to the intervention. By the sixth week, Mark correctly read 100% of words presented when prior to intervention he was only reading 55% to 60% accurately. Figure 4 shows that Mark improved in reading fluency as well. Prior to word attack intervention, the effects of the fluency intervention had leveled off. With the addition of the word attack intervention, Mark's fluency steadily improved until he met the second-grade goal. By the end of May, Mark met the PALS summed score benchmark. His end-of-the-year PALS (58 summer score) showed him meeting the benchmark, reading instructionally at second-grade level with comprehension, and reading at a rate of about 60 WCPM.

Step 5: Decision-Making Process to Determine Eligibility for Special Education Services

Despite falling below the second-grade benchmark in September, Mark demonstrated growth on accuracy, fluency, and decoding as a result of the efforts of school personnel. The team reviewed Mark's intervention data and determined that special education services were not necessary. However, Julie voiced concerns about Mark and the continued need for support:

> I could see that Mark had made great progress, but I knew that summer could potentially influence his

Figure 3
Mark's Accuracy During Individualized Intervention

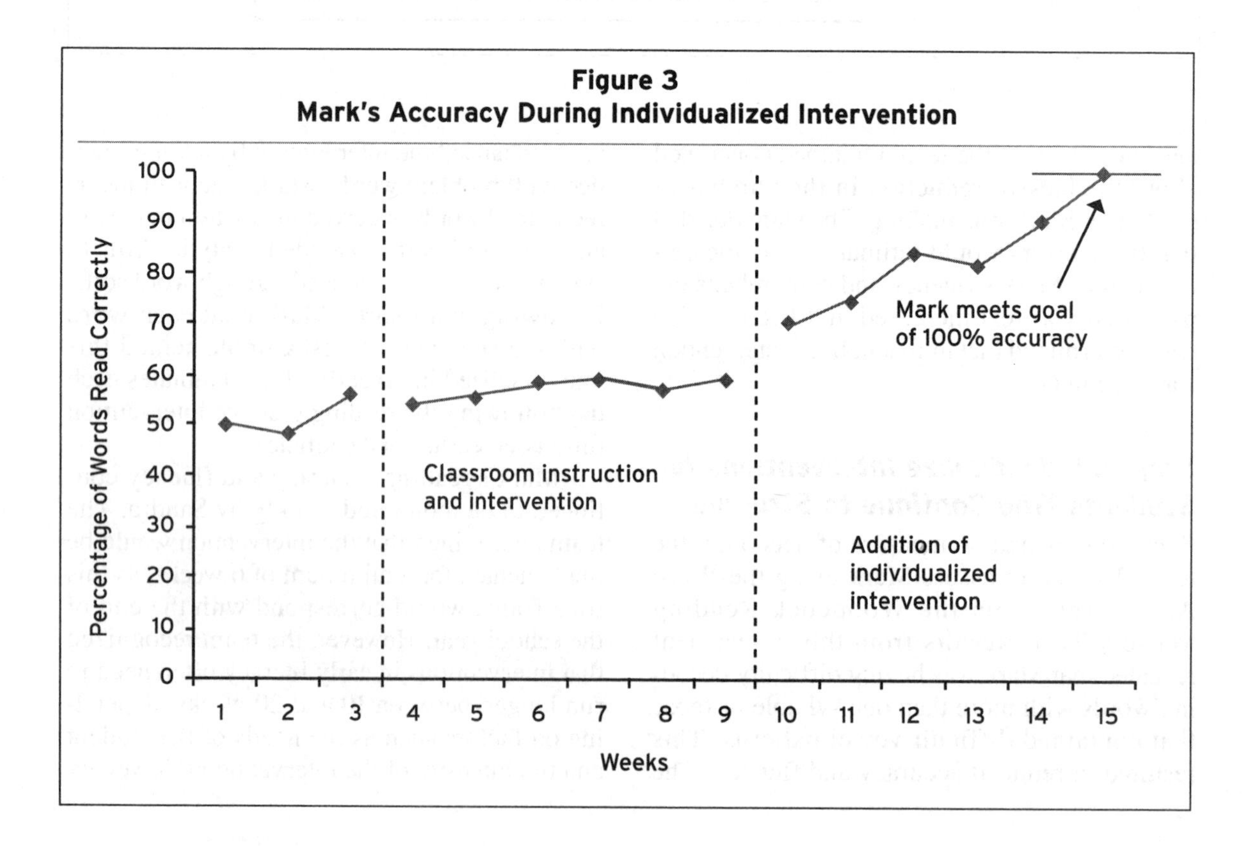

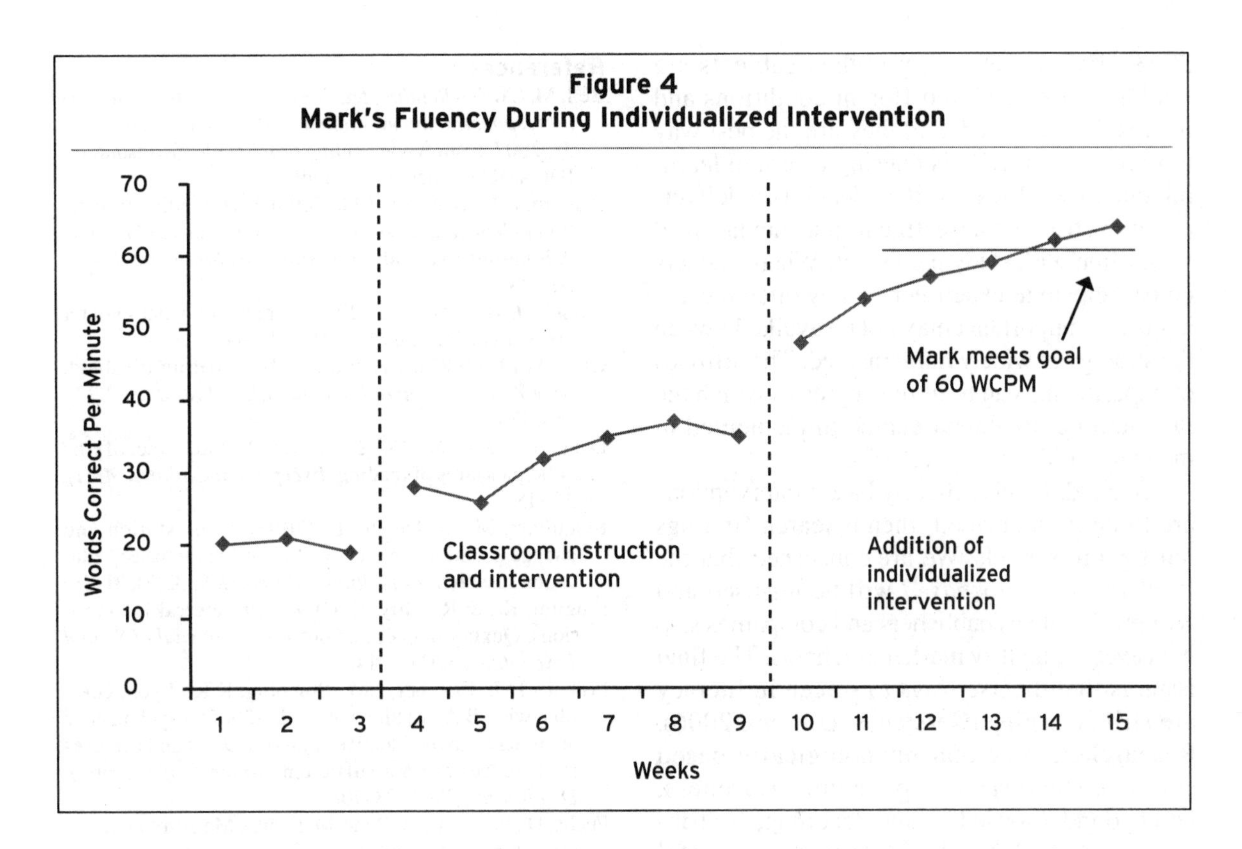

> starting point in the fall and that his progress was the result of substantive instruction *in addition* to the regular classroom. So I insisted that a meeting be scheduled for him in the fall to be proactive about his needs.

Mark's progress was significant relative to where his skills were at the beginning of the year. If the interventions had not met Mark's needs, the team would have been charged with determining whether the lack of response was indicative of a learning disability.

Why RTI?

As illustrated, RTI is a process that incorporates both assessment and intervention so that immediate benefits come to the student. Assessment data are used to inform interventions and determine the effectiveness of them. As a result of the intervention-focused nature of RTI, eligibility services shift toward a supportive rather than sorting function. A testing model that identifies and sorts students into programs or services is predicated upon the effectiveness of those services. Unfortunately, the effectiveness of special education, particularly placement of students in separate classrooms, has been variable at best (Bentum & Aaron, 2003; Kavale, 1990), even as an increasing percentage of students have been identified as learning disabled over the past 30 years (Gresham, 2002). Within the RTI model, instruction can at last be addressed.

Queries, Concerns, and Future Research

We have worked with state departments of education, school districts, schools, and teachers long enough to have questions about RTI. The first issue is that definitions of scientific research privilege experimental and quasi-experimental research (Eisenhart & Towne, 2003; Pressley,

2003). Experiments occur when subjects are randomly assigned to different conditions and the results measured, and they are the best way to know if a practice is causing a certain learning outcome. However, they depend on delivering an instructional treatment in a standardized way, often with study personnel. When teachers do participate in experiments, they often receive intensive support that may not be available when the strategy is widely implemented. The artifices of experiments can limit the degree to which the instructional treatment can be implemented in the real world (Pressley, 2003).

Second, if scientifically based interventions are to be implemented, then research findings must get to schools. We are concerned that the label *scientifically based* will be misused and will proliferate as publishers and companies slap it on everything they market to schools. The final issue is that diverse ways to screen in literacy are still emerging (Gersten & Dimino, 2006). Researchers note that phonologically based competencies, such as phoneme awareness, letter/sound knowledge, and decoding, contribute to part of what makes a student a successful reader (Gersten & Dimino, 2006; Paris, 2005; Scarborough, 2005). Readers must also have a deep knowledge of word meanings and be able to comprehend text. We know oral reading fluency is a good predictor of grade 1 comprehension (Riedel, 2007) but powerful, direct screenings in the areas of vocabulary and comprehension have yet to be developed for elementary learners. Nonetheless, intervening in these areas is important despite the fact that few screening tools exist.

Despite the challenges with RTI, we have seen this approach increase the quantity and quality of instruction for struggling readers. RTI is an initial attempt to provide an alternative to the dominant and damaging discrepancy model in which so much time is spent admiring the student's reading problem. By this we mean people discuss the problem, collect data on it, and write about it, months before they *do* anything about it. IDEA 2004 provides school districts with a choice to opt out of the discrepancy model.

References

Bell, M. (2007). *Reading teachers play key role in successful response to intervention approaches.* Retrieved May 31, 2007, from www.reading.org/downloads/resources/IDEA_RTI_teachers_role.pdf

Bentum, K.E., & Aaron, P.G. (2003). Does reading instruction in learning disability resource rooms really work? A longitudinal study. *Reading Psychology, 24*(3–4), 361–382.

Cassidy, J., & Cassidy, D. (2008). What's hot, what's not for 2008? *Reading Today, 25*(4), 1, 10–11.

Clay, M.M. (1987). Learning to be learning disabled. *New Zealand Journal of Educational Studies, 22*(2), 155–173.

Deno, S.L., Mirkin, P.K., & Chiang, B. (1982). Identifying valid measures of reading. *Exceptional Children, 49*(1), 36–45.

Eisenhart, M., & Towne, L. (2003). Contestation and change in national policy on "scientifically based" education research. *Educational Researcher, 32*(7), 31–38.

Flugum, K., & Reschly, D. (1994). Prereferral interventions: Quality indices and outcomes. *Journal of School Psychology, 32*(1), 1–14.

Francis, D.J., Fletcher, J.M., Stuebing, K.K., Lyon, G.R., Shaywitz, B.A., & Shaywitz, S.E. (2005). Psychometric approaches to the identification of LD: IQ and achievement scores are not sufficient. *Journal of Learning Disabilities, 38*(2), 98–108.

Fuchs, D., Fuchs, L., & Bahr, M. (1990). Mainstream assistance teams: A scientific basis for the art of consultation. *Exceptional Children, 57*(2) 128–139.

Fuchs, D., Mock, D., Morgan, P.L., & Young, C.L. (2003). Responsiveness-to-intervention: Definitions, evidence, and implications for the learning disabilities construct. *Learning Disabilities: Research & Practice, 18*(3), 157–171.

Fuchs, L.S., & Deno, S.L. (1981). *The relationship between curriculum-based mastery measures and standardized achievement tests in reading* (Research Report No. 57). Minneapolis: University of Minnesota Institute for Research on Learning Disabilities. (ERIC Document Reproduction Service No. ED212662)

Gersten, R., & Dimino, J.A. (2006). RTI (Response to Intervention): Rethinking special education for students with reading difficulties (again). *Reading Research Quarterly, 41*(1), 99–108.

Good, R., & Kaminski, R. (2002). *DIBELS oral reading fluency passages for first through third grades* (Technical Report 10). Eugene: University of Oregon.

Gresham, F. (2002). Responsiveness to intervention: An alternative approach to the identification of learning disabilities. In R. Bradley, L. Danielson, & D. Hallahan (Eds.), *Identification of learning disabilities: Research to practice* (pp. 467–519). Mahwah, NJ: Erlbaum.

Illinois State Board of Education. (2008). *Illinois Snapshots of Early Literacy.* Retrieved June 5, 2007, from www.isbe.state.il.us/curriculum/reading/html/isel.htm

International Reading Association. (2007). *Implications for reading teachers in Response to Intervention (RTI).* Retrieved May 31, 2007, from www.reading.org/downloads/resources/rti0707_implications.pdf

Invernizzi, M., Juel, C., Swank, L., & Meier, J. (2005). *Phonological awareness literacy screening.* Charlottesville: University of Virginia Press.

Kavale, K. (1990). Effectiveness of special education. In T.B. Gutkin & C.R. Reynolds (Eds.), *Handbook of school psychology* (2nd ed., pp. 868–898). New York: Wiley.

Lyon, G.R. (1995). Research initiatives in learning disabilities: Contributions from scientists supported by the National Institute of Child Health and Human Development. *Journal of Child Neurology, 10*(Suppl. 1), S120–S126.

Lyons, C., & Beaver, J. (1995). Reducing retention and learning disability placement through reading recovery: An educationally sound cost-effective choice. In R. Allington & S. Walmsley (Eds.), *No quick fix: Rethinking literacy programs in America's elementary schools* (pp. 116–136). New York: Teachers College Press.

National Center on Student Progress Monitoring. (2007). *Common questions for progress monitoring.* Retrieved May 20, 2007, from www.studentprogress.org/progresmon.asp#2

O'Connor, R.E., Fulmer, D., Harty, K.R., & Bell, K.M. (2005). Layers of reading intervention in kindergarten through third grade: Changes in teaching and student outcomes. *Journal of Learning Disabilities, 38*(5), 440–455.

O'Malley, K., Francis, D.J., Foorman, B.R., Fletcher, J.M., & Swank, P.R. (2002). Growth in precursor and reading-related skills: Do low-achieving and IQ-discrepant readers develop differently? *Learning Disabilities Research & Practice, 17*(1), 19–34.

Paris, S.G. (2005). Reinterpreting the development of reading skills. *Reading Research Quarterly, 40*(2), 184–202.

Parker, R., Hasbrouck, J., & Tindal, G. (1992). Greater validity for oral reading fluency: Can miscues help? *The Journal of Special Education, 25*(4), 492–503.

Powell-Smith, K., & Ball, P. (2002). Best practices in reintegration and special education exit decisions. In A. Thomas & J. Grimes (Eds.), *Best practices in school psychology-IV* (pp. 541–557). Bethesda, MD: National Association of School Psychologists.

Pressley, M. (2003). A few things reading educators should know about instructional experiments. *The Reading Teacher, 57*(1), 64–71.

Riedel, B. (2007). The relation between DIBELS, reading comprehension, and vocabulary in urban first grade students. *Reading Research Quarterly, 42*(4), 546–567.

Scarborough, H. (2005). Developmental relationships between language and reading: Reconciling a beautiful hypothesis with some ugly facts. In H.W. Catts & A.G. Kamhi (Eds.), *The connections between language and reading disabilities* (pp. 3–24). Mahwah, NJ: Erlbaum.

Shinn, M. (1989). *Curriculum-based measurement: Assessing special children.* New York: Guilford.

Stanovich, K. (2005). The future of a mistake: Will discrepancy measurement continue to make the learning disabilities field a pseudoscience? *Learning Disability Quarterly, 28*(2), 103–106.

Taylor-Greene, S., Brown, D., Nelson, L., Longton, J., Cohen, J., Swartz, J., et al. (1997). School-wide behavioral support: Starting the year off right. *Journal of Behavioral Education, 7*(1), 99–112.

Texas Education Agency & University of Texas System. (2006). *Texas Primary Reading Inventory.* Retrieved from www.tpri.org/products/

University of Texas Center for Reading and Language Arts. (2003). *Three-tier reading model: Reducing reading difficulties for kindergarten through third grade students.* Austin, TX: Author.

U.S. Department of Education. (1977). *1977 code of federal regulations.* Washington, DC: Author.

U.S. Department of Education. (2006). *Assistance to states for the education of children with disabilities and preschools grants for children with disabilities, final rule.* Retrieved May 17, 2007, from eric.ed.gov/ERICDocs/data/ericdocs2sql/content_storage_01/0000019b/80/1b/e9/95.pdf

Vaughn, S., & Fuchs, L.S. (2003). Redefining learning disabilities as inadequate response to instruction: The promise and potential problems. *Learning Disabilities Research & Practice, 18*(3), 137–146.

Vellutino, F.R., Scanlon, D.M., & Lyon, G.R. (2000). Differentiating between difficult-to-remediate and readily remediated poor readers: More evidence against the IQ-discrepancy definition of reading disability. *Journal of Learning Disabilities, 33*(3), 223–238.

Walmsley, S., & Allington, R. (2007). *No quick fix, the RTI edition: Rethinking literacy programs in America's elementary schools.* New York: Teachers College Press; Newark, DE: International Reading Association.

Wanzek, J., & Vaughn, S. (2008). Response to varying amounts of time in reading intervention for students with low response to intervention. *Journal of Learning Disabilities, 41*(2), 126–142.

Questions for Reflection

- In this article, a reading teacher, special educator, second-grade teacher, and school psychologist work collaboratively to design and implement an intervention for Mark. Are any of the thoughts, frustrations, or beliefs expressed by these professionals familiar to you? In your experience, what are the barriers to school psychologists, special educators, classroom teachers, and reading specialists working together? Can RTI help or hinder collaborative efforts? What can your school do to foster effective collaboration that benefits struggling readers?
- The article describes specific reasons behind the introduction of RTI, including addressing the "waiting to fail" phenomenon, the failure of an IQ-ability discrepancy to inform instructional improvements for struggling readers, and the skyrocketing numbers of students identified for special education. Have your experienced any of these phenomena yourself with struggling readers? Have you felt uncomfortable with decisions made about any of your struggling learners? How might RTI help avoid bad decisions that harm students? What pitfalls might exist in RTI that could harm students?

A Child's Response to Intervention Requires a Responsive Teacher of Reading

Mary K. Lose

The revised Individuals with Disabilities Education Act (IDEA) offers U.S. schools confronting rising enrollments of students with learning disabilities (LD) two options for managing this increasing population. The first option is that local education agencies can use as much as 15% of their special education funds to pay for early intervening services (EIS) and to support professional development and literacy instruction. The second option offered by IDEA is Response to Intervention (RTI) that can be used to provide early interventions without labeling students at risk for school failure as learning disabled. RTI encourages early identification and prereferral intervention to determine if a child responds to the intervening instruction. The goal is to limit referrals based on inadequate instruction or limited English proficiency and to reduce the number of children identified for LD services. In order to do this, the lowest performing children must be identified early so that appropriately intensive interventions and tiers of support can be provided within a comprehensive approach to literacy instruction at the first indication of the child's difficulty.

Fundamental Principles

The U.S. Department of Education does not require or endorse any particular model of RTI. State education agencies may establish the criteria for identifying children with specific learning disabilities, but the state criteria must permit local agencies to choose an RTI model. In this column, I will present the fundamental principles of an appropriate RTI approach and review the evidence on early literacy interventions as provided by the U.S. Department of Education. The following points that are central to the provision of RTI and EIS within the IDEA are based on those identified by Lose et al. (2007) and are elaborated upon here:

Ensure Early Identification and Early Intervention for All Children Struggling With Literacy Learning

Research has shown that signs of a child's literacy learning difficulties usually surface after one year in school. If schools expect children to meet literacy achievement benchmarks, a child must be identified and intensive interventions provided at the first indication of a difficulty.

Provide a Way to Appropriately Identify Children With LD

Assessments must explore a child's multiple knowledge sources and literacy experiences. Assessments should examine all aspects of a child's control over literacy, including oral language skill; knowledge of letters, words, and sound-letter correspondences; concepts of print; and text reading and writing.

Reprinted from Lose, M.K. (2007). A child's response to intervention requires a responsive teacher of reading. *The Reading Teacher, 61*(3), 276–279.

Provide Effective, Intensive, Evidence-Based Early Intervening Services

An intervention must show accelerative learning and steady progress over time on the part of the child or else it has failed. The U.S. Department of Education Institute for Education Sciences identified one-to-one tutoring by qualified tutors in grades 1–3 as meeting the gold standard for effectiveness for the most at-risk learners. Other researchers have documented the importance of individual lessons for the lowest-performing students at the onset of their literacy learning difficulties (Pinnell, Lyons, DeFord, Bryk, & Seltzer, 1994; Snow, Burns, & Griffin, 1998; Vellutino et al., 1996; Wasik & Slavin, 1993).

Ensure Monitoring of Student Progress and Data-Based Documentation for Each Student

Student progress is best monitored by a teacher who is a skilled diagnostician and who also designs and delivers the intervention in response to the child. Assessment information and sensitive observation on the part of the teacher are used to refine teaching decisions in response to changes in the child's control over literacy processing.

Report Annual Yearly Progress, Which Depends on Accelerated Growth of Struggling Readers

Yearly reports of progress ensure that struggling readers will receive interventions that support their accelerative progress regardless of their economic status, race, or ethnicity. Annual reporting also helps schools, systems, and the community monitor the quality of their intervention services for children and advocate for equity in appropriately and responsively serving all their low-performing students.

Provide the Highest Quality of Professional Development for Teachers of Low Achievers

Research has shown that every dollar spent on teachers' professional development yields greater student achievement outcomes than any other expenditure of school dollars (Darling-Hammond, 1996). Because they are the learners most vulnerable to instruction, regardless of the approach to instruction in our schools, the lowest-performing learners need the most skilled teachers (McEneaney, Lose, & Schwartz, 2006).

Create a Multitiered Problem-Solving Team to Support Comprehensive Literacy Efforts

For optimum child learning, all members of the school team—administrators, teachers, and intervention specialists—must acknowledge the range of students' learning abilities and assume responsibility for children's success. Intervention effectiveness may be seriously compromised by fractured approaches to children's learning. Collegial communication within a comprehensive approach to literacy and shared accountability for children by members of the school team can ensure that students' needs are quickly identified and strategies formulated to meet those needs.

Fundamental Principles of a Successful RTI Approach

What principles do we, as teachers of reading, need to keep in mind to ensure that struggling literacy learners will achieve success within the provisions of the IDEA for RTI? Unfortunately, many RTI approaches place emphasis on prescriptive instruction delivered by teachers-as-technicians who focus on what children don't know as the starting point for instruction. Such approaches lack the necessary decision making on the part of teachers to respond effectively to differing challenges posed by individual children (Clay, 2005a). In contrast, I now highlight several fundamental principles that I consider foundational to any successful RTI approach.

A Child, Not a Group, Learns to Read

Anecdotal and research evidence supports the notion that children come "by different paths to common outcomes" in literacy (Clay, 1998). A skilled responsive teacher will observe the different paths taken by individual children and will design instruction that supports their literacy learning progress.

The Only Valid RTI Approach Is One in Which the Child Responds Successfully

The intervention must be appropriately intensive, delivered without delay, and tailored precisely to the individual child. A child who has been provided with the intervention he or she needs will respond successfully, making progress daily and learning how to lift his or her own literacy performance with skilled support from a knowledgeable teacher (Clay, 2001, 2005b). While many children respond quite well to whole-class and small-group instruction, the most struggling literacy learner needs the most intensive instruction delivered individually and tailored precisely to his or her needs.

To Be Successful, the Most Struggling Child Requires the Most Expert Teacher

Teachers, not programs, teach children to read. The child who is challenged by literacy learning requires a knowledgeable teacher who can make moment-by-moment teaching decisions in response to his or her idiosyncratic literacy competencies. The struggling child is likely to be harmed by a one-size-fits-all, prescriptive intervention that fails to acknowledge his or her abilities as a starting point for instruction.

Teacher Expertise Requires High-Quality, Sustained Professional Development

Teaching the lowest-performing learners is difficult. Because no two children ever respond quite the same, teachers of the lowest-performing children must be the most tentative, skilled, and responsive in their interactions with children. Sustained continual professional development is required to continuously develop highly expert teachers (Darling-Hammond, 1996; Darling-Hammond & McLaughlin, 1995).

Given the federal requirement for evidence-based interventions, the most reliable source for teachers, administrators, researchers, and policymakers seeking effective reading interventions is the What Works Clearinghouse (WWC; [ies.ed.gov/ncee/wwc/]). Established in 2002 by the U.S. Department of Education's Institute for Education Sciences, the WWC's mission is to provide "a central and trusted source of scientific evidence of what works in education." The WWC provides information on the relative effectiveness of a variety of beginning reading programs in four key domains: alphabetics (phonemic awareness, phonological awareness, letter identification, print awareness, and phonics), reading fluency, comprehension (vocabulary development and reading comprehension), and general reading achievement (a combination of two or more of the previous domains). Ratings are based on the statistical significance of the empirical effect estimate and the quality of the research design generating the effect estimate. They are reported at the following six levels of effects from highest to lowest: "positive effects" (+), "potentially positive effects" (+?), "mixed effects" (±), "no discernable effects" (?), "potentially negative effects" (-?), and "negative effects" (-).

Of the 20 interventions reviewed by the WWC, only one intervention, Reading Recovery, an early intervention and prevention for the lowest-performing, first-grade students, has qualifying research evidence in all four domains. Reading Recovery received the highest ratings of any of the 20 programs with two "positive effects"

(+) ratings for alphabetics and general reading achievement and two "potentially positive effects" (+?) ratings for reading fluency and comprehension. Reading Recovery, developed by researcher and developmental psychologist Marie Clay, is implemented as a not-for-profit collaborative among schools and universities (Clay, 2005a, 2005b). Reading Recovery students participate in 30-minute daily lessons in reading and writing activities tailored to their individual needs and delivered one-to-one by a certified Reading Recovery teacher. Reading Recovery teachers initially receive one year of graduate-level coursework and are required to participate in continual professional development each year thereafter to remain certified.

Of the 19 remaining beginning reading programs, only 3 are rated as providing evidence for either "positive effects" (+) or "potentially positive effects" (+?) in, at most, three of the four domains. Out of those programs, only one, Kaplan SpellRead, exhibited a positive (+) rating. The program has one rating of "positive effects" (+) in alphabetics and two ratings of "potentially positive effects" (+?) in fluency and comprehension. According to the developers, Kaplan SpellRead is a literacy program for struggling students in grades 2 and above who are two or more years below grade level in reading, are receiving special education, or are English-language learners. The program is delivered in small groups of five students with one instructor; takes five to nine months to complete; and "consists of 140 lessons implemented in three distinct phases that interweave phonemics, phonetics, and instruction in language-based reading and writing" [ies.ed.gov/ncee/wwc/reports/beginning_reading/spellread/]. Teachers who implement the program receive five days of instruction, two follow-up workshops, and regular on-site coaching visits from Kaplan K12 staff and a Web-based instructor support system to monitor student progress. The next highest rated programs with potentially positive effects (+?) in alphabetics, fluency, and comprehension are Peer-Assisted Learning Strategies (PALS) and Start Making a Reader Today (SMART).

It is clear that the emphasis today is (as it should be) on evidence-based approaches to early literacy intervention, and we, as teachers, administrators, and policymakers, have a responsibility to children to implement highly rated evidence-based approaches. We all agree that children are the focus of our work, and children who struggle with literacy learning do not deserve unproven programs when we already know what works. As indicated in the title of this column, a child's response to intervention requires a skilled, responsive teacher, and reading professionals already have enough information to make an appropriate, informed, and timely response to the challenges of RTI.

References

Clay, M.M. (1998). *By different paths to common outcomes.* York, ME: Stenhouse.

Clay M.M. (2001). *Change over time in children's literacy development.* Portsmouth, NH: Heinemann.

Clay, M.M. (2005a). *Literacy lessons designed for individuals: Part one: Why? when? and how?* Portsmouth, NH: Heinemann.

Clay, M.M. (2005b). *Literacy lessons designed for individuals: Part two: Teaching procedures.* Portsmouth, NH: Heinemann.

Darling-Hammond, L. (1996). What matters most: A competent teacher for every child. *Phi Delta Kappan, 78,* 193–200.

Darling-Hammond, L., & McLaughlin, M.W. (1995). Policies that support professional development in an era of reform. *Phi Delta Kappan, 76*(8), 597–604.

Lose, M.K., Schmitt, M.C., Gomez-Bellenge, F.X., Jones, N., Honchell, B., & Askew, B.J. (2007). Reading Recovery and IDEA legislation: Early intervening services (EIS) and response to intervention (RTI). *The Journal of Reading Recovery, 6*(2), 42–47.

McEneaney, J.E., Lose, M.K., & Schwartz, R.M. (2006). A transactional perspective on reading difficulties and Response to Intervention. *Reading Research Quarterly, 41*(1), 117–128.

Pinnell, G.S., Lyons, C.A., DeFord, D.E., Bryk, A.S., & Seltzer, M. (1994). Comparing instructional models for the literacy education of high-risk first graders. *Reading Research Quarterly, 29*(1), 8–39.

Snow, C.E., Burns, S., & Griffin, P. (1998). *Preventing reading difficulties in young children.* Washington, DC, National Academy Press.

Vellutino, F.R., Scanlon, D.M., Sipay, E.R., Small, S.G., Pratt, A., Chen, R., et al. (1996). Cognitive profiles of difficult-to-remediate and readily remediated poor readers: Early intervention as a vehicle for distinguishing between cognitive and experiential deficits as basic causes of specific reading disability. *Journal of Educational Psychology*, *88*(4), 601–638.

Wasik, B.A., & Slavin, R.E. (1993). Preventing early reading failure with one-to-one tutoring: A review of five programs. *Reading Research Quarterly*, *28*(2), 178–200.

Questions for Reflection

- Lose suggests that struggling readers, especially in RTI plans, need the most expert teachers. Is your RTI model staffed by expert teachers of reading? If not, how can you work with school or district administrators to ensure appropriate opportunities for professional development and resulting increases in teacher effectiveness?
- The author also emphasizes individual instruction for the students who struggle most with reading. This obviously can pose organizational challenges in finding the time and resources needed to devote appropriate personal attention to the small number of students who need one-to-one instruction. What ideas do you have for organizational structures and classroom management that might facilitate individual instruction?

The Benefits of Sustained Silent Reading: Scientific Research and Common Sense Converge

Elaine M. Garan and Glenn DeVoogd

As reading teachers, we recognize the joy that comes from getting lost in the pages of a good book. We fondly recall the books that inspired and changed us as children and that still influence us as adults. As teachers, we want to awaken that love of literacy in our students and invite them to experience that magic in our classrooms. We want them to grow into "skilled, passionate, habitual, and critical readers" (Atwell, 2007). However, confusion over and misinterpretation of federal research on independent reading in the United States have caused some to question this vision of literacy. Teachers and administrators are now wondering if reading books in school helps students increase their reading skills, much less appreciate the value of reading.

There are many misconceptions about the role Sustained Silent Reading (SSR) should play in reading instruction. Much of the confusion stems from the research on SSR in the report of the National Reading Panel (NRP; National Institute of Child Health and Human Development [NICHD], 2000). Although it was published in 2000, the report still has clout. In fact, *Guidance for the Reading First Program* requires five "Effective Components of Reading Instruction" based on the NRP's findings (U.S. Department of Education Office of Elementary and Secondary Education, 2002, p. 3). The document also cites the NRP's research methodology as the gold standard for scientifically based reading research (SBRR). Clearly, it is SBRR that both defines and confines the curricula in Reading First schools. Touted as the definitive research on reading instruction, the NRP report still influences education policy in the United States and the materials and methods schools adopt.

It is not surprising that the NRP report has generated spirited and even angry debate among educators and researchers, ranging from criticism of its methodology to contradictions in the panel's summary of its findings to charges of conflicts of interest among NRP and Reading First panel members (Coles, 2003; Cunningham, 2001; Garan, 2001; Krashen, 2005; U.S. Department of Education Office of the Inspector General, 2006). In the midst of a storm of controversy, one of the most divisive criticisms of the NRP is the claim that its findings do not support SSR in schools (Stahl, 2004). In this article, we will clarify the panel's research with the words of the NRP report and those of its panel members and contributors. We will then offer suggestions on variations of pure SSR and how teachers can use them in their classrooms.

On Defining SSR or Any Instructional Method

It's tempting to accept research at face value, especially if it's labeled as *scientific* and involves quantitative methods. However, as consumers of

Reprinted from Garan, E.M., & DeVoogd, G. (2008). The benefits of sustained silent reading: Scientific research and common sense converge. *The Reading Teacher, 62*(4), 336-344.

research, teachers must approach all studies with careful scrutiny rather than unquestioning acceptance. This is true even with—or, some might suggest, particularly with—research based on a scientific, medical model that strives to establish firm causal relationships between teaching methods and results. There are just too many confounding factors that can and do contaminate the research process and make it nearly impossible to apply findings to all children in all schools and to effectively standardize instruction. We will examine some of those general challenges to educational research and then apply them to the studies on SSR in particular.

One of the biggest obstacles in applying an experimental model to educational research is that classrooms are not laboratories. Therefore, conditions cannot be controlled or variables completely refined. There is a slipperiness, an illusiveness, to even the very definitions of teaching methods that create roadblocks to the goal of scientific certainty right from the beginning.

That is, although teaching methods may be defined at their inception and in the literature, they seldom remain pure as teachers adjust them to fit their own beliefs and teaching styles. Therefore, at the outset, researchers are faced with the challenge of finding pure examples of any method they wish to study. This can be particularly problematic in SBRR because it is based on an experimental research model that must isolate and refine variables, as cleanly as possible, so the findings can be directly attributed to the method being studied. However, because teachers tweak methods, the best that can be said when defining most teaching methods is "sometimes" or "often, such and such is the case."

And so it is with SSR. Like other instructional methods, it can and does operate along a continuum. At one end of the continuum is pure SSR as a time devoted to free reading during which students read books of their own choice, without assessment, skills work, monitoring, or instruction from the teacher. In fact, often the teacher reads a book along with the students, thus providing a model of literacy for the class. Other teachers implement SSR by monitoring the type and the number of books students read; they may also administer assessments, keep reading checklists, and ask questions or encourage student discussion about books (Atwell, 2007; Gambrell, 2007; Reutzel, Jones, Fawson, & Smith, 2008).

Regardless of the amount of teacher involvement, however, the distinguishing feature of SSR is that every day for at least 15 to 30 minutes, students are permitted a block of time to read a book, usually of their own choice (Stahl, 2004). SSR can also be found under a variety of labels including, but not limited to, DEAR (Drop Everything and Read) and SQUIRT (Super Quiet Reading Time), as listed in the NRP report (NICHD, 2000, p. 3-24). Now, we will examine the problems the NRP experienced in attempting to gather significant research on SSR and why any statements opposed to independent reading—even those made by panel members—cannot be based on sound research.

The NRP on SSR

There has been considerable criticism of the methodology behind, inherent flaws in, and reporting of the NRP's findings, and it is not our purpose to revisit that general debate here. Rather, we will now focus on how the narrow, questionable selection criteria for studies on SSR led to a misinterpretation of the role research plays in reading.

First, as consumers of research, teachers must understand that the NRP did not find that SSR is ineffective. Nowhere did the report state that having children read in school is a bad idea. What it claimed was that there were not enough studies meeting the panel's methodological requirements to draw any conclusions. In fact, the panel found only 14 studies that met their research criteria, and of those, "several...could not be analyzed because of serious methodological or reporting flaws that undermined their results" (NICHD, 2000, p. 3-24).

Perhaps one reason the NRP had problems finding enough experimental studies on SSR and the reason its findings have not been unanimously embraced by the reading community is because it relied on a component-skills model of reading (Paris, 2005). That is, the panel operated on the assumption that reading skills can be taught in isolation, one at a time, and that once children accumulate knowledge of the individual letters and sounds that produce language, they will then be able to comprehend connected text as competent readers. That paradigm lends itself to the research methodology the panel chose to consider, and also to exclude, in its deliberations. Recall that the NRP sought causality from research and decided a priori on the selection criteria for the studies it would analyze (Cunningham, 2001, p. 327). In their quest for scientific certainty, the panel chose to rely solely on a medical model, using experimental treatments and control groups, even though few education researchers adopted such a model (NICHD, 2000, p. 5).

Nevertheless, the NRP chose an experimental model they believed would result in a direct relationship between methods and results. Thus, the NRP's "methodological standards did not arise from the research literature on reading, but rather, were imposed upon it" (Cunningham, 2001, p. 326). It's not surprising, then, that few studies conformed to their opinions on how reading research should be conducted.

Given the lack of evidence as cited by the NRP, and given that the evidence the panel *did* use was weak and poorly designed, any conclusions that SSR does not benefit children cannot be a derivation of sound data. If the research is flawed, then so are any conclusions based on it. In point of fact, the NRP report itself did not draw any conclusions one way or the other about SSR:

> It should be made clear that these findings [on the effectiveness of SSR] do not negate the positive influence SSR *may* have on reading fluency, nor do the findings negate the possibility that wide independent reading significantly influences vocabulary development and reading comprehension. Rather, there are simply not sufficient data from well-designed studies capable of testing questions of causation to substantiate causal claims. (NICHD, 2000, p. 13)

Yet another reason the NRP had problems finding enough studies on SSR is because independent silent reading was inappropriately placed in the fluency subgroup, rather than in the section on comprehension. In other words, the panel viewed independent silent reading as a "treatment whose effectiveness could be measured with an oral reading dependent measure" (Cunningham, 2001, p. 333). As Cunningham noted, "No wonder they couldn't find a single study that evaluated...silent reading with an oral reading fluency test...at that point, they should have realized that perhaps they had put the research on [SSR] in the wrong subgroup" (p. 333).

Nevertheless, so committed was the panel to imposing a medical research model on reading methods that it described, in detail, the results of each and every one of the 14 experimental studies on SSR that it had already declared were weak in design and of no use to its analysis of SSR (NICHD, 2000, pp. 3-24–3-27). On the other hand, it essentially ignored the "literally hundreds of correlational studies that find that the best readers read the most and poor readers read the least" (NICHD, 2000, p. 3-21). Among those studies the panel dismissed were the findings of the National Assessment for Educational Progress (NAEP), showing that "the more you read the better your vocabulary, your knowledge of the world, your ability to read and so on" (NICHD, 2000, p. 3-21). In other words, there were hundreds of studies to support SSR, but because they did not meet the panel's narrow selection criteria, the NRP excluded them.

Another reason the panel dismissed "literally hundreds" of studies correlating time spent reading with reading ability is that correlation is not causation. In other words, "it could be that if you read more, you are a better reader; but it also seems possible that better readers choose to read more" (NICHD, 2000, p. 3-21). However, there are flaws in that reasoning that educators should consider before eliminating SSR from their classrooms.

The Illusion of Certainty in Research

First, causality can seldom be determined absolutely, even when the physical sciences use the medical model the NRP adopted for its methodology. Consider, for example, that if the medical profession dismissed correlational studies, it would not have concluded that smoking is hazardous to our health (Peace, 1985; Siepmann, 1999). Furthermore, humans bring a variety of physical characteristics, allergies, and unexplained resistance to treatments that make certainty—even in medicine—nearly impossible. How much more unpredictable then, are the social sciences, in which a myriad of human, as opposed to physical, factors come into play? Human interactions are complicated and messy. Therefore, simplistic and reductionist research methods are not always appropriate in spite of their appeal, and the results of such approaches are often arbitrary at best (Cronbach, 1975).

What's more, because the benefits of SSR are not immediate but evolve throughout a process, experimental studies are not always practical or even ethical, a consideration that may further deter researchers from implementing such methods. Consider, for instance, that to conduct an effective experiment on independent reading, researchers would need to establish a treatment group (one that reads independently) and a control group (one that doesn't read). What's more, the conditions imposed on these groups would need to be sustained over an extended period of time—the longer, the better. The amount of reading done by each group of students would have to be controlled as strictly as possible; the less reading done in the control group, the more accurate the results would be and vice versa. These methodological imperatives raise a question: What administrator or parent would allow children to participate in a study that prohibits, discourages, or drastically controls the amount of reading children can do over a long period of time?

It's no wonder, then, that there are so few "well-designed" experimental studies on independent reading. Although it's not impossible to conduct such research, it is difficult. It is nearly impossible to refine the variables and to exclude all confounding factors, such as students' motivation, their emotional problems, and other human characteristics, that can contaminate the results. In terms of the time and the conditions that must be controlled, then, researchers can seldom draw definitive conclusions and proclaim, "If you do this, then you *will* produce that."

The Lack of Consensus in the Field and Among Panel Members

As Cunningham (2001) stated, "The best science has the power to change the thinking of those who previously disagreed with it but are fair-minded enough to admit they were wrong once the case has been made" (p. 334). In other words, good science results in a reasonably strong consensus among open-minded professionals in a given field. Though there is a general consensus among many literacy experts concerning the benefits of having children read books of their own choice in school (Allington & McGill-Franzen, 2003; Gambrell, 2007; Krashen, 2001, 2005; Trelease, 2001), there is a noteworthy lack of scientific consensus among the NRP members themselves about the role SSR should play in reading instruction.

For example, one NRP member stated that SSR is "probably not a good idea" (Shanahan, 2006, p. 12). On the other hand, other panel members and contributors disagree with that opinion (Pressley, Dolezal, Roehrig & Hilden, 2002; Stahl, 2004; Wu & Samuels, 2004). It is essential, then, that educators are aware of the varying interpretations of data that derive even from scientific research and that we cannot accept the findings, or the opinions of researchers, as absolutes. We will now examine some of the differing opinions of panel members and contributors about the benefits of SSR and scientific research subsequent to the release of the NRP report.

It is obvious from the impact of the No Child Left Behind Act of 2001 and Reading First, and from their reliance on SBRR, that not all research—and not all researchers—are given equal credence in the framing of educational policy. Clearly, SBRR is hot (Cassidy & Cassidy, 2008, p. 10). Conversely, qualitative research and researchers not federally sanctioned are not. Although we may not agree that one paradigm should prevail over other voices, and although it's not our intention to ignore the importance of qualitative studies in our discussion of SSR, we must acknowledge the power of federal research to regulate education policy. In the prevailing climate, clearly some researchers are given more credence than others. Therefore, in the following section of this article, we emphasize the connections of the researchers we cite to federally sanctioned studies, including the NRP report.

In 2004, a volume titled *The Voice of Evidence in Reading Research* (McCardle & Chhabra, 2004) was published under the auspices of several federal agencies including the NICHD, which also funded the NRP report (NICHD, 2000). The purpose of McCardle and Chhabra's (2004) book was to explain the scientific evidence on reading instruction, including the findings of the NRP report, to teachers and parents. NRP contributor Steven Stahl wrote the chapter explaining the findings of the Fluency subgroup, including the role of SSR in reading instruction. In that chapter (Stahl, 2004), he refuted the notion that SSR should not be part of the school curriculum.

First, Stahl (2004) agreed with Krashen (2001), noting that the "best studies" in independent reading are not experimental, but are, in fact, correlational (p. 206). Stahl also revealed that the NRP omitted a large body of *experimental* [emphasis added] longitudinal studies, known as the "book flood" studies (Elley, 2000; Elley & Mangubhai, 1983). Those studies showed that increasing the amount of reading material available to children can "dramatically increase reading achievement" (Stahl, 2004, p. 206). Stahl stated that the NRP excluded this series of studies because, "This work was done with second-language learners, generally in the South Pacific, so it was outside the purview of the NRP" (Stahl, 2004, p. 206). However, the omission of these studies represented an internal inconsistency in the NRP's methodology, because the Phonemic Awareness section included studies done not only in other countries but in languages other than English (NICHD, 2000, p. 2-16).

Thus, we see that even in federal research, even within the very same report, the participating researchers do not always agree. There are no absolutes. And we see a lack of consensus among panel members about the methodology, as well as about how to interpret the findings, that renders definitive statements based on such studies highly questionable.

Consider that in his Fluency chapter, Stahl (2004) also cited Krashen (2001), Berliner (1981), and other researchers who advocated that the more time students spend with "eyes on text," the better readers they will become (p. 190). After noting the omission of the book flood studies and citing researchers and literacy experts who advocate for more time spent reading, Stahl (2004) concluded,

> Although the research reviewed by the NRP does not support the use of SSR, common sense suggests that children should have some time during the day to read books of their own choosing, if only for motivational purposes (see Turner, 1995). However, I suggest that teachers actively monitor children's reading, both by going around the room to make sure children are on task and by asking questions about what children are reading, and encourage children to read books at an appropriate level. (p. 207)

Stahl (2004) recommended that students should spend 15 to 30 minutes of each day reading books of their own choice as an essential component of reading instruction (p. 201). Thus, in his chapter of the book written to interpret and implement the panel's findings (McCardle & Chhabra, 2004), Stahl (2004), the NRP contributor, clearly refuted interpretations of the research that would discourage independent reading time in schools.

Samuels is another NRP member who advocates for independent reading in school. Samuels was co-chair of the Fluency subgroup that consisted of only three members. In 2004 at the IRA annual convention, Wu and Samuels (2004) presented a paper based on their research, "How the Amount of Time Spent on Independent Reading Affects Reading Achievement: A Response to the National Reading Panel." Their research was the result of a six-month, quasi-experimental study. Wu and Samuels (2004) reported the following:

> Data analysis found that more time spent reading had a significant effect on achievement compared to a control condition where less time was allocated for independent reading. In addition, results found that poor readers showed significantly greater gains in word recognition and vocabulary than good readers. Third grade showed greater gains in comprehension than fifth grade. Furthermore, the results also showed that poor readers tended to have greater gains in vocabulary with 15 minutes of reading, but they had better gains on reading comprehension with 40 minutes of reading. (p. 2)

In addition to his coauthored, quasi-experimental study, Samuels also conducted a meta-analysis with Lewis that further established the benefits of SSR on student reading achievement (Lewis & Samuels, 2003).

Again, although we acknowledge and respect the contributions of many other well-known researchers showing the benefits of wide reading on students' reading achievement (Allington & McGill-Franzen, 2003; Fisher & Frey, 2007; Krashen, 2001; Kuhn, 2004), we reiterate that we focused on NRP members and contributors because it is the federal research and researchers that frame school policy in the United States. It is important for teachers to recognize the lack of consensus among federally sanctioned researchers, as evidenced in the studies and reports subsequent to the NRP cited above. They provide strong evidence that time spent reading is *class time* well spent.

In summary then, given the following four pieces of evidence—(1) the insufficient data on SSR in the NRP report, (2) the lack of consensus among the panel's members on the methodology and interpretations of the findings, (3) the overwhelming body of correlational evidence supporting SSR, and (4) the experimental or quasi-experimental studies completed subsequent to the NRP report that support SSR—we conclude there is a convergence of research and the views of NRP researchers to support SSR in schools.

SBRR Meets Common Sense

In life, common sense routinely prevails over research. Few of us conduct experiments to inform every decision we make. Sometimes, common sense just makes sense. In education, however, there is a disconnect that derives from the assumption that conclusions resulting from SBRR are somehow sacrosanct. There is a mistaken notion that the findings of research are absolute. And therefore, so the reasoning goes, teachers must abrogate their own experience, professional judgment, and common sense to mandates that have not even met with consensus among the researchers who served on the panels that reported the studies.

The fracture in that logic becomes obvious if we base our approach to other areas of our lives strictly on what research "proves." For example, if we accept the lack of experimental research as a reason to eliminate SSR from schools, then we should also call a halt to practicing sports, or musical instruments, or phonics worksheets, or math homework, or preparing students to take standardized tests for that matter. Either we believe practice helps or we don't.

There is yet another consideration, and that is the message we as educators communicate to children. Students attend not only to what we preach but also to what we do. As a matter of course, schools do not just encourage but often aggressively promote reading by rewarding students with points, stickers, pizzas, or other external and even silly inducements to read, such as having the principal kiss a pig when students have read a certain number of books. If we don't allow students to read in school at the same time that we tout the wonders of reading, what message are we sending to students about our values?

Furthermore, if we really believe that reading is probably not a good idea in school, then why assign it for homework or encourage it at all for that matter? Would any researcher, teacher, or administrator seriously tell parents they should not encourage their children to read because there's not enough scientific evidence—using a medical model of research—to tell us that it helps? If reading is not worth doing in school, then it's not worth the sacrifice of family time at home either. Our society values books. Certainly, it would be a betrayal of those values if we did not promote or allow real books and real reading in schools.

Therefore, having addressed the obstacles presented by misinterpretations of the research, we will now examine other questions that teachers have about independent reading and offer practical variations on pure SSR that can make the process less daunting.

Free Fall

Garan (2007) observed that allowing pure SSR in classrooms feels like free fall for teachers because it means letting go and giving up control. It means trusting that students with a book in front of them are actually reading. That loss of control can be daunting, particularly in the present climate of standards, mandated curricula, and accountability.

One looming question teachers face is, Should students really be left to read unmonitored? If a teacher permits students to read as she sits at her desk and reads too, will students actually read? Some research supports that they will (Cohen, 1999; Herda & Ramos, 2001; Von Sprecken & Krashen, 1998). Other research suggests that many students won't (Stahl, 2004) and that some teacher monitoring may actually enhance students' comprehension of and their appreciation for literature. Consequently, teachers have developed a number of innovations to pure SSR that resolve the tension between their need to monitor and establish accountability and students' autonomy.

The Role of Common Sense and Teacher Praxis in SSR

Gambrell (2007) suggested that many newer innovations to SSR may actually enhance the benefits of silent reading. In addition, such innovations can afford teachers some degree of student monitoring so they are not pushed too far outside their comfort zone and compliance with standards and mandates. For example, many teachers and researchers have documented the importance of conversations as a way of extending students' thinking, even as book clubs for adults can deepen *their* appreciation for and understanding of literature (Atwell, 2007; Cole, 2003; McLaughlin & DeVoogd, 2004). Other modifications to traditional SSR can include conferences and minilessons to increase its effectiveness (Kelley & Clausen-Grace, 2006; Pilgreen, 2000).

Kelley and Clausen-Grace (2006) found that some of the students in Clausen-Grace's third-grade class engaged in "fake" reading—looking at the book superficially without actually attempting to read it. Their unique adaptation of SSR, R^5 (read, relax, reflect, respond, rap), requires the students to stay in one place anywhere in the classroom and read. Clausen-Grace arranged bathroom breaks before SSR time to preempt avoidance behaviors. She also made other modifications, such as peer sharing and conference logs, to focus the students and make sure they were on task. Clausen-Grace acted in praxis as a professional. She reflected on the challenges in her classroom; discussed them with Kelley, a university professor; and then subsequently refined her practice as a result of ongoing professional dialogues. Thus, theory, teaching methods, and common sense converged, in fact, after the second year of R^5, Kelley and Clausen-Grace reported that the students gained 1.6 years on the Developmental Reading Assessment 4–8 (First edition, 2004).

Yet another promising innovation to traditional SSR is Scaffolded Silent Reading (ScSR; Reutzel et al., 2008). In this approach, "students were held accountable for reading widely across selected literary genres, setting personal goals for completing the reading of books within a timeframe, conferring with their teacher, and completing response projects to share the books they read with others" (p. 196). At the end of a year-long controlled experiment, the findings showed that the students engaged in ScSR made as much progress as those who participated in the more traditional Guided Repeated Oral Reading with feedback (GROR), thus assuaging the concerns of the principal who resisted SSR because of the perceived findings of the NRP report. Furthermore, both students and teachers involved in ScSR responded positively to the approach, as documented by surveys and journal responses.

Thus, SSR was more than just an enjoyable activity for students. These teacher-researchers reported that its use resulted in demonstrable growth in many areas of reading. Furthermore, it provided the participating teachers with hard data to support their innovations. This can serve as encouragement for other teachers to document student progress so they meet accountability requirements and district standards.

Other modifications to SSR provide opportunities for teachers to contribute to the process by modeling how mature readers approach books. Although some students come to school already familiar with books, many do not. For them, some intervention by and interaction with the teacher during SSR can provide the kind of modeling they've missed at home with their parents. Teachers can engage students by asking the kinds of questions parents ask as they read with children and by commenting on and extending the text to make stories relevant to the lives of young readers (Heath, 1982).

Although such modeling of story interactions and language can occur at other junctures in the school day and is typically associated with shared reading using Big Books, it can also support naive (not *necessarily* struggling) readers and help them to engage more meaningfully with the text. As literate and literature-loving adults, teachers can scaffold children by providing an important middle step between total dependence on the teacher and true independent reading.

Teachers have yet more options to help them negotiate some of the roadblocks that may discourage them from implementing SSR. For example, often young children don't read silently. They don't always think silently either. As Vygotsky (1978) demonstrated, young children speak out loud as they think. For them, talk is essential to thought and action until they eventually develop "inner speech" (Vygotsky, 1978). Therefore, first-grade students who often don't read silently anyway may benefit from buddy reading or subvocalizing instead of the more orthodox version of SSR. Yet another advantage of buddy reading is that it provides children with an audience. By taking turns, each student has an opportunity to show off at reading, to perform a bit, thus promoting fluency in a natural way. When the buddy readers switch and the reader becomes the listener, she or he can then assume the role of the teacher, and in guiding the partner, internalize the supportive reading strategies that have been modeled by the teacher. And so by helping her or his partner, each internalizes and solidifies those teaching/scaffolding behaviors that are reflective of sound reading strategies.

Such extensions of SSR do not detract from the value of independent reading. Rather, they can be unobtrusive and natural and serve to increase student engagement as well as afford teachers a way of monitoring student involvement. Research shows it is possible to successfully adjust literacy frameworks and instructional methods to meet the unique needs of the students as well as the beliefs and teaching styles of teachers (Fisher & Frey, 2007).

Kersten and Pardo (2007) observed that although policymakers envision uniformity and fidelity to mandated methods and materials, teachers "hybridize" and bring their own unique styles and beliefs to their instruction. In our view, that's not just how it is. That's how it should be. Certainly, sound research should inform practice. However, because—as we've demonstrated—research can be subject to error and misinterpretation, it should not supplant common sense and professional experience.

It is our hope that we have helped teachers and administrators untangle data from opinion, and that having reviewed the evidence from federal studies and federally sanctioned researchers, they now have a deeper understanding of the support for SSR. We hope we have helped to remove some of the road-blocks to SSR and that teachers will strive to implement it, whether it's pure, a variation we've described here, or their own unique adaptation of it. The body of evidence on SSR reveals an alignment of research with what the professional judgment of many teachers has determined—Sustained Silent Reading benefits students, and so we see that SBRR and common sense converge.

References

Allington, R., & McGill-Franzen, A. (2003). The impact of summer setback on the reading achievement gap. *Phi Delta Kappan, 85*(1), 68–75.

Atwell, N. (2007). *The reading zone: How to help kids become skilled, passionate, habitual, critical readers.* New York: Scholastic.

Berliner, D.C. (1981). Academic reading time and reading achievement. In J.T. Guthrie (Ed.), *Comprehension and teaching: Research reviews* (pp. 203–226). Newark, DE: International Reading Association.

Cassidy, J., & Cassidy, D. (2008, February/March). What's hot, what's not for 2008. *Reading Today, 25*(4), 1, 10–11.

Cohen, K. (1999). Reluctant eighth grade readers enjoy sustained silent reading. *California Reader, 33*(1), 22–25.

Cole, A.D. (2003). *Knee to knee, eye to eye: Circling in on comprehension.* Portsmouth, NH: Heinemann.

Coles, G. (2003). *Reading the naked truth: Literacy, legislation, and lies.* Portsmouth, NH: Heinemann.

Cronbach, L.J. (1975). Beyond the two disciplines of scientific psychology. *American Psychologist, 30*(2), 116–127.

Cunningham, J.W. (2001). The National Reading Panel Report. *Reading Research Quarterly, 36*(3), 326–335.

Elley, W.B. (2000). The potential of book floods for raising literacy levels. *International Review of Education, 46*(3–4), 233–255.

Elley, W.B., & Mangubhai, F. (1983). The impact of reading on second language learning. *Reading Research Quarterly, 19*(1), 53–67.

Fisher, D., & Frey, N. (2007). Implementing a schoolwide literacy framework: Improving achievement in an urban elementary school. *The Reading Teacher, 61*(1), 32–43.

Gambrell, L. (2007, June/July). Reading: Does practice make perfect? *Reading Today, 24*(6), 16.

Garan, E. (2001). Beyond the smoke and mirrors: A critique of the National Reading Panel report on phonics. *Phi Delta Kappan, 82*(7), 500–506.

Garan, E. (2007). *Smart answers to tough questions: What to say when you're asked about fluency, phonics, grammar, vocabulary, SSR, tests, support for ELLs, and more.* New York: Scholastic.

Heath, S.B. (1982). What no bedtime story means: Narrative skills at home and school. *Language in Society, 11*(1), 49–76.

Herda, R., & Ramos, F. (2001). How consistently do students read during Sustained Silent Reading? A look across the grades. *California School Library Journal, 24*(2), 29–31.

Kelley, M., & Clausen-Grace, N. (2006). R^5: The Sustained Silent Reading makeover that transformed readers. *The Reading Teacher, 60*(2), 148–156.

Kersten, J., & Pardo, L. (2007). Finessing and hybridizing: Innovative literacy practices in Reading First classrooms. *The Reading Teacher, 61*(2), 146–154.

Krashen, S. (2001). More smoke and mirrors: A critique of the National Reading Panel report on fluency. *Phi Delta Kappan, 83*(2), 119–123.

Krashen, S. (2005). Is in-school free reading good for children? Why the National Reading Panel Report is (still) wrong. *Phi Delta Kappan, 86*(6), 444–447.

Kuhn, M. (2004). Helping students become accurate, expressive readers: Fluency instruction for small groups. *The Reading Teacher, 58*(4), 338–344.

Lewis, M., & Samuels, S.J. (2003). *Read more—Read better? A meta-analysis of the literature on the relationship between exposure to reading and reading achievement.* Unpublished manuscript, University of Minnesota Twin Cities. Retrieved from [www.tc.umn.edu/~samue001/final%20version.pdf]

McCardle, P., & Chhabra, V. (Eds.). (2004). *The voice of evidence in reading research.* Baltimore, MD: Paul H. Brookes.

McLaughlin, M., & DeVoogd, G. (2004). *Critical literacy: Enhancing student comprehension of texts.* New York: Scholastic.

National Institute of Child Health and Human Development. (2000). *Report of the National Reading Panel. Teaching children to read: An evidence-based assessment of the scientific research literature on reading and its implications for reading instruction* (NIH Publication No. 00-4769). Washington, DC: U.S. Government Printing Office.

Paris, S.G. (2005). The reinterpreting the development of reading skills. *Reading Research Quarterly, 40*(2), 184–202.

Peace, L.R. (1985). A time correlation between smoking and lung cancer. *The Statistician, 34*(4), 371–381.

Pilgreen, J. (2000). *The SSR handbook: How to organize and manage a Sustained Silent Reading program.* Portsmouth, NH: Heinemann.

Pressley, M., Dolezal, S., Roehrig, A.D., & Hilden, K. (2002). Why the National Reading Panel's Recommendations are not enough. In R. Allington (Ed.), *Big brother and the national reading curriculum: How ideology trumped evidence* (pp. 75–89). Portsmouth, NH: Heinemann.

Reutzel, R., Jones, C., Fawson, P., & Smith, J. (2008). Scaffolded silent reading: A complement to Guided Repeated Oral Reading that works! *The Reading Teacher, 62*(3), 196.

Shanahan, T. (2006, June/July). Does he really think kids shouldn't read? *Reading Today, 23*(6), 12.

Siepmann, J.P. (1999, October/November). Smoking does not cause lung cancer (according to WHO/CDC data). *Journal of Theoretics*, (1–4). Retrieved from www.journaloftheoretics.com/Editorials/Vol-1/e1-4.htm

Stahl, S. (2004). What do we know about fluency? Findings of the National Reading Panel. In P. McCardle & V. Chhabra (Eds.), *The voice of evidence in reading research* (pp. 187–211). Baltimore, MD: Paul H. Brookes.

Trelease, J. (2001). *The read-aloud handbook* (5th ed.). New York: Penguin.

Turner, J.C. (1995). The influence of classroom contexts on young children's motivation for literacy. *Reading Research Quarterly, 30*(3), 410–441.

U.S. Department of Education Office of Elementary and Secondary Education. (2002, April). *Guidance for the Reading First program.* Retrieved from www.ed.gov/programs/readingfirst/guidance.pdf

U.S. Department of Education Office of the Inspector General. (2006, September). *The Reading First program's grant application process: Final inspection report* (ED-OIG/I13-F0017). Retrieved from www.ed.gov/about/offices/list/oig/aireports/i13f0017.pdf

Von Sprecken, D., & Krashen, S. (1998). Do students read during sustained silent reading? *California Reader, 32*(1), 11–13.

Vygotsky, L.S. (1978). *Mind in society: The development of higher psychological processes* (M. Cole, V. John-Steiner, S. Scribner, & E. Souberman, Eds. & Trans.). Cambridge, MA: Harvard University Press.

Wu, Y., & Samuels, S.J. (2004, May). *How the amount of time spent on independent reading affects reading achievement: A response to the National Reading Panel.* Paper presented at the 49th annual convention of the International Reading Association, Lake Tahoe, NV. Retrieved from www.tc.umn.edu/~samue001/web%20pdf/time_spent_on_reading.pdf

Questions for Reflection

- Helping students acquire the abilities needed to read independently is one of the major goals of reading instruction. Consider your school. Is encouraging independent reading a focus of your reading instruction? How can we foster independent reading if that isn't part of our school reading plan?
- The authors point out that it could be the case that some students do not actually read during SSR, and that poorer readers may read less than proficient readers. What can you do to support the struggling readers in your class during SSR? What suggestions can you make to them and to their parents regarding texts for independent reading, either at home or in school?

Summary Reading Loss

Maryann Mraz and Timothy V. Rasinski

"I know my students covered important reading skills last school year, but I still need to spend so much time reviewing those same skills at the start of the new school year." Comments like this reflect the all too common laments of teachers who, after having worked so hard during the academic year to establish a solid foundation for continued literacy learning, find that when a new school year begins too many of their students seem to be starting from scratch. Often, it is the students who can least afford to lose the reading gains they've achieved during the school year who fall the farthest behind when they return to the classroom after a summer break away from formal literacy instruction.

The achievement gap between high-socioeconomic and low-socioeconomic students has long been a source of concern for educators and policymakers. The passage of the first Elementary and Secondary Education Act (ESEA) and accompanying Title I legislation back in 1964 assured unprecedented funding to support and improve reading programs for children across socioeconomic lines. Seeking to provide equitable resources for impoverished school districts, the U.S. Congress continually revised the ESEA over four decades, creating programs to assist migrant, neglected, and limited English proficient children.

The passage of the No Child Left Behind Act of 2001 (2002), including the Reading First and Early Reading First programs in 2001, has intensified the attention focused on accountability and achievement in literacy education. Mandatory testing of student performance has also increased notably over the past several years. High-stakes tests, the results of which carry potentially significant rewards and penalties for schools, districts, individual teachers, administrators, and students, are, to the concern of many educators, administered to students at younger and younger ages and with greater frequency than ever before (Hoffman et al., 1999).

Despite the increased attention focused on literacy achievement across socioeconomic lines, The National Assessment of Educational Progress (NAEP; 2002) reported that proficient readers are improving while struggling readers are continuing to lose ground. For example, 58% of fourth-grade students eligible for free-lunch programs fell below basic reading proficiency levels. By contrast, 27% of fourth-grade students from higher income areas fell below basic proficiency levels. NAEP data released in 2005 indicated that, while the percentage of fourth graders performing at or above a proficient level increased between 1992 and 2003, the percentage of fourth graders at or above a basic level was not found to have changed significantly during that same period of time (NAEP, 2005). The achievement gap persists. Questions remain about the extent to which summer reading loss contributes to this gap and what educators can do to lessen its impact.

How Does Summer Loss Affect Students' Reading Achievement?

Summer reading loss refers to the decline in children's reading development that can occur during summer vacation times when children are away from the classroom and not participating in formal literacy programs (Allington &

Reprinted from Mraz, M., & Rasinski, T.V. (2007). Summer reading loss. *The Reading Teacher*, 60(8), 784–789.

McGill-Franzen, 2003). Far from being an intuitive perception in the minds of educators, the reality of summer reading loss is well documented—and it is more persistent among students from lower socioeconomic backgrounds who are already at risk for academic failure. Researchers have uncovered evidence to suggest that the impact of summer reading loss on students in general, and on at-risk students in particular, is significant.

A review of 13 empirical studies representing approximately 40,000 students found that, on average, the reading proficiency levels of students from lower income families declined over the summer months, while the reading proficiency levels of students from middle-income families improved modestly. In a single academic year, this decline resulted in an estimated three-month achievement gap between more advantaged and less advantaged students. Between grades 1 and 6, the potential cumulative impact of this achievement gap could compound to 1.5 years' worth of reading development lost in the summer months alone (Cooper, Nye, Charlton, Lindsay, & Greathouse, 1996).

In their review of reading achievement gains in Title I reading programs, Borman and D'Agostino (1996) found that achievement gains were significantly higher from fall to spring when students were enrolled in school reading classes, but they were lower from spring to spring, when the summer months, in which students were not participating in school reading programs, were considered.

In other studies, the reading achievement of both high- and low-income students was found to improve during the academic year, yet the overall achievement gap between the two groups remained high. A longitudinal study of high- and low-income students found that, while both groups of students made comparable gains in reading achievement during the academic year, by the end of sixth grade the achievement gap between high- and low-income students had grown to approximately three grade-level years (Entwisle, Alexander, & Olson, 1997).

After examining 3,000 students over a two-year period, Heyns (1987) found that the top quartile made rapid gains during the academic year and slower, albeit continued, growth over the summer months. The reading achievement of average students remained steady or fell slightly over the summers. The bottom quartile of students made comparatively slower gains in reading achievement during the academic year and then lost a significant portion of those gains over each summer. Some have suggested that nearly 80% of the achievement difference between high-income and low-income students may be attributable to summer reading loss (Hayes & Grether, 1983).

Our research with 116 first, second, and third graders in a school in a middle class neighborhood found that the decoding skills of nearly 45% of the participants and the fluency skills of 25% declined between May and September. Lower achieving students exhibited a sharper decline than higher achieving students.

While working in a lower socioeconomic-status, urban school whose students were already performing, on average, significantly below expectations, we found declines over summer in word decoding among fourth graders and declines in both word decoding and reading fluency among sixth graders.

At a time when the policy climate is intensely focused on raising the achievement levels of all students, summer reading loss seems to have its greatest impact on low-achieving students and at-risk students—those who can least afford to fall further behind.

Why Does Summer Reading Loss Occur?

Access to reading materials has been consistently identified as a vital element in enhancing the reading development of children. Of all the activities in which children engage outside of school, time spent actually reading is the best predictor of reading achievement—the more students read, the better readers they become (Allington, 2006; Anderson, Wilson, & Fielding, 1988). The research indicates also that students, on average, spend pitifully little time reading outside of school—about 10 minutes (Anderson, Wilson, & Fielding).

All too often, however, low-performing readers are offered little or no opportunity beyond the classroom to improve their reading proficiency (Coats & Taylor-Clark, 2001). Children from low-income households have a limited selection of books to read both within their homes and their communities (McQuillan, 1998). Wealthier communities have been found to have up to three businesses selling children's books for every one such business that existed in poorer communities (Neuman & Celano, 2001). Other barriers to reading at home include parents' lack of awareness of the benefits of reading to children and lack of confidence in reading, particularly in the case of adults who are themselves English-language learners or who possess a low literacy level.

In an effort to respond to the lack of access to reading materials and to the need for continued reading instruction, some school districts offer formal summer intervention programs or summer book lists with suggested or required titles. While these initiatives can be effective for some students, for others participation in them is not probable. Even if formal reading instruction cannot be part of all students' summer schedules, there are recommendations that teachers can make to help families support children's reading development when school is not in session.

What Can Be Done to Curb Summer Reading Loss?

The value placed on literacy in the home, time spent reading with children, and the availability and use of reading materials have been identified as important elements in children's reading success (Snow, Burns, & Griffin, 1998). Supporting reading development over the summer months can be done in ways that tap into children's own interests and imaginations. It is not enough, however, to simply tell parents that it is important to read to children. Parents, particularly lower socioeconomic-status parents, need to be offered concrete, specific programs and suggestions on how to participate in family literacy, and they need to be supported in their attempts to do so (Edwards, 2004).

Schools and teachers can do much to set the stage for children's continued engagement in literacy over the summer. Schools can host workshops for parents in the weeks before the start of summer vacation in which teachers make the case for summer reading and share suggestions for keeping children engaged over the summer months. This would be a wonderful time to coordinate with the local public library on its summer reading program. Perhaps the library could arrange to sign up parents and children for library cards and the summer reading program at one of the school workshops.

A required summer reading list of three to five proven favorites for which children will be accountable when school begins again may be appropriate for some schools. Teachers need to be sure that the books assigned are readily available at the local library. Perhaps the school library could remain open over the summer, on a limited basis, to facilitate student reading and access to materials.

Some schools may want to initiate a variation of the Reading Millionaires program that is most often implemented during the school year (Rasinski & Padak, 2004). In a school of 400 students, if each student read 30 minutes a day over the course of a 75-day summer vacation, the total amount of reading done by the student body would be about a million minutes. The school parent–teacher association could arrange to run the program with students submitting weekly logs of the number of minutes read to the school. A team of parents would tally the minutes by student, grade level, and whole school. Outside, the school could display the cumulative total of minutes read. Reminders could be sent periodically to children and parents about the program. The school year would then begin with a celebration of achieving the summer reading goal and with recognition given to individual students and grade levels that achieved or exceeded their goals.

At the family level, the International Reading Association (1998) suggested that parents look for reading materials that relate to interests that a child enjoys, such as baseball, swimming, animals, or nature. Families may need to be assured that useful reading materials come in many forms. In addition to books, children's magazines may link to a child's interest or hobby. While reasonable limits should be set for television viewing, television programs and age-appropriate movies that are based on books can serve as a catalyst for reading. Moreover, when watching television, parents should be advised to engage the captioning feature (and reduce the volume) so that students have access to and are encouraged to read the words on the television screen. Every word that is read counts.

Daily routines provide reading opportunities. Cooking, using the phone book, reading the television listing in a local newspaper, looking for information on the World Wide Web, reading directions for using a new gadget, or reading a brochure or article about a place to which the family may travel during the summer can all provide authentic reading experiences.

The value of modeling reading for children needs to be reiterated to families. All too often families unwittingly send the message to children that reading is a chore: something that must be finished before one can proceed to more active and enjoyable pursuits. Instead, it is important to remind families of the need to create a positive climate for reading so that children look forward to reading. Encourage parents or caregivers to show their children how family members use reading to extend their own interests and acquire information. Let children see family members reading and talking together about what they have read.

Books and other reading materials can be made available during transition times. Children can read on the way to a destination, at the park, at the beach, or while waiting for an appointment. A local library can, of course, help to suggest reading materials. Encourage families to make regular visits to the library and allow children to explore different reading materials. Librarians can offer suggestions that might be a good match for a child's interests and reading level. Keep in mind that reading books that seem slightly below a child's reading level or books that have become "old favorites" can help a developing reader to build confidence and fluency. Table 1 outlines additional suggestions that teachers can make to families of early readers and more advanced readers.

What Elements Contribute to Family Literacy Participation?

There is little doubt that family participation in children's literacy experiences is valuable and needed, especially if attempting to increase children's literacy experiences over the summer months. Educators seek to establish an effective climate for family literacy programs and to elicit substantive family participation in those programs. The following elements have been identified in literacy programs that successfully engage families in participating (Neuman, Caperelli, & Kee, 1998).

An Established Sense of Community

Family members can offer insights for understanding individual children as well as information to enhance specific units of study. Recognize that every member has something useful to contribute.

Teachers' Effective Interpersonal Skills

A teacher's interpersonal skills, along with his or her perceived professional competence, affects parents' willingness to participate. Simple gestures that convey welcome and an appropriate level of concern can enhance teacher–parent rapport.

Ongoing and Varied Communication

Parent–teacher communication can and should take a variety of forms. Those forms can include face-to-face contact, phone calls (those calls can convey positive messages as well as express concern), classroom newsletters sent home on a consistent basis, as well as opportunities for

Table 1
Literacy Advice for Families

Literacy tips for early readers	• Point out print in the child's environment: on cereal boxes, food labels, toys, restaurants, and traffic signs. • Sing songs, say short poems or nursery rhymes, and play rhyming words games with your child. • Tell stories to your child. • Read aloud to your child. Point to the words on the page as you read. • Read a short passage several times to your child until your child can read it with you. Then encourage your child to read the passage to you. • Encourage older children to read with younger children. • Encourage your child to read (or pretend read) to you. Make this reading enjoyable. Don't worry if your child does not read all of the words correctly but, rather, applaud your child's efforts to read. • Go to the library together. • Have books, magazines, and newspapers around the house. Let your child see you reading. • Encourage your child to write messages such as grocery lists, to-do lists, postcards, or short messages to family members or friends. Don't worry about conventional spelling at this point but, rather, encourage your child's first efforts at authorship. • When watching television, have the captioning feature enabled so that the children view the words while hearing them performed aloud.
Literacy tips for more advanced readers	• Talk to your child about what he or she is reading. Ask open-ended questions such as "What do you think about that story?" "What would you have done if you were that character?" • Make reading and writing a regular part of your daily home activities. Let your child see you using reading and writing for real purposes. • Visit the public library. Help your child to get his or her own library card. • Read to your child regularly, even after your child is able to read some books independently. • Listen to your child read. Use strategies to help your child with tricky words. For example, when your child comes to an unfamiliar word, you might say, "Skip it and read to the end of the sentence. Now try again—what makes sense and looks like the word that you see?" • Praise your child's efforts at reading. • Play word games such as thinking of different words to describe the same things. • Support your child's writing. Have writing materials such as paper, markers, and pencils available. Read what your child writes. • Set reasonable limits for television viewing.

Note. Adapted from Mraz, Padak, & Baycich (2002).

parents to visit the classroom and learn firsthand about what is happening there.

Consistent Recruitment of Family Participation

Requesting and encouraging family participation needs to happen consistently over the course of the school year. The more opportunities families have to interact with one another, the more likely their participation in school programs is to increase.

The Suggestion of a Variety of Literacy Activities for the Home

Families need concrete suggestions about how to support literacy development at home. The ideas presented in this article can serve as a starting point. When making suggestions to parents, teachers need to keep in mind that effective family literacy interactions should seek to promote the natural and enjoyable interactions between parents and children, not to make the home environment a structured extension of the classroom.

Teachers' Understanding of Family Challenges

The vast majority of families want to provide a home environment that will allow younger members to thrive. Life circumstances often make this hope a difficult reality to accomplish. Be aware of circumstances that may make literacy participation challenging for some families. When possible, offer suggestions and resources that may aid families in overcoming these challenges

Summer reading loss is a documented reality for many students. It is often of greatest concern for those students who are already at risk—who typically have limited access to reading materials at home and parents or caregivers who may be reluctant to or unsure of how to help. By raising parents' awareness of the importance of supporting their children's reading development during the summer months and by providing concrete guidelines on how to do so, teachers and students may be better able to start anew instead of starting from scratch when the next school year begins.

References

Allington, R.L. (2006). *What really matters for struggling readers: Designing research-based programs* (2nd ed.). Boston: Allyn & Bacon.

Allington, R.L., & McGill-Franzen, A. (2003). The impact of summer reading setback on the reading achievement gap. *Phi Delta Kappan, 85*, 68–75.

Anderson, R.L., Wilson, P., & Fielding, L. (1988). Growth in reading and how children spend their time outside of school. *Reading Research Quarterly, 23*(3), 285–303.

Borman, G.D., & D'Agostino, J.V. (1996). Title I and student achievement: A meta-analysis of federal results. *Educational Evaluation and Policy Analysis, 18*(4), 309–326.

Coats, L.T., & Taylor-Clark, P. (2001). Finding a niche for reading: A key to improving underachievers' reading skills. *Reading Improvement, 38*, 70–73.

Cooper, H., Nye, B., Charlton, K., Lindsay, J., & Greathouse, S. (1996). The effects of summer vacation on achievement test scores: A narrative and meta-analytic review. *Review of Educational Research, 66*(3), 227–268.

Edwards, P.A. (2004). *Children's literacy development: Making it happen through school, family, and community involvement.* Boston: Allyn & Bacon.

Entwisle, D.R., Alexander, K.L., & Olson, L.S. (1997). *Children, schools, and inequality.* Boulder, CO: Westview.

Hayes, D.P., & Grether, J. (1983). The school year and vacations: When do students learn? *Cornell Journal of Social Relations, 17*, 56–71.

Heyns, B. (1987). Schooling and cognitive development: Is there a season for learning? *Child Development, 55*, 6–10.

Hoffman, J.V., Au, K.H., Harrison, C., Paris, S.G., Pearson, P.D., Santa, C.M., et al. (1999). High-stakes assessments in reading: Consequences, concerns, and common sense. In S.J. Barrentine (Ed.), *Reading assessment: Principles and practices for elementary teachers* (pp. 247–260). Newark, DE: International Reading Association.

International Reading Association. (1998). *Summer reading adventure: Tips for parents of young readers.* Newark, DE: Author.

McQuillan, J. (1998). *The literacy crisis: False claims, real solutions.* Portsmouth, NH: Heinemann.

Mraz, M., Padak, N., & Baycich, D. (2002). *Literacy tips for children.* Ohio Literacy Resource Center. Retrieved January 18, 2007, from http://literacy.kent.edu/Oasis/Pubs/child_lit_tips.pdf

National Assessment of Educational Progress. (2002). *NAEP reading: National trends in reading.* Washington, DC: National Center for Educational Statistics.

National Assessment of Educational Progress. (2005). *Reading: The nation's report card.* Retrieved on August 16, 2005, from http://nces.ed.gov/nationsreportcard/reading

Neuman, S.B., & Celano, D. (2001). Access to print in low-income and middle-income communities. *Reading Research Quarterly, 36*(1), 8–26.

Neuman, S.B., Caperelli, B.J., & Kee, C. (1998). Literacy learning: A family matter. *The Reading Teacher, 52*, 244–252

No Child Left Behind Act of 2001, Pub. L. No. 107-110, 115 Stat. 1425 (2002).

Rasinski, T.V., & Padak, N.D. (2004). *Effective reading strategies: Teaching children who find reading difficult* (3rd ed.). Columbus, OH : Merrill/Prentice Hall.

Snow, C.E., Burns, M.S, & Griffin, P. (Eds.). (1998). *Preventing reading difficulties in young children.* Washington, DC: National Academy Press.

Questions for Reflection

- As the authors point out, summer reading is important for all children but perhaps most so for poor children and for those who struggle. Consider the tips the authors provide in Table 1 in this article, and the elements they describe as supporting family participation in students' independent reading. How can you use this information to design ways to encourage and support students' reading outside of school, particularly during the long summer vacation?
- Read this article in conjunction with the preceding piece by Garan and DeVoogd on SSR. How might you use SSR in your classroom to build reading habits among your students—habits they can carry into their out-of-school time? What additional support may need to be provided to your struggling learners?

"She's My Best Reader; She Just Can't Comprehend": Studying the Relationship Between Fluency and Comprehension

Mary DeKonty Applegate, Anthony J. Applegate, and Virginia B. Modla

Our graduate students are for the most part reading specialist candidates, and in the course designed to sharpen their assessment skills, we require them to administer an informal reading inventory to several students. To broaden the scope of their experience, we ask that they not limit themselves to struggling readers but test at least one student who has been identified by teachers or parents as a strong reader. Last year, one of our students waited until class was over to share with us how distraught she was about the poor overall performance of her "strong reader." Unfortunately, we were quite familiar with the scenario she was describing. We encouraged her to speak with the child's teacher to gain more insight into the child's day-to-day performance in reading. The following week she came back equally distressed. It seems that the teacher had told her, "Oh, she's my best reader, for sure. She's just not a good comprehender."

As disconcerting as this story may be, even more disconcerting were the responses to the tale that we encountered from nearly a dozen practicing professionals: They were not surprised at all. A large proportion of both our students and our professional colleagues had an opinion as to the reason behind this incident and others like it. They cited as the chief cause an overemphasis in their schools on the development of oral reading indicators such as rate and accuracy without an accompanying emphasis on comprehension. Our curiosity about how widespread the problem might be led to this formal investigation into the relationship between fluency and reading comprehension.

Fluency and Comprehension

Fluency was once famously described as a "neglected goal" of American reading education (Allington, 1983), but that is clearly no longer the case. The origins of the resurgence of interest in reading fluency can be traced earlier than the report of the National Reading Panel (NRP; National Institute of Child Health and Human Development [NICHD], 2000), but there is little doubt that the report's recognition of fluency as one of its five pillars of reading served as a flashpoint for an explosive increase of interest in fluency and its instructional corollaries.

The fact remains that variations in the definition of reading fluency still abound in the literature (Keehn, 2003), but there seems to be a sizeable consensus on two of its key components: (1) accurate and automatic word recognition and (2) reading at an appropriate rate of speed. Reading with appropriate prosody or expression has been regularly added to the definition of fluency by many theorists, but it should be noted that there is some conflict in the findings of researchers who have investigated links between prosody and comprehension. Some researchers have reported links between the two (Meyer & Felton, 1999; Miller & Schwanenflugel, 2006),

Reprinted from Applegate, M.D., Applegate, A.J., & Modla, V.B. (2009). "She's my best reader, she just can't comprehend": Studying the relationship between fluency and comprehension. *The Reading Teacher, 62*(6), 512–521.

while others have failed to verify a relationship (Schatschneider et al., 2004).

Still other theorists add to these components the essential elements of comprehension and the construction of meaning (Eldredge, 2005; LaBerge & Samuels, 1974; Pikulski & Chard, 2005; Rasinski, 2003, Samuels, 2007). However, in most of the studies that we reviewed, the most common definition of fluency did not specifically include the concept of comprehension; instead, researchers seemed to be attempting to determine if links between fluency and comprehension could be established. Consequently, we will use *fluency* in this paper in the same way that we found it most frequently used in the literature, as an indicator of the speed, accuracy, and prosody of oral reading.

Fluency as a Predecessor of Comprehension

LaBerge and Samuels (1974) proposed the idea that reading requires two central tasks of our inherently limited cognitive resources: word recognition and comprehension. If readers have not developed automaticity in word recognition, then the efforts they must expend in decoding will almost necessarily limit the efforts they can direct to comprehension. Conversely, the more automatic the decoding, the more attentional resources they will have available to direct toward comprehension.

Based on the ideas of LaBerge and Samuels, some researchers have suggested that once they are freed up, attentional resources depleted by basic word recognition can then be directed toward comprehension (Hudson, Lane, & Pullen, 2005; NICHD, 2000). Consequently, they concluded that increases in student fluency should result in increases in reading achievement, particularly comprehension.

Fluency and Comprehension Intertwined

Other researchers and theorists argue that the relationship between fluency and comprehension is much more complex than meets the eye (Dowhower, 1991; Rasinski, 1984; Strecker, Roser, & Martinez, 1998). Some, for example, have called attention to the fact that readers' comprehension and fluency strategies are affected by the extent to which they find the material interesting (Walczyk & Griffith-Ross, 2007). Others have insisted that the fluency instruction given to struggling readers must be multidimensional if they are to achieve the ultimate goal of reading: the ability to respond to text reflectively and intelligently (Gaskins, 1999; Pikulski & Chard, 2005; Pressley, Gaskins, & Fingeret, 2006). Still others have suggested that the development of fluency requires opportunities to engage in critical and meaningful discussions of text (Griffith & Rasinski, 2004). Such interactive conceptualizations insist that skills such as fluency and comprehension be developed simultaneously (Schwanenflugel et al., 2006) so that the reciprocal relationship between them becomes obvious and conscious to readers and can be incorporated into their internal monitoring system.

Rationale

We were mindful of a sizeable number of studies in which children trained in the acquisition of reading fluency also demonstrated growth in comprehension (Breznitz, 1987; Flood, Lapp, & Fisher, 2005; Greenwood, Tapia, Abbott, & Walton, 2003; Griffith & Rasinski, 2004; Keehn, 2003; O'Connor et al., 2002; O'Connor, White, & Swanson, 2007; Reutzel, Hollingworth, & Eldredge, 1994; Schwanenflugel et al., 2006; Young, Bowers, & MacKinnon, 1996). In our study, however, the children had already acquired a high level of fluency as evidenced by their rate, accuracy, and prosody. In addition, they had been identified by their classroom teachers or parents as strong readers, and all were members of the top reading group in their classroom. We reasoned that if fluency promotes reading comprehension, then these students should be expected to demonstrate reasonably high performance levels when comprehension was assessed at their current grade level.

We were also mindful of the fact that most studies that reported gains in comprehension as a function of fluency improvement assessed comprehension by means of either standardized multiple-choice tests (Breznitz, 1987; Jenkins, Fuchs, van den Broek, Espin, & Deno, 2003; Keehn, 2003; O'Connor et al., 2007; Schwanenflugel et al., 2006) or on the basis of literal retellings (Keehn, 2003; Young et al., 1996). Some of these same researchers called for replication of their findings using a broader range of comprehension measures (Schwanenflugel et al., 2006). We set out to assess reading comprehension as complex, higher-level, thoughtful response to text.

To investigate the nature of the relationship between fluency and comprehension, we identified a sizeable number of children who had been identified as strong and fluent readers. We reasoned that if these students performed well at their current grade level in a measure of reading comprehension, such a result would lend support to the idea that fluency contributes to comprehension. If, however, a significant proportion of highly fluent and highly regarded readers should experience difficulties with comprehension, we may need to take a closer look at the relationship between fluency and comprehension.

Our study examined two issues:

1. Is there support in our findings for the idea that the development of a high level of fluency will be accompanied by a high degree of reading comprehension?
2. Will a high degree of fluency be accompanied by a high degree of reading comprehension when that comprehension is assessed as thoughtful response to text?

Assessing Reading Comprehension

We selected the Critical Reading Inventory-2 (CRI-2; Applegate, Quinn, & Applegate, 2008) as our measure of reading comprehension for several reasons. First, we needed a tool that could be used to assess a wide range of specific grade levels since our study included students from grades 2 through 10. The CRI-2 includes passages at grade levels preprimer through 12th grade. We also sought a measure of a reader's ability to not only recall text but to also respond thoughtfully to it. The CRI-2 is rooted in widely accepted definitions of reading that we found in the professional literature, definitions that reflect a remarkable level of agreement on the thoughtful, interactive nature of comprehension (Flippo, 2001). Much of this agreement is reflected in the NRP's definition of reading: "an active process that requires an intentional and thoughtful interaction between the reader and the text" (NICHD, 2000). In addition, Applegate, Applegate, McGeehan, Pinto, and Kong (2009) conducted an examination of the fourth-grade instructional and assessment frameworks from all 50 states and found that no state defines the ability to read as the simple ability to extract meaning from text. All state assessments expect at least some level of thoughtful response on the part of the reader.

The CRI-2 includes narrative and informational text selections that were leveled on the basis of the Flesch-Kincaid readability formula and followed by an extensive analysis of actual test data, aimed at validating these grade levels. The CRI-2 incorporates a retelling rubric structured to resemble a typical story grammar and includes credit for a reader's well-supported personal response to the text. Analysis of retelling data was aimed toward maximizing the relationship between retelling scores and comprehension and distinguishing between and among scoring categories. A computerized automated scoring and interpretation interview includes a program that accurately calculates retelling scores and requires only that the user indicate those story elements that were present or absent in the retelling. In the standardization study for the CRI-2, narrative retellings were found to correlate at 0.51 with total comprehension item score for narrative text. Descriptions of narrative retelling scores are included in Table 1.

Finally the fluency rubric that accompanies the CRI-2 is designed to assess pacing, accuracy, and prosody of oral reading (see Figure 1).

The CRI-2 was developed to measure reading along three dimensions:

Table 1
Descriptions of Narrative Retelling Scores

Score	Description
4.0	A virtually perfect retelling that includes all story elements and a well-supported personal response
3.5	An exceptionally strong retelling that omits a small but significant part of the problem-solving process but still includes a well-supported personal response
3.0	A very strong retelling that includes all story elements, including all five steps in the problem-solving process, but does not include a personal response
2.5	A strong retelling that includes many story elements in a variety of combinations and may include a personal response; a reader who achieves this score has clearly comprehended the primary gist of the story
2.0	A solid retelling that includes most key story elements but that is also characterized by some key omissions and that may include a personal response
1.5	A fairly weak retelling that includes some story elements but also omits a good deal of key information and may contain some factual distortions and that may include a personal response
1.0	A weak retelling that includes a few story elements but is also characterized by some glaring omissions and factual distortions and that does not include a personal response
.5	A very weak retelling that includes little more than a few disjointed story elements and factual distortion and that does not include a personal response
.0	A retelling that may include nothing more than a vague idea of the topic of the story or a character in the story and that does not include a personal response

Note. From Applegate, Quinn, and Applegate, 2008, p. 80. Reprinted by permission of Pearson Education, Upper Saddle River, New Jersey, USA.

1. Text-based—These items include both literal questions whose answers are stated explicitly (verbatim) in the text and low-level inferences whose answers are not stated verbatim in the text but may be so close to literal as to be obvious. One such example (Leslie & Caldwell, 2006, p. 314) occurred when the text read "Pele had a dream. He wanted to become a professional soccer player." The question was "What was Pele's main goal?" Despite the fact that this item was labeled as assessing implicit comprehension (interaction of text information and prior knowledge), we categorized such items as text-based because they required only that the reader translate a response from one linguistic form to another.
2. Inference—These items call for the reader to link experiences with the text and to draw a logical conclusion. Answers to these items require significantly more complex thinking than low-level inferences. For example, a story describes a father's effort to teach his children to fish. His daughter is very successful, but his frustrated son will not listen to his father's advice. The inference question is "Why would Pat's sister be better at fishing than Pat?" To answer the question successfully, the reader must note that Pat's sister is listening to the advice she is given and avoiding the kind of behavior that might lead to failure (Applegate, Quinn, & Applegate, 2008, p 111).

Figure 1
Oral Reading Fluency Rubric From the *Critical Reading Inventory*

Rate the reader's fluency in each of the four categories below. Check only one box in each category.

Oral reading

______ (5 pts.) Reading is fluent, confident, and accurate.

______ (4 pts.) Reading is fluent and accurate for the most part, but reader occasionally falters or hesitates.

______ (3 pts.) Reader lacks confidence at times, and reading is characterized by frequent pauses, miscues, and hesitations.

______ (2 pts.) Reader consistently lacks confidence and occasionally lapses into word-by-word reading with frequent meaning-violating miscues.

______ (1 pt.) Reader demonstrates largely word-by-word reading with little or no inflection and numerous meaning-violating miscues, some of which may be nonwords.

Intonation

______ (5 pts.) Intonations consistently support meaning of the text.

______ (4 pts.) Intonations are largely meaningful but may include exaggerations or inflections inappropriate for the text.

______ (3 pts.) Intonation is characterized by some joining of words into meaningful phrases, but this element often breaks down when the reader encounters difficulties.

______ (2 pts.) Intonation is largely flat with lack of enthusiasm.

______ (1 pt.) Intonation is almost completely absent.

Punctuation

______ (5 pts.) Reader demonstrates a natural use of and appreciation for punctuation.

______ (4 pts.) Reader demonstrates a solid use of punctuation as an aid to intonation.

______ (3 pts.) Reaction to punctuation marks results in pauses that are inappropriately long or short.

______ (2 pts.) Punctuation is occasionally ignored and meaning may be distorted.

______ (1 pt.) Reader demonstrates frequent ignoring of punctuation.

Pacing

______ (5 pts.) Pacing is rapid but smooth and unexaggerated.

______ (4 pts.) Reading is well paced with only occasional weakness in response to difficulties with the text.

______ (3 pts.) Pacing relatively slow and markedly slower (or markedly faster) when reader encounters difficult text.

______ (2 pts.) Pacing is either very slow or inappropriately fast.

______ (1 pt.) Pacing is painfully slow and halting.

______ Total score

Note. From Applegate, Quinn, and Applegate, 2008, p. 76. Reprinted by permission of Pearson Education, Upper Saddle River, New Jersey, USA.

3. Critical response—These items call for a reader to link text and experience and to express and defend an idea related to the actions of characters or the outcome of events. Critical response items differ from high-level inference items in that they are directed toward broader ideas or underlying themes that relate to the significance of the passage. They require analysis, reaction, and response to text, based on personal experience and values (Nilsson, 2008), and demand that the reader react to the underlying meaning of the passage as a whole. For the passage described above, a critical response item asks, "How well do you think Dad taught the children to fish?" The reader can respond either positively or negatively but must support the response with information from the text and demonstrate a solid understanding of the essence of the story (Applegate, Quinn, & Applegate, 2008, p. 111).

We designed this type of assessment to enable users to distinguish between readers who can recall information from the text and those who can think about it. No less than 60% of the comprehension questions in the CRI-2 assess the higher-level thinking included in inference and critical response items. Our intent in this regard was to emulate national and international assessments that are heavily weighted with such items. Most prominent among these is the National Assessment of Educational Progress, often referred to as "the nation's report card." Included in its 2007 framework for test development (National Assessment Governing Board, 2006) are four aspects of reading: (1) forming a general understanding, (2) developing interpretation, (3) making reader-text connections, and (4) examining content and structure. Only the first of these focuses on text-based comprehension.

Sample and Methodology

The sample for this study consisted of 171 children, ranging from grade 2 through grade 10 and residing in Pennsylvania, New Jersey, and Delaware. The sample included 60 males and 111 females, a rather heavy weighting in favor of females. Eighty-six percent of the children in the sample were Caucasian while 14% were members of minority groups. One hundred and nine attended public schools, 45 attended parochial schools, 17 attended private schools, and two were home-schooled. Table 2 includes a breakdown of the sample in light of grade-level categories.

All subjects were tested by graduate or undergraduate examiners as part of the course work in the diagnosis and correction of reading difficulties. All examiners were trained in the administration and scoring of the CRI-2 via classroom demonstrations and web-based tutorials for the scoring of comprehension items, miscues, and retellings. Examiners were instructed to audiotape oral readings of passages as well as retellings. All retellings were scored by comparing the child's retelling to a retelling rubric unique to each passage and based largely on the recall of key elements drawn from a modified story grammar structure. Retelling scores were calculated by a computer program available to CRI-2 users. The use of the program has been

Table 2
Number of Subjects in Grade-Level Categories

Primary grades (2–3)	Intermediate grades (4–5)	Middle and high school grades (6–10)	Total
n = 60	*n* = 57	*n* = 54	*N* = 171

shown to significantly increase the reliability of the scoring of retellings (Applegate, Quinn, & Applegate, 2008).

As indicated earlier, we asked examiners to test a reader who had been identified by a parent or teacher as a strong reader. We reasoned that parents would be most likely to identify their children as strong readers if their teachers had done so. The results of the parent interview of the CRI-2 confirmed those assumptions. A large number of parents cited teacher feedback and grades as the source of their characterization of the reading skills of their children. In addition, only children placed by their teachers in the high reading group in their classrooms were included in the study. From among the strong readers identified, we selected for this study only those who earned a score of 16 or higher on the CRI-2 Reading Fluency Rubric, indicating strong fluency performance in terms of accuracy, pace, and prosody.

All examiner scores for retellings and comprehension items were cross-checked independently by two experienced CRI-2 users and any discrepancies were resolved by discussion. In the case of fluency scores, the experts cross-checked a random sample of 30 audiotapes to ensure the accuracy of assigned scores. In 97% of the cases sampled, the experts agreed that subjects met the minimum criteria in speed, accuracy, and prosody of oral reading for inclusion in the study.

Results

Each subject was tested at his or her current grade level on two narrative passages from the CRI-2, with one read orally and the other read silently. Each passage was followed by a retelling and a series of 10 open-ended comprehension questions. Text-based comprehension at each child's current grade level was assessed by a total of eight comprehension items and higher order comprehension was assessed by a total of 12 comprehension items. We combined inference and critical response items because both item types assess the ability to link text and experience and because such a combination of items would enable us to measure higher order thinking with a higher degree of reliability. The mean scores for all subjects are presented in Table 3.

Of more interest than raw mean scores is the proportion of the sample that was judged to be functioning as advanced, proficient, or struggling comprehenders in their current grade-level placement. For the purpose of this study, we defined advanced comprehenders as those achieving a total comprehension score of 85% or higher. Proficient comprehenders achieved a total score ranging between 63% and 80%. Struggling comprehenders received a total score of 58% or lower. Table 4 includes the number of readers in the sample classified at each level and the mean comprehension, retelling, and fluency scores they achieved at their current grade level.

As might be expected, a significant number (30%) of our fluent and strong readers achieved a high level of reading comprehension, both literal and higher order, at their current grade levels. An even larger number (36%) of these readers scored at a level that suggested that they are proficient readers but still have some instructional needs in comprehension. The most startling finding, however, was the fact that fully one third of our fluent and "strong" readers struggled mightily with comprehension at their current grade level. It is difficult to escape the conclusion that many of

Table 3
Mean Scores in Text-Based and Higher Order Items

Mean score text-based	Mean score higher order	Mean score all items
80.70	66.12	70.07

Table 4
Comprehension, Retelling, and Fluency Scores for Advanced, Proficient, and Struggling Readers

	Total comprehension	Text-based	Higher order	Average retelling	Average fluency
Advanced comprehenders (*n* = 52)	91.64	96.74	88.23	2.45	17.87
Proficient comprehenders (*n* = 62)	71.28	82.42	63.85	1.73	18.03
Struggling comprehenders (*n* = 57)	49.46	70.75	35.31	1.00	17.40

these children had been judged strong readers on the basis of their pacing, accuracy, and prosody alone.

Our experiences with comprehension questioning following reading led us to investigate another possible explanation for these results. The data in Table 4 suggest that the average text-based comprehension of struggling comprehenders reached an instructional level, suggesting that much of the problem lies with higher order comprehension. From among the 57 struggling comprehenders in this sample, we identified those whose percentage score on text-based comprehension exceeded their score on higher order comprehension by a margin of 30 percentage points or more. We found that 29 of the 57 struggling comprehenders we identified fit this pattern of differential scores. This finding sheds some light on the overall results and may reveal a problem that is more widespread than is apparent. In his discussion of thoughtful literacy, Allington (2001) identified numerous studies of classrooms where researchers found an overwhelming proportion of tasks that emphasize remembering and reciting with very few tasks that engage children in thinking about what they read. If our subset of struggling readers were to be placed in such classrooms, their high levels of speed, accuracy, and prosody, coupled as they were with the ability to answer factual questions, would make them reading stars. And if the assessment of reading comprehension remained largely literal, it may be years before their struggles with comprehension are discovered.

An examination of the pattern of scores included in Table 4 suggests that the differences in performance between text-based and higher order comprehension cannot be ascribed simply to the fact that one type of item is easier than another (Jennings, Caldwell, & Lerner, 2006). It is clear that nearly a third of all the readers in our sample were able to perform very well on challenging, open-ended items.

Disaggregation of our results into grade-level groups revealed some inconsistency in results for text-based comprehension but very little with respect to higher order or total comprehension (see Table 5). Thus it appears that in this study, grade level of subjects was not a factor in the relationship between fluency and comprehension.

Discussion

The most obvious and disturbing element of these findings is that there may be a considerable number of teachers who are judging the reading proficiency of their students based solely on speed, accuracy, and prosody, divorced from thoughtful comprehension. In retrospect, this should not come as a surprise to savvy

Table 5
Comprehension, Retelling, and Fluency Scores for Advanced, Proficient, and Struggling Readers by Grade Level

Grade level	Comprehension performance	Text-based	Higher order	Total comprehension	Average retelling	Average fluency
Grades 2-3	Advanced (*n* = 15)	98.80	86.97	91.70	2.42	17.20
Grades 4-5	Advanced (*n* = 19)	97.36	88.37	91.97	2.43	18.21
Grades 6-10	Advanced (*n* = 18)	93.93	89.14	91.07	2.50	18.06
Grades 2-3	Proficient (*n* = 18)	74.14	66.63	69.63	1.81	18.16
Grades 4-5	Proficient (*n* = 21)	87.00	62.83	72.50	1.54	17.81
Grades 6-10	Proficient (*n* = 23)	85.25	62.41	71.55	1.91	18.14
Grades 2-3	Struggling (*n* = 27)	62.00	35.22	45.93	0.99	17.33
Grades 4-5	Struggling (*n* = 17)	67.33	36.56	48.87	1.12	17.47
Grades 6-10	Struggling (*n* = 13)	75.92	33.85	50.68	0.83	17.46

observers of reading education. Much of the recent literature in the field emphasizes the sizeable correlation that exists between fluency and reading achievement. Many of the articles that we reviewed encouraged teachers to work on the speed, phrasing, or prosody of their students' oral reading while giving little or no attention to comprehension (Devault & Joseph, 2004; Hudson et al., 2005; Richards, 2000; Speece & Ritchey, 2005). As we discussed earlier, even in many of those cases when comprehension was incorporated into fluency instruction, the type of comprehension assessed was purely text based and, if these results are in any way representative, largely unable to detect their subjects' levels of thoughtful comprehension.

LaBerge and Samuels (1974), in their oft-cited description of attentional resources, suggest that automaticity in word recognition frees up an individual's attention for use in comprehension. Our data suggest that for many of the students in our sample, the freed-up resources that result from automaticity and fluency do not necessarily or automatically flow toward comprehension. The fact that we know little about the type of reading instruction these children received is both a limitation of the current study and a challenge to future research. However, it is clear that a significant number of these children have developed a distorted conceptualization of reading, focusing their energies on a high level of word recognition and fluency without also developing high levels of comprehension. A second challenge to future research is to investigate whether females are more likely to be overcategorized as strong readers based on their fluency alone.

Thus it seems that treating word recognition and fluency as skills that exist separate and distinct from comprehension may open the door for a great deal of confusion on the part of students and teachers alike. Even many researchers have "treated all reading skills as similar components compiled in expert reading" (Paris, 2005, p. 199), opening the door to conceptual misinterpretations of the nature of skill development. If, as it seems, the processes of automaticity and comprehension are interactive and intertwined in their effects upon each other, there is no rationale for partitioning them in our instructional schemata. To do so is to run the risk that some students and teachers will come to accept the notion that automaticity and fluency are ends in themselves and not means to the ultimate goal—a thoughtful response to text. Instead, we believe that fluency must take its rightful place among many other cognitive processes that affect the quality of comprehension, such as background knowledge, vocabulary, motivation, selective attention, and schemata organization.

Few of the authors we reviewed would go so far as to suggest that the correlation between fluency and comprehension is linear or causal. Indeed many writers specifically warn against this oversimplification of such a complex interrelationship (Pikulski & Chard, 2005; Strecker, Roser, & Martinez, 1998). Translating such complexity into simple instructional prescriptions, no matter how good the intent, opens the door for what Rasinski (2004) calls "the corruption of the definition of fluency" (p.49).

In fact, the dangers of confusing curricular means and ends in the use of such assessments as the Dynamic Indicators of Basic Elementary Literacy Skills (DIBELS) have been discussed at length by Pearson (2006), Samuels (2007), and Allington (2009). Our data lend support to the notion that assessments of fluency without concurrent assessments of thoughtful comprehension are potentially misleading and damaging. What may ultimately be even more detrimental is the establishment of programs of instruction that divorce fluency and word recognition from comprehension.

It is clear that many theorists believe that fluency is a facilitator of comprehension and precedes its development. At the other end of the spectrum, some believe that fluency is an "outcome" of comprehension. Both positions are challenged by these data. In the former case, fluency did not produce in all of these students a high level of comprehension. Some may argue that since fluency has been achieved in these children it is now time to focus on comprehension. The problem is that nearly one quarter of our struggling comprehenders are attending middle school and high school. For those who view fluency as an outcome of comprehension, a high level of comprehension was clearly not necessary to produce fluency in all of these students. It seems to us that the answer to the relationship between fluency and comprehension lies elsewhere in a complex interaction that is not clearly understood and needs much more investigation and research.

It is our hope that these findings give us all reason to pause and consider the consequences of developing sets of reading skills in our children without an uncompromising diligence in assessing whether these skills are working together as they should. In the old nursery rhyme, Humpty Dumpty fell off the wall and broke into many pieces. In the cases of many of the children whom we assessed, it will be a daunting task to reassemble the pieces and help them to become the thoughtful and intelligent readers that we need them to be.

References

Allington, R.L. (1983). Fluency: The neglected reading goal. *The Reading Teacher, 36*(6), 556–561.

Allington, R.L. (2001). *What really matters for struggling readers: Designing research-based programs.* New York: Longman.

Allington, R.L. (2009). *What really matters in fluency: Research-based practices across the curriculum.* Boston: Allyn & Bacon.

Applegate, A.J., Applegate, M.D., McGeehan, C.M., Pinto, C.M., & Kong, A. (2009). The assessment of thoughtful literacy in NAEP: Why the states aren't measuring up. *The Reading Teacher, 62*(5), 372–381.

Applegate, M.D., Quinn, K.B., & Applegate, A.J. (2008). *The critical reading inventory: Assessing students' reading and thinking* (2nd ed.). Upper Saddle River, NJ: Pearson.

Breznitz, Z. (1987). Increasing first graders' reading accuracy and comprehension by accelerating their reading rates. *Journal of Educational Psychology, 79*(3), 236–242.

Devault, R., & Joseph, L.M. (2004). Repeated readings combined with word boxes phonics technique increases fluency levels of high school students with severe reading delays. *Preventing School Failure, 49*(1), 22–27.

Dowhower, S.L. (1991). Speaking of prosody: Fluency's unattended bedfellow. *Theory Into Practice, 30*(3), 165–175.

Eldredge, J.L. (2005). Foundations of fluency: An exploration. *Reading Psychology, 26*(2), 161–181.

Flippo, R.F. (2001). *Reading researchers in search of common ground.* Newark, DE: International Reading Association.

Flood, J., Lapp, D., & Fisher, D. (2005). Neurological Impress Method Plus. *Reading Psychology, 26*(2), 147–160.

Gaskins, I.W. (1999). A multidimensional reading program. *The Reading Teacher, 53*(2), 162–164.

Greenwood, C.R., Tapia, Y., Abbott, M., & Walton, C. (2003). A building-based case study of evidence-based literacy practices: Implementation, reading behavior, and growth in reading fluency, K-4. *The Journal of Special Education, 37*(2), 95–110.

Griffith, L.W., & Rasinski, T.V. (2004). A focus on fluency: How one teacher incorporated fluency with her reading curriculum. *The Reading Teacher, 58*(2), 126–137.

Hudson, R.F., Lane, H.B., & Pullen, P.C. (2005). Reading fluency assessment and instruction: What, why, and how? *The Reading Teacher, 58*(8), 702–714.

Jenkins, J.R., Fuchs, L.S., van den Broek, P., Espin, C., & Deno, S.L. (2003). Sources of individual differences in reading comprehension and reading fluency. *Journal of Educational Psychology, 95*(4), 719–729.

Jennings, J.H., Caldwell, J.S., Lerner, J.W., & Richek, M.A. (2006). *Reading problems: Assessment and teaching strategies* (5th ed.). Boston: Allyn & Bacon.

Keehn, S. (2003). The effect of instruction and practice through Readers Theatre on young readers' oral reading fluency. *Reading Research and Instruction, 42*(4), 40–61.

LaBerge, D., & Samuels, S.J. (1974). Toward a theory of automatic information processing in reading. *Cognitive Psychology, 6*(2), 293–323.

Leslie, L., & Caldwell, J. (2006). *Qualitative reading inventory-4.* Boston: Allyn & Bacon.

Meyer, M.S., & Felton, R.H. (1999). Repeated readings to enhance fluency: Old approaches and new directions. *Annals of Dyslexia, 49*(1), 283–306.

Miller, J., & Schwanenflugel, P.J. (2006). Prosody of syntactically complex sentences in the oral reading of young children. *Journal of Educational Psychology, 98*(4), 839–853.

National Assessment Governing Board. (2006). *Reading framework for the 2007 National Assessment of Educational Progress.* Retrieved December 18, 2007, from www.nagb.org/frameworks/reading_07.pdf

National Institute of Child Health and Human Development. (2000). *Report of the National Reading Panel. Teaching children to read: An evidence-based assessment of the scientific research literature on reading and its implications for reading instruction* (NIH Publication No. 00-4769). Washington, DC: U.S. Government Printing Office.

Nilsson, N.L. (2008). A critical analysis of eight informal reading inventories. *The Reading Teacher, 61*(7), 526–536.

O'Connor, R.E., Bell, K.M., Harty, K.R., Larkin, L.K., Sackor, S.M., & Zigmond, N. (2002). Teaching reading to poor readers in the intermediate grades: A comparison of text difficulty. *Journal of Educational Psychology, 94*(3), 474–485.

O'Connor, R.E., White, A., & Swanson, H.L. (2007). Repeated reading versus continuous reading: Influences on reading fluency and comprehension. *Exceptional Children, 74*(1), 31–46.

Paris, S. (2005). Reinterpreting the development of reading skills. *Reading Research Quarterly, 40*(2), 184–202.

Pearson, P.D. (2006). Foreword. In K.S. Goodman (Ed.), *The truth about DIBELS: What it is—What it does* (pp. v–xix). Portsmouth, NH: Heinemann.

Pikulski, J.J., & Chard, D.J. (2005). Fluency: Bridge between decoding and reading comprehension. *The Reading Teacher, 58*(6), 510–519.

Pressley, M., Gaskins, I.W., & Fingeret, L. (2006). Instruction and development of reading fluency in struggling readers. In S.J. Samuels & A.E. Farstrup (Eds.), *What research has to say about fluency instruction* (pp. 47–69). Newark, DE: International Reading Association.

Rasinski, T.V. (1984). *Developing models of reading fluency.* Newark, DE: International Reading Association.

Rasinski, T.V. (2003). *The fluent reader.* New York: Scholastic.

Rasinski, T.V. (2004). Creating fluent readers. *Educational Leadership, 61*(6), 46–51.

Reutzel, D.R., Hollingworth, P.M., & Eldredge, J.L. (1994). Oral reading instruction: The impact on student reading development. *Reading Research Quarterly, 29*(1), 40–62.

Richards, M. (2000). Be a good detective: Solve the case of oral reading fluency. *The Reading Teacher, 53*(7), 534–539.

Samuels, S.J. (2007). Commentary: The DIBELS test is speed of barking at print: What we mean by reading fluency. *Reading Research Quarterly, 42*(4), 563–566.

Schatschneider, C., Buck, J., Torgeson, J., Wagner, R., Hassler, L., Hecht, S., et al. (2004). *A multivariate study of individual differences in performance on the reading portion of the Florida comprehensive assessment test: A brief report.* Tallahassee, Florida: Center for Reading Research. Retrieved December 4, 2008, from www.fcrr.org/technicalreports/multi_variate_study_december2004.pdf

Schwanenflugel, P.J., Meisinger, E.B., Wisenbaker, J.M., Kuhn, M.R., Strauss, G.P., & Morris, R.D. (2006). Becoming a fluent and automatic reader in the early elementary school years. *Reading Research Quarterly, 41*(4), 496–522.

Speece, D.L., & Ritchey, K.D. (2005). A longitudinal study of the development of oral reading fluency in young children at risk for reading failure. *Journal of Learning Disabilities, 38*(5), 387–399.

Strecker, S.K., Roser, N.L., & Martinez, M.G. (1998). Toward understanding oral reading fluency. In T. Shanahan & F. Rodriguez-Brown (Eds.), *47th yearbook of the National Reading Conference* (pp. 295–310). Chicago: National Reading Conference.

Walczyk, J.J., & Griffith-Ross, D.A. (2007). How important is reading skill fluency for comprehension? *The Reading Teacher, 60*(6), 560–569.

Young, A.R., Bowers, P.G., & MacKinnon, G.E. (1996). Effects of prosodic modeling and repeated reading on poor readers' fluency and comprehension. *Applied Psycholinguistics, 17*(1), 59–84.

Questions for Reflection

- What practices and assessments in your classroom might contribute to a view that your fluent readers are also automatically high achievers in reading? What alternative assessments and practices might you put in place to help prevent mislabeling of readers?
- How do you classroom practices connect fluency and comprehension? How do you assess fluency? What about comprehension? How can you ensure that the two are linked—both to give you a complete picture of your students' achievement and to help your students develop into proficient comprehenders who are also fluent readers?

What Every Teacher Needs to Know About Comprehension

Laura S. Pardo

Comprehension is a complex process that has been understood and explained in a number of ways. The RAND Reading Study Group (2002) stated that comprehension is "the process of simultaneously extracting and constructing meaning through interaction and involvement with written language" (p. 11). Duke (2003) added "navigation" and "critique" to her definition because she believed that readers actually move through the text, finding their way, evaluating the accuracy of the text to see if it fits their personal agenda, and finally arriving at a self-selected location. A common definition for teachers might be that comprehension is a process in which readers construct meaning by interacting with text through the combination of prior knowledge and previous experience, information in the text, and the stance the reader takes in relationship to the text. As these different definitions demonstrate, there are many interpretations of what it means to comprehend text. This article synthesizes the research on comprehension and makes connections to classroom practice. I begin by introducing a visual model of comprehension.

How Comprehension Works

Comprehension occurs in the transaction between the reader and the text (Kucer, 2001; Rosenblatt, 1978). The reader brings many things to the literacy event, the text has certain features, and yet meaning emerges only from the engagement of that reader with that text at that particular moment in time. Figure 1...presents a visual model of this process. Each of the elements in the model (reader, text, context, and transaction) is described in more detail later in this article, along with specific suggestions for how teachers can interact with the model to help children become strong comprehenders, beginning in kindergarten.

The Reader

Any literacy event is made up of a reader engaging with some form of text. Each reader is unique in that he or she possesses certain traits or characteristics that are distinctly applied with each text and situation (Butcher & Kintsch, 2003; Fletcher, 1994; Narvaez, 2002). The most important of these characteristics is likely the reader's world knowledge (Fletcher, 1994). The more background knowledge a reader has that connects with the text being read, the more likely the reader will be able to make sense of what is being read (Butcher & Kintsch, 2003; Schallert & Martin, 2003). The process of connecting known information to new information takes place through a series of networkable connections known as schema (Anderson & Pearson, 1984; Narvaez, 2002). In schema theory, individuals organize their world knowledge into categories and systems that make retrieval easier. When a key word or concept is encountered, readers are able to access this information system, pulling forth the ideas that will help them make connections with the text so they can create meaning. Schema theory involves the storage of various kinds of information in long-term

Reprinted from Pardo, L.S. (2004). What every teacher needs to know about comprehension. *The Reading Teacher*, 58(3), 272–280.

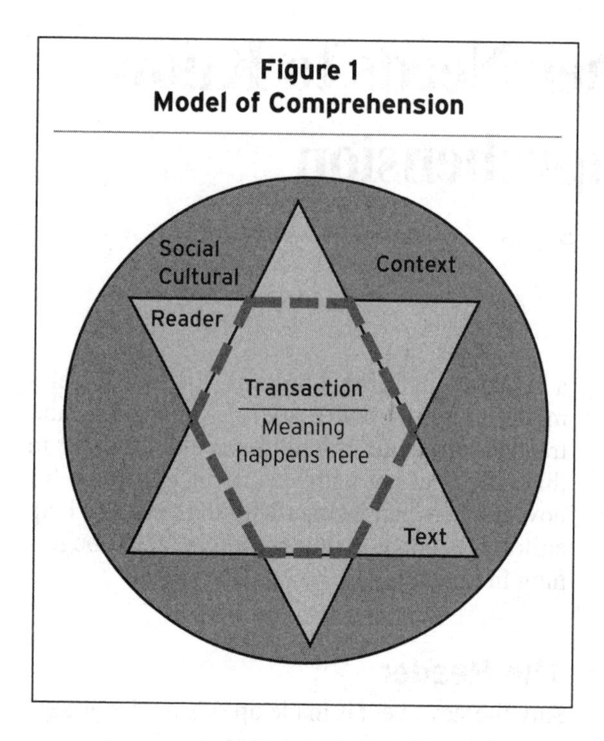

Figure 1
Model of Comprehension

memory. Because long-term memory appears to have infinite capacity (Pressley, 2003), it is likely that readers have many ideas stored in long-term memory. When a key word or concept is presented to the reader (through a title, heading, or someone who has recommended the text), some of this stored information is brought forward and temporarily placed into short-term memory so that the reader can return to it quickly as he or she reads. Short-term memory has limited capacity, and often the information pulled from long-term memory prior to or during reading is only available for a short time and then is placed back in long-term memory. Short-term memory shifts and juggles information, using what is immediately pertinent and allowing less pertinent information to slip back into long-term memory (Schallert & Martin, 2003).

The amount and depth of a reader's world knowledge vary as do other individual characteristics. Readers vary in the skills, knowledge, cognitive development, culture, and purpose they bring to a text (Narvaez, 2002). Skills include such things as basic language ability, decoding skills, and higher level thinking skills. Knowledge includes background knowledge about content and text and relates to the available schema a reader has for a particular text. A reader's cognitive development causes that reader to evaluate text in different ways—for example, to make moral judgments. Comprehension is affected by a reader's culture, based on the degree to which it matches with the writer's culture or the culture espoused in the text. Readers also read in particular ways depending on the purpose for reading. Another individual difference that exists in readers is motivation. Motivation can influence the interest, purpose, emotion, or persistence with which a reader engages with text (Butcher & Kintsch, 2003; Schallert & Martin, 2003). More motivated readers are likely to apply more strategies and work harder at building meaning. Less motivated readers are not as likely to work as hard, and the meaning they create will not be as powerful as if they were highly motivated.

Teachers Support Readers

If readers have all these individual differences, how do teachers best support elementary-age readers to become competent comprehenders? They teach decoding skills, help students build fluency, build and activate background knowledge, teach vocabulary words, motivate students, and engage them in personal responses to text.

Teach Decoding Skills

In order to comprehend, readers must be able to read the words. Some level of automatic decoding must be present so that short-term memory can work on comprehending, not on decoding, words. Teachers help students get to this level of automatic decoding by providing instruction in phonemic awareness and phonics at all grade levels. If students put too much mental energy into sounding out the words, they will have less mental energy left to think about the meaning. While teachers in the primary grades work with phonemic awareness and phonics, teachers in the intermediate grades support students' continued development of automatic decoding through spelling, vocabulary, and high-frequency word activities.

Help Students Build Fluency

As word reading becomes automatic, students become fluent and can focus on comprehension (Rasinski, 2003). Teachers help students become more fluent by engaging them in repeated readings for real purposes (like performances and Readers Theatre). Teachers also model fluent reading by reading aloud to students daily so that they realize what fluent reading sounds like. Some research indicates that reading aloud to students is the single most effective way to increase comprehension (see Morrow & Gambrell, 2000, for a review of this literature).

Build and Activate Prior Knowledge

Background knowledge is an important factor for creating meaning, and teachers should help students activate prior knowledge before reading so that information connected with concepts or topics in the text is more easily accessible during reading (Keene & Zimmermann, 1997; Miller, 2002). If students do not have adequate background knowledge, teachers can help students build the appropriate knowledge. Duke (2003) suggested that one way to add to world knowledge is to use informational books with all students, particularly very young students. By using information books, students build world knowledge so that they will have the appropriate information to activate at a later time. Teachers also support students' acquisition of world knowledge by establishing and maintaining a rich, literate environment, full of texts that provide students with numerous opportunities to learn content in a wide variety of topics.

Another way teachers help students build background knowledge is to create visual or graphic organizers that help students to see not only new concepts but also how previously known concepts are related and connected to the new ones (Keene & Zimmermann, 1997; Miller, 2002). Teachers teach students how to make text-to-text, text-to-self, and text-to-world connections so that readers can more easily comprehend the texts they read.

Reading aloud and teacher modeling show students how to activate schema and make connections. For example, a first-grade teacher read aloud *from Ira Says Goodbye* (Waber, 1991). She began the lesson by thinking aloud about the title and cover of the book. "Oh I see that the author is Bernard Waber and the title is *Ira Says Goodbye*. I think this book is about the same Ira as in *Ira Sleeps Over* (Waber, 1973). I can activate my schema from that book. I am making a text-to-text connection. I remember that...." She continued modeling for her students how to activate schema and make connections that helped her make meaning from this text. As she read the book to her students, she stopped occasionally to model and think aloud how she activated her own schema to make connections.

Teach Vocabulary Words

If there are too many words that a reader does not know, he or she will have to spend too much mental energy figuring out the unknown word(s) and will not be able to understand the passage as a whole. Teachers help students learn important vocabulary words prior to reading difficult or unfamiliar texts. When teaching vocabulary words, teachers make sure that the selected words are necessary for making meaning with the text students will be reading and that they help students connect the new words to something they already know. Simply using the word lists supplied in textbooks does not necessarily accomplish this task (Blachowicz & Fisher, 2000). Many teachers consider the backgrounds and knowledge levels of their students and the text the students will be engaging in and then select a small number of words or ideas that are important for understanding the text. Once teachers have decided on the appropriate vocabulary words to use, students must actively engage with the words—use them in written and spoken language—in order for the words to become a part of the students' reading and writing vocabularies. For example, asking students to create graphic organizers that show relationships among new words and common and known words helps them assimilate new vocabulary. Asking students to look up long lists of unrelated, unknown words is unlikely to help students access the text more appropriately or to increase personal vocabularies.

Motivate Students

Many individual reader factors (e.g., cognitive development, culture) are not within a teacher's control. However, teachers can motivate students by providing them with interesting texts, allowing them choices in reading and writing, and helping students set authentic purposes for reading (e.g., generating reports, writing letters, demonstrating some new ability or skill; Pressley & Hilden, 2002). Many teachers actively seek out students' interests so that they can select texts, topics, themes, and units that will more likely engage students. Teachers also provide and promote authentic purposes for engaging in reading and writing. Authentic literacy events are those that replicate or reflect reading and writing purposes and texts that occur in the world outside of schools. Some teachers do this by providing pen pals, using students' authentic questions for in-depth study, responding to community needs, or having students solve problems.

Engage Students in Personal Responses to Text

Teachers encourage students to read both efferently and aesthetically (Rosenblatt, 1978). Researchers (McMahon, Raphael, Goatley, & Pardo, 1997) building on the ideas of Rosenblatt developed a literature-based approach to teaching reading comprehension through the Book Club program. In this instructional approach students read authentic literature; write personal, critical, and creative responses; and talk about books with their classmates (Pardo, 2002). Teachers help students learn and apply comprehension strategies while reading, through writing, and during student-led discussion groups called Book Clubs, where students explore the individual meanings that have emerged as they engage with the text over a period of time. While this program initially focused on the intermediate grades, many teachers have found that students in first and second grades are successful comprehenders when they read and engage in Book Clubs (Grattan, 1997; Raphael, Florio-Ruane, & George, 2001; Salna, 2001).

The Text

Understanding the reader is one important piece of the comprehension puzzle, but features of the text also influence the transaction where comprehension happens. The structure of the text—its genre, vocabulary, language, even the specific word choices—works to make each text unique. Some would even argue that it is at the word or micro-structure level that meaning begins (Butcher & Kintsch, 2003). How well the text is written, whether it follows the conventions of its genre or structure, and the language or dialect it is written in are all factors of the text. The content of a specific text, the difficulty or readability of it, and even the type font and size are factors of a text that can influence a reader's interaction. These features collectively are referred to as "surface features," and studies have shown that the quality of the text at the surface level is important for readers to be able to make meaning effectively (Tracey & Morrow, 2002).

The author's intent in writing the text can influence how a reader interacts with that text, particularly if this intent is made known through a foreword, back-cover biography, or knowledgeable other (as in the case of teachers in schools). Some texts are promoted as carrying a certain message or theme by those who have encountered the book previously (Rosenblatt, 1978). The inherent message that some texts carry with them, often related to the author's intent, is referred to as *gist* and has been defined as "what people remember...the main ideas in the text" (Pressley, 1998, p. 46). Gist is frequently assessed through basal workbooks and standardized reading tests; therefore, the author's intent is a key feature of text.

Teachers Support Texts

Because certain features make some texts more easily comprehensible, teachers help young readers understand those features so they can comprehend effectively. Teachers teach text structures, model appropriate text selection, and provide regular independent reading time.

Teach Text Structures

Because features of the text are beyond a teacher's control, teachers select texts that have an obvious structure. They teach a variety of narrative genres and some expository text structures. With narrative works teachers help students understand basic story grammar, including the literary elements that are common across narrative pieces, such as plot, characters, and setting. They teach specific elements that make each genre unique (e.g., talking animals in folk tales). By doing this, students will be able to access a schema for a certain narrative genre when they begin to read a new text and can begin to make text-to-text connections for a particular story genre, which will help them more easily make meaning. Likewise, teachers share some common expository text structures with students, such as sequence, description, comparison, and cause and effect. Teachers discuss the idea of "inconsiderate texts" (Armbruster, 1984) with students and show them how to use cues when reading nonfiction (such as reading tables, charts, graphs, and the captions under pictures; using bold print and italics to determine big or important ideas). Inconsiderate texts do not adhere strictly to one structure, but might be a combination of several structures. Many textbooks have a varied and mixed set of structures, and teachers can address specific features and demands of informational text so that students are more likely to engage in informational text with a repertoire of strategies and schema to help them construct meaning (Duke, 2003).

Model Appropriate Text Selection

Teachers teach students how to select appropriate texts by showing them what features to consider. Some teachers use the Goldilocks approach (Tompkins, 2003), while others suggest that teachers level books and tell students which level books they may select (Fountas & Pinnell, 1996). In the Goldilocks approach, readers look for books that are not too hard or too easy, but just right. Just-right books are those that look interesting, have mostly decodable words, have been read aloud previously, are written by a familiar author, or will be read with a support person nearby (Tompkins, 2003). Teachers have a wide variety of genres and levels of books available for students to select for independent reading, and they support students throughout the year with appropriate book selection.

Provide Regular Independent Reading Time

Teachers can make sure they provide students with time to read independently every day. Reading becomes better with practice, and comprehending becomes better with more reading practice (Pressley, 2003). Many teachers use programs such as DEAR (Drop Everything And Read) or SSR (Sustained Silent Reading) to ensure that students read independently every day.

Teachers Create and Support a Sociocultural Context

Reading takes place somewhere between a specific reader and a specific text. A sociocultural influence likely permeates any reading activity (Kucer, 2001; Schallert & Martin, 2003). Depending on the place, the situation, and the purpose for reading, the reader and the text interact in ways that are unique for that specific context. The same reading at another time or in a different place might result in a different meaning. The context also involves the activity that occurs around the transaction. If a teacher assigns his or her students to read a certain text for a specific reason, the transaction that occurs will be based on this context. If students are asked to discuss a text, generate questions from it, or come up with a big idea, these kinds of activities form a context within which the reader and text interact for a specific reason, one that is unlikely to occur in exactly the same manner ever again. Teachers create contexts and learning opportunities that will support the construction of meaning. Environments that value reading and writing, that contain a wide variety of texts, that allow students to take risks, and that find time for reading aloud and reading independently are contexts that effectively promote the construction of meaning (Keene & Zimmermann, 1997; Miller, 2002; Pardo, 2002).

The Transaction

As we consider the reader's individual and unique differences, the characteristics of the context, and the features of the text, we are left to wonder exactly what happens when these three come together. At the most basic level microstructures (words, propositions) are being decoded and represented by mental images (Butcher & Kintsch, 2003). This is most likely happening quickly, automatically, and in short-term memory. These mental images are calling forth ideas and information stored in long-term memory to assist the reader in building a series of connections between representations (van den Broek, 1994). These connections occur between the reader and the text and between different parts of the text. This representation is fine-tuned by the reader as more information is encountered in the text and more connections are made. Readers exit the transaction maintaining a mental representation or gist of the text.

How do these connections lead to mental representations? One way is through making inferences. A reader is quite intentional as he or she engages with the text, asking, "What is it I'm looking at here?" Readers are searching for coherence and for a chain of related events that can lead them to infer or make meaning. As readers continue moving through the text, they continue to build inferences, drawing from long-term memory specific ideas that seem to create coherence and answer the question posed earlier, "What is it I'm looking at here?" As this answer emerges, meaning is realized. Inferencing is most likely done automatically and is one of the most important processes that occur during comprehension (Butcher & Kintsch, 2003; van den Broek, 1994).

The mental representation needs to make sense to the reader as it emerges; therefore, readers monitor the emerging meaning as they read, using metacognitive and fix-up strategies, sometimes discarding ideas in the text if they do not add to the coherence that the reader is trying to build (Pressley & Afflerbach, 1995). If the reader's background knowledge or personal experiences agree with the text, the reader assimilates this new information and creates new meaning. If, however, the reader's background knowledge and personal experiences do not agree with the new information presented in the text, readers either adjust the information to make it fit (accommodation), or they reject that information and maintain their previous understanding (Kucer, 2001). Readers apply a variety of strategies throughout this process to support their construction of meaning such as summarizing, clarifying, questioning, visualizing, predicting, and organizing. It is through the application of these strategies at various moments throughout the interaction that meaning emerges.

Teachers Support Transaction

At this point, it seems fairly obvious that comprehension occurs in the transaction between a reader and a text within a sociocultural context. That makes the transaction crucial to comprehension and the teacher's role within this transaction very important. Teachers provide explicit instruction of useful comprehension strategies, teach students to monitor and repair, use multiple strategy approaches, scaffold support, and make reading and writing connections visible to students.

Provide Explicit Instruction of Useful Comprehension Strategies

Good readers use strategies to support their understanding of text. Teachers help students become good readers by teaching them how to use the strategies of monitoring, predicting, inferring, questioning, connecting, summarizing, visualizing, and organizing (Keene & Zimmermann, 1997; Miller, 2002; Pardo, 2002). Teachers are explicit and direct in explaining what these strategies are and why good readers use them (Duffy, 2002; Pressley & McCormick, 1995). They model the strategies (often by thinking aloud) for the students and provide them with numerous opportunities to practice and apply the strategies. In order for strategies to transfer so that students use them on their own or in assessment situations, contexts need to remain similar. Therefore, teachers use texts and classroom structures that are easily maintained for teaching, practicing and applying independently, and assessing. Teachers help students think metacognitively about strategies, considering when and where to apply each strategy, how to use it, and the impact it can have. In addition, teachers occasionally provide students with difficult text. If students encounter only texts that they can read easily, there will be no reason to practice and apply strategies. It is when readers encounter challenging texts that they put strategies to use (Kucer, 2001).

Teach Students to Monitor and Repair

Knowing what is understood and not understood while reading and then applying the appropriate strategy to repair meaning are vital for comprehension to occur. Good readers monitor while reading to see if things make sense, and they use strategies to repair the meaning when things stop making sense (Duke, 2003; Pressley & Hilden, 2002). While some studies support that monitoring is important (Baker, 2002; Pressley & Afflerbach, 1995), other studies indicate that readers often mismonitor (Baker, 1989; Baker & Brown, 1984; Kinnunen, Vauras, & Niemi, 1998). Readers have been found to both over- and underestimate their comprehension of text. So, while monitoring is important and good readers seem to monitor successfully, effective teachers realize that mismonitoring can affect meaning for less able students, and they provide additional support as needed so that all readers comprehend text successfully.

Use Multiple Strategy Approaches

Researchers have found that teaching multiple strategies simultaneously may be particularly powerful (Trabasso & Bouchard, 2002; National Institute of Child Health and Human Development, 2000; Pressley, 2000).

> There is very strong empirical, scientific evidence that the instruction of more than one strategy in a natural context leads to the acquisition and use of reading comprehension strategies and transfer to standardized comprehension tests. Multiple strategy instruction facilitates comprehension as evidenced by performance on tasks that involve memory, summarizing, and identification of main ideas. (Trabasso & Bouchard, 2002, p.184)

Perhaps the most frequently used multiple strategies approach is transactional strategy instruction (TSI), created and studied by Pressley and colleagues (Brown, Pressley, Van Meter, & Schuder, 1996; Gaskins, Anderson, Pressley, Cunicelli, & Satlow, 1993). TSI teachers encourage readers to make sense of text by using strategies that allow them to make connections between text content and prior knowledge. Teachers and students work in small reading groups to collaboratively make meaning using several teacher-identified strategies. Teachers model and explain the strategies, coach students in their use, and help students use them flexibly. Throughout the instruction, students are taught to think about the usefulness of each strategy and to become metacognitive about their own reading processes.

Scaffold Support

When teaching strategies to elementary-age students, teachers gradually release responsibility for comprehending to students. An effective model that has been used by some teachers is the Gradual Release of Responsibility model (Pearson & Gallagher, 1983). In this model, teachers take all the responsibility for applying a newly introduced strategy by modeling, thinking aloud, demonstrating, and creating meaning. As time passes and students have more exposure to and practice with using the strategy, teachers scaffold students by creating activities within students' Zone of Proximal Development (Vygotsky, 1978) and slowly withdrawing more and more responsibility. Teachers work collaboratively with the students and the strategy, giving and taking as much as necessary to create meaning. Eventually, students take on more and more responsibility as they become more confident, knowledgeable, and capable. Finally, students are able to work independently. Teachers and students do not always progress in a linear way, but often slip back and forth between more and less responsibility depending on the task, the text, and the strategy. While adaptations may be made with students of different ages, teachers use this model with students in all elementary grades.

Make Reading/Writing Connections Visible

Teachers help students see that reading and writing are parallel processes and that becoming good writers can help them become good readers (Kucer, 2001). Composing a text can be thought of as writing something that people will understand. Writing can bring understanding about a certain topic to the writer, who will have to be clear about the topic he or she is writing about. Meaning matters in comprehending, and becoming a clear writer is all about how the reader will make meaning of the text that is being created. Recalling the earlier discussion of authentic purposes is important here as well; students will likely become engaged with the task of writing if asked to write for authentic and important purposes.

Closing Comments

Comprehending is a complicated process, as we have discovered and explored in this article. Yet it is one of the most important skills for students to develop if they are to become successful and productive adults. Comprehension instruction in schools, beginning in kindergarten, is therefore crucial. Teachers use their knowledge and understandings of how one learns to comprehend to inform classroom practices so they can most effectively help readers develop the abilities to comprehend text. It is hoped that the discussion in this article can open a dialogue with teachers and teacher educators toward this end.

References

Anderson, R.C., & Pearson, P.D. (1984). A schemathematic view of basic processes in reading comprehension. In P.D. Pearson, R. Barr, M.L. Kamil, & P. Mosenthal (Eds.), *Handbook of reading research* (pp. 255–291). New York: Longman.

Armbruster, B.B. (1984). The problem of "inconsiderate texts." In G.G. Duffy, L.R. Roehler, & J. Mason (Eds.), *Theoretical issues in reading comprehension* (pp. 202–217). New York: Longman.

Baker, L. (1989). Metacognition, comprehension monitoring, and the adult reader. *Educational Psychology Review, 1*, 3–38.

Baker, L. (2002). Metacognition in comprehension instruction. In C.C. Block & M. Pressley (Eds.), *Comprehension instruction: Research-based best practices* (pp. 77–95). New York: Guilford.

Baker, L., & Brown, A.L. (1984). Metacognitive skills and reading. In P.D. Pearson, R. Barr, M. Kamil, & P. Mosenthal (Eds.), *Handbook of reading research* (pp. 353–394). New York: Longman.

Blachowicz, C.L.Z., & Fisher, P. (2000). Vocabulary instruction. In M.L. Kamil, P.B. Mosenthal, P.D. Pearson, & R. Barr (Eds.), *Handbook of reading research* (Vol. 3, pp. 503–523). Mahwah, NJ: Erlbaum.

Brown, R., Pressley, M., Van Meter, P., & Schuder, T. (1996). A quasi-experimental validation of transactional strategies instruction with low-achieving second-grade students. *Journal of Educational Psychology, 88*(1), 18–37.

Butcher, K.R., & Kintsch, W. (2003). Text comprehension and discourse processing. In A.F. Healy & R.W. Proctor (Vol. Eds.) & I.B. Weiner (Ed.-in-Chief), *Handbook of psychology, Volume 4, Experimental psychology* (pp. 575–595). New York: Wiley.

Duffy, G.G. (2002). The case for direct explanation of strategies. In C.C. Block & M. Pressley (Eds.), *Comprehension instruction: Research-based best practices* (pp. 28–41). New York: Guilford.

Duke, N. (2003, March 7). *Comprehension instruction for informational text.* Presentation at the annual meeting of the Michigan Reading Association, Grand Rapids.

Fletcher, C.R. (1994). Levels of representation in memory for discourse. In M.A. Gernsbacher (Ed.), *Handbook of psycholinguistics* (pp. 589–607). San Diego: Academic Press.

Fountas, I.C., & Pinnell, G.S. (1996). *Guided reading: Good first teaching for all children.* Portsmouth, NH: Heinemann.

Gaskins, I.W., Anderson, R.C., Pressley, M., Cunicelli, E.A., & Satlow, E. (1993). Six teachers' dialogue during cognitive process instruction. *The Elementary School Journal, 93,* 277–304.

Grattan, K.W. (1997). They can do it too! Book Club with first and second graders. In S.I. McMahon, T.E. Raphael, V.J. Goatley, & L.S. Pardo (Eds.), *The Book Club connection: Literacy learning and classroom talk* (pp. 267–283). New York: Teachers College Press.

Keene, E.O., & Zimmermann, S. (1997). *Mosaic of thought: Teaching comprehension in a reader's workshop.* Portsmouth, NH: Heinemann.

Kinnunen, R., Vauras, M., & Niemi, P. (1998). Comprehension monitoring in beginning readers. *Scientific Studies of Reading, 2,* 353–375.

Kucer, S.B. (2001). *Dimensions of literacy: A conceptual base of teaching reading and writing in school settings.* Mahwah, NJ: Erlbaum.

McMahon, S.I., Raphael, T.E., Goatley, V.J., & Pardo, L.S. (1997). *The Book Club connection: Literacy learning and classroom talk.* New York: Teachers College Press.

Miller, D. (2002). *Reading with meaning: Teaching comprehension in the primary grades.* Portland, ME: Stenhouse.

Morrow, L.M., & Gambrell, L.B. (2000). Literature-based reading instruction. In M.L. Kamil, P.B. Mosenthal, P.D. Pearson, & R. Barr (Eds.), *Handbook of reading research* (Vol. 3, pp. 563–586). Mahwah, NJ: Erlbaum.

Narvaez, D. (2002). Individual differences that influence reading comprehension. In C.C. Block & M. Pressley (Eds.), *Comprehension instruction: Research-based best practices* (pp. 158–175). New York: Guilford.

National Institute of Child Health and Human Development. (2000). *Report of the National Reading Panel: Teaching children to read: An evidence-based assessment of the scientific research literature on reading and its implications for reading instruction* (NIH Publication No. 00-4769). Washington, DC: U.S. Government Printing Office.

Pardo, L. S. (2002). Book Club for the twenty-first century. *Illinois Reading Council Journal, 30*(4), 14–23.

Pearson, P.D., & Gallagher, M. (1983). The instruction of reading comprehension. *Contemporary Education Psychology, 8,* 317–344.

Pressley, M. (1998). *Reading instruction that works: The case for balanced teaching.* New York: Guilford.

Pressley, M. (2000). What should comprehension instruction be the instruction of? In M.L. Kamil, P.B. Mosenthal, P.D. Pearson, & R. Barr (Eds.), *Handbook of reading research* (Vol. 3, pp. 545–561). Mahwah, NJ: Erlbaum.

Pressley, M. (2003, March 7). *Time to revolt against reading instruction as usual: What comprehension instruction could and should be.* Presentation at the annual meeting of the Michigan Reading Association, Grand Rapids.

Pressley, M., & Afflerbach, P. (1995). *Verbal protocols of reading: The nature of constructively responsive reading.* Hillsdale, NJ: Erlbaum.

Pressley, M., & Hilden, K. (2002). How can children be taught to comprehend text better? In M.L. Kamil, J.B. Manning, & H.J. Walberg (Eds.), *Successful reading instruction: Research in educational productivity* (pp. 33–51). Greenwich, CT: Information Age.

Pressley, M., & McCormick, C. (1995). *Advanced educational psychology for researchers, educators, and policymakers.* New York: HarperCollins.

RAND Reading Study Group. (2002). *Reading for understanding: Toward a research and development program in reading comprehension.* Santa Monica, CA: Office of Education Research and Improvement.

Raphael, T.E., Florio-Ruane, S., & George, M. (2001). Book Club Plus: A conceptual framework to organize literacy instruction. *Language Arts, 79,* 159–168.

Rasinski, T. (2003, March 7). *Fluency: Chasing the illusive reading goal.* Presentation at the annual meeting of the Michigan Reading Association, Grand Rapids.

Rosenblatt, L.R. (1978). *The reader, the text, the poem: The transactional theory of the literary work.* Carbondale: Southern Illinois University Press.

Salna, K. (2001). Book Clubs as part of a balanced curriculum. *Illinois Reading Council Journal, 29*(4), 40–47.

Schallert, D.L., & Martin, D.B. (2003). A psychological analysis of what teachers and students do in the language arts classroom. In J. Flood, D. Lapp, J.R. Squire, & J.M. Jensen (Eds.), *Handbook of research on teaching the English language arts* (pp. 31–45). Mahwah, NJ: Erlbaum.

Tompkins, G.E. (2003). *Literacy for the 21st century: Teaching reading and writing in pre-kindergarten through grade 4.* Upper Saddle River, NJ: Merrill Prentice Hall.

Trabasso, T., & Bouchard, E. (2002). Teaching readers how to comprehend text strategically. In C.C. Block & M. Pressley (Eds.), *Comprehension instruction: Research-based best practices* (pp. 176–200). New York: Guilford.

Tracey, D.H., & Morrow, L.M. (2002). Preparing young learners for successful reading comprehension. In C.C. Block & M. Pressley (Eds.), *Comprehension instruction: Research-based best practices* (pp. 319–333). New York: Guilford.

van den Broek, P. (1994). Comprehension and memory of narrative texts: Inferences and coherences. In M.A. Gernsbacher (Ed.), *Handbook of psycholinguistics* (pp. 539–588). San Diego, CA: Academic Press.

Vygotsky, L.S. (1978). *Mind in society.* Cambridge, MA: Harvard University Press.

Waber, B. (1973). *Ira sleeps over.* Boston: Houghton Mifflin.

Waber, B. (1991). *Ira says goodbye.* Boston: Houghton Mifflin.

Questions for Reflection

- Compare this article and the preceding piece by Applegate et al. How do you feel about sequencing skill development, from phonics and phonemic awareness to comprehension? What has worked best for you and your colleagues' students? At what grade level is it best to begin emphasizing comprehension instruction? Does this change when you consider your struggling readers? Why or why not?
- Think about your role in ensuring the "gradual release" of responsibility as Pardo describes it. Does your teaching incorporate this feature? How could you strengthen this component? What approaches can you use particularly with struggling readers to provide sufficient support while also encouraging independent growth?

How Important Is Reading Skill Fluency for Comprehension?

Jeffrey J. Walczyk and Diana A. Griffith-Ross

Dwain and Tammy are third graders of normal intelligence. Dwain can read aloud fluently most texts assigned to him by his teacher, Ms. Lopez (all names are pseudonyms). However, she often notices that he misses key points when asked to summarize the passage just read. Tammy, on the other hand, reads comparable passages slowly, pauses quite often, and regularly mispronounces words. Even so, when asked to summarize, she frequently surprises Ms. Lopez with what she noticed and remembers from the passage. Along these lines, a central goal of this article is to help clarify the relationship between word reading fluency and comprehension.

Word reading fluency is the ability to identify written words quickly and accurately (Perfetti, 1985, 1999; Stanovich, 1986). In recent years, there has been an emphasis by reading teachers and researchers on developing fluent word reading in struggling readers to improve their comprehension (Fuchs, Fuchs, Hosp, & Jenkins, 2001; Perfetti, 1999). In this article, the scientific rationale for this emphasis is reconsidered, and compensatory-encoding theory is presented to help clarify the relationship between reading fluency and comprehension.

Individual Differences in Reading Skills

The scientific basis for the current emphasis on word reading fluency can be partially traced to automaticity theory (AT; LaBerge & Samuels, 1974; Samuels & Flor, 1997) and verbal efficiency theory (VET; Perfetti, 1985, 1999). Both theories highlight the harmful effects of inefficient skills on comprehension and maintain that if word reading demands too much attention, little remains for higher level comprehension. According to both, beginning readers first concentrate on word reading and gradually shift attention to understand what they read (LaBerge & Samuels; Samuels & Flor; Perfetti, 1985). By this view, repeated practice makes word recognition automatic and frees attention for comprehension.

Consistent with AT and VET, several studies have shown that fluent word reading helps comprehension (e.g., Bell & Perfetti, 1994; Fuchs et al., 2001). Even so, 10 to 15% of children have comprehension difficulties that are not due to poor word reading (Yuill & Oakhill, 1991), and many of them have deficits in spoken language processing (Nation & Snowling, 1997; Stothard & Hulme, 1995).

Gough and Tunmer (1986) and Hoover and Gough (1990) proposed that reading consists of word recognition, with listening comprehension added on. In support of that theory, word reading fluency and listening comprehension are largely independent (Oakhill, Cain, & Bryant, 2003; Storch & Whitehurst, 2002). For instance, in early elementary school, visual and auditory analysis (e.g., phonemic awareness) determine the speed and accuracy of word reading (Pazzaglia, Cornoldi, & Tressoldi, 1993). Even so, older children can comprehend well, even when word or pseudoword reading skills are poor (Shankweiler et al., 1995; Thompson & Johnston, 2000).

Reprinted from Walczyk, J.J., & Griffith-Ross, D.A. (2007). How important is reading skill fluency for comprehension? *The Reading Teacher, 60*(6), 560-569.

Adults, too, can overcome poor word reading. For instance, college students diagnosed with dyslexia in childhood or with persistent problems in phonological processing, spelling, or rapid word reading, often comprehend adequately (Bruck, 1998; Jackson & Doellinger, 2002).

As noted above, comprehension problems can arise due to deficits in understanding spoken language. For instance, some struggling readers have difficulty acting out sentences others have read to them (Crain, Shankweiler, Macaruso, & Bar-Shalom, 1990). They frequently have small listening verbal working memory capacities (information in consciousness) and quickly forget to whom *he* refers or the meaning of a sentence heard a minute before (Perfetti, 1985; Walczyk, Marsiglia, Johns, & Bryan, 2004). Grammatical complexity is often a source of confusion, including temporal terms (e.g., *before*) or relative clauses in sentences (Shankweiler et al., 1995). Even when texts challenge listening comprehension skills, however, readers can compensate.

Compensatory-Encoding Theory

Though reading and listening are certainly related, a fundamental difference between them is often overlooked. When listening to teachers or parents, children typically have little control over how quickly and in what order verbal information enters their minds compared to reading (Walczyk, 2000). This fact is crucial for understanding compensatory-encoding theory (C-ET), which explains how readers with weak skills can comprehend well by adjusting reading. Specifically, the theory describes how poor word readers, those who quickly forget sentence meanings or with other weak skills, prevent reading problems and overcome those that occur. Thus, it complements AT and VET by identifying how weak readers can understand well.

How Readers Can Overcome Weak Skills

Struggling readers often experience significant improvements in comprehension when taught reading strategies (Shearer, Ruddell, & Vogt, 2001; Vogt & Nagano, 2003). C-ET identifies actions, some used spontaneously and others learned, which can overcome weak skills. They include strategies that are components of Reading Recovery (Clay, 1979) and other successful interventions for helping struggling readers. C-ET adds to this literature by mapping compensatory actions onto the problems, by describing when and how they work, and by other ways discussed later.

All readers have occasions that challenge their skills. These cases create "confusions": instances of reader uncertainty over the meaning of a word, a phrase, or another part of text. A confusion can result from poor word reading, an unfamiliar word, a small verbal working memory capacity, or other sources. For example, readers may forget to whom the pronoun *she* refers in a narrative.

To overcome confusion, readers can employ "compensations": reader actions that help automatic reading to succeed or that provide information to working memory by an alternative means when automatic reading fails. In other words, readers can take actions to help their skills succeed (e.g., slowing reading rate, pausing, reading aloud) or can take other actions (e.g., sounding out, rereading) when automatic processes cannot provide readers with the information needed to understand text.

Common Compensations and Sources of Confusion

The following are the most frequently used compensations, which are described and ranked by how disruptive they are of reading. The compensations that appear at the end of the list take longer to perform. As a general rule, readers will use the least disruptive compensations first. If they fail to prevent or resolve confusion, later ones serve as backups.

1. Slowing Reading Rate. As readers become more skilled, their control over reading rate increases (Baker & Brown, 1984; Chall, 1996). Moreover, readers become more aware of cues to text difficulty, signaling the need to read slowly (Kucan & Beck, 1997). Slowing reading helps to prevent many confusions by allowing inefficient readers to read text at a pace that their skills can handle, whereas faster reading might overwhelm skills (Baker & Brown; Chall; Walczyk, Wei, Griffith-Ross, Goubert, Cooper, & Zha, 2006).

2. Pause. Less skilled readers pause longer and more often than do skilled readers (Haviland & Clark, 1974; Perfetti, 1985, 1999; Walczyk, Marsiglia, Bryan, & Naquin, 2001; Walczyk et al., 2004). A pause is compensatory if it is an uncommonly long delay during reading that allows an inefficient reading subcomponent (e.g., reading a word by sight) sufficient time to succeed. When slowing reading does not allow enough time, pausing may be its backup. Furthermore, when the source of confusion is unclear, pausing can occur as readers try to understand its nature and select other compensations for resolving it (Pressley & Afflerbach, 1995; Walczyk et al., 2006).

3. Look Back. Looking back occurs when readers briefly glance to text previously read. Walczyk et al. (2001) defined it as the reprocessing of three words or less, which is slightly more disruptive of word reading than slowing reading rate or pausing (Cataldo & Oakhill, 2000). Looking back is compensatory when it resolves confusion by restoring information forgotten from working memory or by providing information overlooked on the first pass through text (e.g., what *it* refers to). It can aid poor word reading by uncovering textual cues to an unfamiliar word's meaning (Ehri, 1994). With pausing and reading aloud, it can help overcome confusions due to difficult words, small verbal working memories, unfamiliar concepts, verbosity, or abstractly written text (Kucan & Beck, 1997; Pressley & Afflerbach, 1995).

4. Read Aloud. Reading aloud often occurs spontaneously to difficult text or noisy reading environments (Chall, 1996), suggesting that it is compensatory. Researchers have noted marked improvement in comprehension when reading is done aloud. For instance, Miller and Smith (1985) tested 94 second through fifth graders and found that the 33 poorest readers comprehended best when they read aloud. Reading aloud helps focus attention when readers are tired or bored (see Pressley & Afflerbach, 1995) and facilitates comprehension monitoring (Bereiter & Bird, 1985; Ericsson, 1988). It also helps automatic reading to succeed by drowning out distractions. It is especially helpful for less fluent readers, providing auditory feedback on the accuracy of their word reading attempts (Ehri, 1994; Walker, 2005). Reading aloud provides less fluent readers with more opportunities to learn about words and assists those more fluent to read with prosody (National Institute of Child Health and Human Development, 2000).

5. Sounding Out, Analogizing to Known Sight Words, or Contextual Guessing. Ehri (1994) described four ways children read words. When skills are fluent or words are familiar, *reading by sight* is possible. Words frequently encountered (e.g., *car*) are eventually recognized as whole units that activate sounds and meanings quickly from memory. This is automatic word reading. The remaining three are compensatory: backups when automatic word reading fails.

1. Phonological recoding (sounding out) is using the rules of phonics to match a letter string to a spoken word in memory.
2. Analogizing to known sight words occurs when readers look at a word's spelling and bring to mind similarly spelled words to cue its meaning.
3. Contextual guessing is using surrounding text to infer an unknown word's meaning.

6. Jump Over. Another way of dealing with word reading confusion can be added to the three mentioned previously. If readers conclude that an unfamiliar word or other confusion involves a minor detail, or that resolving it will take too much time, they can jump over it. For example, if the meaning of an unfamiliar word seems tangential to understanding the overall text, choosing to overlook it makes sense. Older readers know that spending too much time resolving such confusion can cause them to forget important information previously read, making it harder to form connections (Walczyk et al., 2006). Of course, jumping over too often will lower comprehension.

7. Reread Text. Rereading is compensatory when it resolves confusion noted on an earlier pass through text but is more disruptive of reading than the preceding compensations. As a consequence, skilled readers will employ it only after other compensations have not prevented or resolved confusion. Walczyk et al. (2004) defined it as the reprocessing of four or more words. With each rereading, readers become more familiar with words, phrases, and their meanings and can focus more attention on comprehension (Perfetti, 1985; Samuels & Flor, 1997). Rereading can resolve confusion due to poor reading skills, as well as to choppy, verbose, or abstract text (Pressley & Afflerbach, 1995; Walczyk & Taylor, 1996; Walczyk et al., 2001, 2004). Other compensations exist (e.g., using a dictionary) but are beyond the scope of this article.

When and How Less Fluent Skills Lower Comprehension

According to C-ET, readers with poor word reading, small verbal working memory capacities, or poor listening comprehension can comprehend well, as long as they are motivated to understand and free to compensate. On the other hand, restriction on reading discourages or stops children from compensating, which is any aspect of the classroom or task that keeps children from compensating when needed. Restriction is not all or nothing. Some tasks are more restrictive than others. Restriction includes (a) having to read under time pressure (as occurs in most standardized testing), which discourages all compensation use; (b) having to read at a fast or constant rate, which prevents readers from slowing reading rate, pausing, or rereading; and (c) mandatory silent reading, which is common in the classroom (Nagy, Campenni, & Shaw, 2000) and prevents children from receiving auditory feedback on attempts at word reading, which might otherwise activate relevant information from memory (Bereiter & Bird, 1985; Ehri, 1994; Ericsson, 1988; Walczyk et al., 2006; Walker, 2005). In contrast, less restricted reading includes (a) reading without time constraints, which allows students to use all compensations without anxiety over deadlines (Calvo & Carreiras, 1993); (b) reading at a normal, variable rate, which allows students to pause and reprocess difficult portions of text; and (c) freedom to read aloud. As noted previously, reading aloud helps readers to overcome distractions, facilitates comprehension monitoring, and increases auditory feedback (Bereiter & Bird; Chall, 1996; Ehri; Ericsson; Pressley & Afflerbach, 1995; Walker, 2005).

Summary of a Major Recent Test of C-ET

A large-scale test of C-ET, funded by the National Science Foundation, was recently concluded. The design and procedures are now summarized. Table 1 describes the children tested (third, fifth, and seventh graders), the reading fluency measures and passages used, the comprehension tests constructed, and the reading tasks. Additional clarification is presented in the following sections. The findings and those of related research are discussed. Three research questions guided the study: (1) How strongly does comprehension depend on reading skill fluency? (2) How is the fluency–comprehension relationship influenced by development and motivation? (3) How is the relationship influenced by restriction?

The Skill Fluency-Comprehension Relationship When Reading Is Unrestricted

Instructions for the unrestricted reading task, which everyone received, encouraged children to take whatever action they needed to

Table 1
Summary of the NSF research

Sample	Seventy-one third-graders were tested: 38 males and 33 females; 46 Caucasians and 25 African Americans. Sixty-eight fifth graders were tested: 35 males and 33 females; 47 Caucasians, 19 African Americans, and 2 Native Americans. Seventy-two seventh graders participated: 39 males and 33 females; 53 Caucasians, 17 African Americans, and 2 Latino Americans. Approximately half of the students at each grade were enrolled in a university laboratory school in Ruston, Louisiana, which is suburban school of approximately 264 students, grades K-8. The other half were enrolled in a rural school in northern Louisiana of 603 students, grades K-12. Standardized test score results revealed that the school performed 13% below the state average in English language arts in 2003. Students at the laboratory school scored 35% above the state average. Clearly, the skill level of participants was quite diverse, though no one had a reading disability.	
Computerized or group reading fluency tasks taken by all children	Word reading	How quickly and accurately children read words flashed on a computer screen.
	Word meanings	How quickly and accurately children decided if two nouns (e.g., *food, sports*) belonged to the same category.
	Sentence comprehension	How quickly and accurately children decided which of two words best completed a sentence.
	Working memory	How accurately verbal information was retained in working memory.
	Motivation	Students' self-reports.
	Comprehension tests	Multiple-choice tests followed each passage, 8 to 11 items in length. Items were a mixture of literal and inferential.
	Reading tasks	Four reading tasks were individually administered. Tasks 2 through 4 in the following section were true experiments. For each task, practice passages and two challenging test passages (expository and narrative) were used, each about 300 words. 1. Unrestricted reading: For this task, all children at each grade were recorded reading aloud the passages. How often and how they compensated was coded later. 2. Time pressure/no time pressure: Half of the students at each grade were randomly assigned to read under time pressure, the other half under no time pressure. All passages were read aloud. 3. Constant/variable rate: Half of the students at each grade were randomly assigned to read at a constant rate, but were not permitted to a slow reading rate, look back in text, or otherwise compensate. The other half could compensate freely. All passages were read aloud. 4. Read silently/aloud: Half of the students at each grade were randomly assigned to read silently at all times; the other half were asked to read aloud.

understand texts. To assess motivation, readers were asked after each task how interesting they found the texts. Among the important findings, reading fluency measures were weakly related to comprehension across grades. Moreover, reading fluency measures were generally negatively related with compensation use. In other words, within each grade, readers with less fluent skills compensated more often (e.g., slowed reading rate, paused, looked back, reread). More fluent readers compensated less. Similar results have been reported (Walczyk & Taylor, 1996; Walczyk et al., 2001, 2004). However, an interesting developmental trend occurred: fifth and seventh graders were likely to jump over minor words spontaneously. Third graders spent too much time trying to sound them out and often had to be prompted by the experimenter to continue reading. Moreover, analysis of seventh-grade data showed that fluent readers tended to compensate infrequently and comprehend well. Less fluent seventh graders who found the texts interesting tended to compensate frequently and comprehended well. Less fluent readers who did not find the texts interesting tended to compensate infrequently and comprehended poorly. Thus, there are at least two pathways to good comprehension: (a) Fluent skills, infrequent compensation or (b) nonfluent skills, high motivation, frequent compensation, which are all consistent with C-ET.

These findings demonstrate, in the case of challenging texts, that the willingness to compensate depends on children's motivation to understand. Less skilled readers low in motivation, or who do not believe in their ability to understand well, will likely compensate infrequently and comprehend poorly (Butkowsky & Willows, 1980; Johnston & Winograd, 1985). According to C-ET, older and more fluent readers generally will require interesting texts or challenging tasks to stay engaged because, for them, reading often is routine (Chall, 1996). As will be seen in the following sections, interesting or challenging tasks can increase readers' motivation to understand.

Effects of Restriction: Time Pressure

The time pressure imposed in this study was moderate, allowing readers 66% of the average time needed by typical readers of their age to complete test passages. Across grade levels, the comprehension of time-pressured readers was significantly lower than that of nontime-pressured readers. For third and fifth graders reading under time pressure, the relationship between reading fluency and comprehension was strongly positive. Those more fluent comprehended significantly better. Under no time pressure, the relationships were much weaker, indicating that readers with weak skills compensated. For seventh graders, the situation was reversed. Stronger positive relationships between skill fluency and comprehension were observed under no time pressure, partly because the skills of older readers are quite robust in overcoming restriction (Chall, 1996; Perfetti, 1985). Rather than overwhelming their skills, time pressure likely increased seventh graders' reading engagement (mostly those with the weakest skills, such that comprehension was weakly related to skill level). This phenomenon has been observed in adults (Walczyk, Kelly, Meche, & Braud, 1999). Under no time pressure, seventh graders generally were poorly engaged (likely because the task resembled routine reading), and compensation use was infrequent for all. As a consequence, more fluent readers comprehended better.

Effects of Restriction: Constant/Variable Rate

This task was not as restrictive as time pressure and did not prevent all compensation use. Rather, it prevented readers from pausing, looking back, and rereading. However, children generally adopted a reading rate they could handle. Reading at a constant rate significantly lowered comprehension for third and fifth graders but not for seventh graders, whose skills were most robust. The relationship between skill fluency and comprehension was positive for third graders who read at a constant rate and was weaker when reading rate was variable, indicating that when readers could compensate (variable rate reading), they did, and comprehension depended less on skill fluency. For the fifth graders, the skill fluency—comprehension relationship was equally positive whether reading rate was constant or variable. For seventh graders, stronger positive skill fluency—comprehension relationships were observed when reading was variable than when it was constant. As before, because a constant reading rate was a novel challenge, it engaged all seventh graders, but especially the least fluent. The variable rate, resembling routine reading, generally resulted in minimal text engagement and compensation use. As a consequence, more fluent readers had superior comprehension. Fifth graders appeared to be in transition between the third and seventh graders.

Effects of Restriction: Read Silently/Aloud

Reading silently is more restrictive than reading aloud. For third graders, reading aloud produced significantly higher comprehension—evidence that it was compensatory. No comprehension differences were found, however, for fifth or seventh graders, likely because their texts were not sufficiently difficult. It was ironic that, for both third and seventh graders, an identical pattern of relationships was found between reading skill fluency and comprehension. It was strongly positive when reading silently and near zero when reading aloud, as predicted. Reading aloud thus helped less fluent readers and skilled readers to comprehend—not so when reading silently. For fifth graders, this relationship was equally positive whether reading silently or aloud. Again, fifth graders may be in transition. For them, reading silently is not well practiced and may engage them cognitively as much as reading aloud. By seventh grade, reading silently has become routine.

Instructional Implications

This presentation of C-ET suggests ways of helping two groups of poor comprehenders to understand better: (1) those whose reading fluency is low, but without reading disabilities, and (2) fluent readers who understand beneath their potential (word callers). The article concludes with instructional recommendations for both.

Helping Nonfluent Word Readers to Comprehend Better

This study, along with those cited previously, demonstrated that low-fluency readers can comprehend better in relaxed, unrestricted environments that encourage and permit them to compensate freely. However, struggling readers often have negative attitudes toward reading. Lack of success, in many cases, creates a sense of learned helplessness. Such readers often attribute poor comprehension to low ability and ascribe success to easy text. This attribution style discourages task analysis, effort, and perseverance when confusion arises (Butkowsky & Willows, 1980; Johnston & Winograd, 1985). Such readers also tend to be anxious in competitive and restrictive tasks, which undermines their integration of sentences and their elaboration of content (Calvo & Carrieras, 1993). Although many academic tasks, such as standardized testing, require students to read under restriction, by setting aside a little time each week for unrestricted reading teachers may help students to enjoy reading more by creating opportunities for success. More positive experiences with reading, in turn, should encourage students to read more on their own and increase their fluency (Charlesworth, Fleege, & Weitman, 1994; Fleege, Charlesworth, Burts, & Hart, 1992). Although independent reading often occurs silently, students should be encouraged by teachers to read aloud when needed, especially when text is difficult.

Struggling readers only need to compensate when confusions occur or are imminent (e.g., when reading a difficult text). They must, therefore, be taught to recognize such occasions. Struggling readers who do not compensate appropriately can be taught to do so. First they must understand how and why to slow reading rate, pause, look back, and use the other compensations discussed previously. Without direct metacognitive training, struggling readers are unlikely to compensate on their own (Miranda & Villaescusa, 1997). Readers can be taught the advantages of pausing briefly at phrase or sentence markers (e.g., a period, comma, or question mark) to integrate textual information. They can further be taught the importance of reading aloud when text is difficult and be exposed to modeled examples of common sources of confusion successfully resolved (e.g., forgetting to whom *they* refers, resolvable by looking back). As readers practice compensating, teachers or more able peers can provide scaffolding. After applying the compensations, students can discuss which ones worked best for them with their peers and explain to them how they applied such strategies. In this manner, students can learn from others who are experiencing similar problems and can discuss them on a level they understand. Knowing that they are not the only students who have difficulties can improve students' self-esteem, which, in turn, can motivate them to work harder to understand text (Winstead, 2004).

Word Calling

In the anecdote that began this article, Dwain's oral reading was fluent, but his comprehension was low. In the reading literature, such occurrences have been labeled *word calling*. Stanovich (1986) proposed this definition: "when the words in the text are efficiently decoded into their spoken forms without comprehension of the passage taking place" (p. 372) and suggested that it may involve the fluent reading of words whose meanings are not in children's listening vocabularies. Although this certainly accounts for some instances, C-ET identifies another possibility. Some word callers may read words so fluently that they are not cognitively engaged by the text. In other words, their effortless word reading allows their minds to wander. To understand text well, children must focus on meaning, relate content to relevant information from memory, and monitor comprehension (Oakhill, 1993; Oakhill et al., 2003). Fluent word reading, then, may not be sufficient, or even necessary, to comprehend well. Based on the data presented in this article, having to struggle a little with word reading helps students to stay engaged (see Salomon & Globerson, 1987). More fluent word readers are engaged by challenging and interesting tasks (Walczyk et al., 2006); otherwise they may read lackadaisically. For older readers (fifth graders and up), slight restriction on reading (e.g., mild time pressure or other challenges) can increase their cognitive engagement and comprehension (Duffy, Shinjo, & Myers, 1990; Salomon & Sieber-Suppes, 1970).

Helping Word Callers to Comprehend Better

Because more fluent readers may require more challenging and interesting tasks to engage them, classroom activities that help them to comprehend at their best differ from those of struggling readers. Acknowledging that teachers do their best to choose texts and tasks to maximize reader engagement, here are a few research-based suggestions, ranging from directing students to read with unusual purposes to presenting them with game-like challenges (Salomon & Globerson, 1987; Walczyk et al., 1999). Benware and Deci (1984) directed students to learn materials with the intention of explaining it to others at a later time. Wittrock (1986) encouraged students to create mental images of passage content and associate it to their existing knowledge. Both approaches led to better learning. Globerson, Weinstein, and Sharabany (1985) found that when learners were focused on the activity of learning (e.g., through metacognitive training), their engagement and comprehension were enhanced. Reading in cooperative learning groups can also increase cognitive engagement. When students work jointly, they communicate information, discuss their views, and are exposed to alternative interpretations (Baker & Brown, 1984; Salomon & Globerson, 1987). Finally, granting students some choice of texts or tasks can increase engagement as well (Shearer et al., 2001).

Final Thoughts

This article presented compensatory-encoding theory by which nonfluent reading skills do not always lower comprehension. The findings of a major test of C-ET indicated that there is more than one way to comprehend well. Less fluent readers must understand how and why to compensate, be motivated, and unrestricted. Furthermore, older, more fluent readers can benefit by reading under slight restriction or by other engaging tasks or texts. Routine reading tasks allow their minds to wander. In light of differences between these two groups, instructional implications were discussed based on the distinct needs of each to maximize comprehension. We hope that this article helps reading teachers to understand the diverse pathways readers can take to good comprehension and helps clarify the relationship between reading fluency and comprehension.

Notes

This material is based upon work supported by the National Science Foundation under Grant No. 0236791. Any opinions, findings, conclusions, or recommendations expressed in this material are those of the author(s) and do not necessarily reflect the views of the National Science Foundation.

References

Baker, L., & Brown, A.L. (1984). Metacognitive skills and reading. In P.D. Pearson, M. Kamil, R. Barr, & P. Mosenthal (Eds.), *Handbook of reading research* (Vol. 1, pp. 353–394). White Plains, NY: Longman.

Bell, L.C., & Perfetti, C.A. (1994). Reading skill: Some adult comparisons. *Journal of Educational Psychology, 86*(2), 244–255.

Benware, C.A., & Deci, E.L. (1984). Quality of learning with an active versus passive motivational set. *American Educational Research Journal, 21*(4), 755–765.

Bereiter, C., & Bird, M. (1985). Use of thinking aloud in identification and teaching reading of comprehension strategies. *Cognition and Instruction, 2*(2), 131–156.

Bruck, M. (1998). Outcomes of adults with childhood histories of dyslexia. In C. Hulme & R.M. Joshi (Eds.), *Reading and spelling: Development and disorders* (pp. 179–200). Mahwah, NJ: Erlbaum.

Butkowsky, I.S., & Willows, D.M. (1980). Cognitive-motivational characteristics of children varying in reading ability: Evidence for learned helplessness in poor readers. *Journal of Educational Psychology, 72*(3), 408–422.

Calvo, M.G., & Carreiras, M. (1993). Selective influence of test anxiety on reading processes. *British Journal of Psychology, 84*, 375–388.

Cataldo, M.G., & Oakhill, J. (2000). Why are poor comprehenders inefficient searchers? An investigation into the effects of text representation and spatial memory on the ability to locate information in text. *Journal of Educational Psychology, 92*(4), 791–799.

Chall, J.S. (1996). *Stages of reading development* (2nd ed.). Fort Worth, TX: Harcourt Brace.

Charlesworth, R., Fleege, P.O., & Weitman, C.J. (1994). Research on the effects of group standardized testing on instruction, pupils, and teachers: New directions for policy. *Early Education and Development, 5*(3), 195–212.

Clay, M.M. (1979). *The early detection of reading difficulties.* Auckland, New Zealand: Heinemann.

Crain, S., Shankweiler, D., Macaruso, P., & Bar-Shalom, E. (1990). Working memory and comprehension of spoken sentences: Investigations of children with reading disorders. In G. Vallar & T. Shallice (Eds.), *Neuropsychological impairments of short-term memory* (pp. 477–508). Cambridge, England: Cambridge University Press.

Duffy, S.A., Shinjo, M., & Myers, J.L. (1990). The effect of encoding task on memory for sentence pairs varying in causal relatedness. *Journal of Memory and Language, 29*(1), 27–42.

Ehri, L. (1994). Development of the ability to read words: Update. In R. Ruddell, M.R. Ruddell, & H. Singer (Eds.), *Theoretical models and processes of reading* (4th ed., pp. 323–358). Newark, DE: International Reading Association.

Ericsson, K.A. (1988). Concurrent verbal reports on text comprehension: A review. *Text, 8*, 295–325.

Fleege, P.O., Charlesworth, R., Burts, D.C., & Hart, C.H. (1992). Stress begins in kindergarten: A look at behavior during standardized testing. *Journal of Research in Childhood Education, 7*, 20–26.

Fuchs, L.S., Fuchs, D., Hosp, M.K., & Jenkins, J.R. (2001). Oral reading fluency as an indicator of reading competence: A theoretical, empirical, and historical analysis. *Scientific Studies of Reading, 5*(3), 239–256.

Globerson, T., Weinstein, E., & Sharabany, R. (1985). Teasing out cognitive development from cognitive style: A training study. *Developmental Psychology, 21*(4), 682–691.

Gough, P.B., & Tunmer, W.E. (1986). Decoding, reading, and reading disability. *Remedial and Special Education, 7*, 6–10.

Haviland, S.E., & Clark, H.H. (1974). What's new? Acquiring new information as a process in comprehension. *Journal of Verbal Learning and Verbal Behavior, 13*(5), 512–521.

Hoover, W.A., & Gough, P.B. (1990). The simple view of reading. *Reading and Writing: An Interdisciplinary Journal, 2*(2), 127–160.

Jackson, N.E., & Doellinger, H.L. (2002). Resilient readers? University students who are poor recoders but sometimes good text comprehenders. *Journal of Educational Psychology, 94*(1), 64–78.

Johnston, P.H., & Winograd, P.N. (1985). Passive failure in reading. *Journal of Reading Behavior, 17*, 279–301.

Kucan, L., & Beck, I.L. (1997). Thinking aloud and reading comprehension research: Inquiry, instruction, and social interactions. *Review of Educational Research, 67*(3), 271–299.

LaBerge, D., & Samuels, S.J. (1974). Toward a theory of automatic information processing in reading. *Cognitive Psychology, 6*(2), 293–323.

Miller, S.D., & Smith, D.E.P. (1985). Differences in literal and inferential comprehension after reading orally and silently. *Journal of Educational Psychology, 77*(3), 341–348.

Miranda, A., Villaescusa, M.I., & Vidal-Abarca, E. (1997). Is attribution retraining necessary? Use of self-regulation procedures for enhancing the reading comprehension strategies of children with learning disabilities. *Journal of Learning Disabilities, 30*, 503–512.

Nagy, N.M., Campenni, C.E., & Shaw, J.N. (2000). A survey of sustained silent reading practices in seventh-grade classrooms. *Reading Online*. Retrieved November 30, 2006, from http://www.readingonline.org/articles/art_index.asp?HREF=/articles/nagy/index.html

Nation, K., & Snowling, M. (1997). Assessing reading difficulties: The validity and utility of current measures of reading skill. *British Journal of Educational Psychology, 67*, 359–370.

National Institute of Child Health and Human Development. (2000). *Report of the National Reading Panel. Teaching children to read: An evidence-based assessment of the scientific research literature on reading and its implications for reading instruction* (NIH Publication No. 00-4769). Washington, DC: U.S. Government Printing Office.

Oakhill, J.V. (1993). Children's difficulties in reading comprehension. *Educational Psychology Review, 5*(3), 223–237

Oakhill, J.V., Cain, K., & Bryant, P.E. (2003). The dissociation of word reading and text comprehension: Evidence from component skills. *Language and Cognitive Processes, 18*(4), 443–468.

Pazzaglia, F., Cornoldi, C., & Tressoldi, P.E. (1993). Learning to read: Evidence on the distinction between decoding and comprehension skills. *European Journal of Psychology in Education, 8*, 247–258.

Perfetti, C.A. (1985). *Reading ability*. New York: Oxford University Press.

Perfetti, C.A. (1999). Cognitive research and the misconceptions of reading education. In J. Oakhill & R. Beard (Eds.), *Reading development and the teaching of reading: A psychological perspective* (pp. 42–58). London: Blackwell.

Pressley, M., & Afflerbach, P. (1995). *Verbal protocols of reading: The nature of constructively responsive reading*. Hillsdale, NJ: Erlbaum.

Salomon, G., & Globerson, T. (1987). Skill may not be enough: The role of mindfulness in learning and transfer. *International Journal of Educational Research, 11*(6), 623–637.

Salomon, G., & Sieber-Suppes, J. (1970). Relevant subjective response uncertainty as a function of stimulus task interaction. *American Educational Research Journal, 7*(3), 337–349.

Samuels, S.J., & Flor, R.F. (1997). The importance of automaticity for developing expertise in reading. *Reading and Writing Quarterly: Overcoming Learning Difficulties, 13*, 107–121.

Shankweiler, D., Crain, S., Katz, L., Fowler, A.E., Liberman, A.M., Brady, S.A., et al. (1995). Cognitive profiles of reading-disabled children: Comparison of language skills in phonology, morphology, and syntax. *Psychological Science, 6*(3), 149–156.

Shearer, B.A., Ruddell, M.A., & Vogt, M.E. (2001). Successful middle school intervention: Negotiated strategies and individual choices. In. J.V. Hoffman, D.L. Schallert, C.M. Fairbanks, J. Worthy, & B. Maloch (Eds.), *50th yearbook of the National Reading Conference* (pp. 558–571). Chicago: National Reading Conference.

Stanovich, K.E. (1986). Matthew effects in reading: Some consequences of individual differences in the acquisition of literacy. *Reading Research Quarterly, 21*(4), 360–406.

Storch, S.A., & Whitehurst, G.J. (2002). Oral language and code-related precursors to reading: Evidence from a longitudinal structural model. *Developmental Psychology, 38*(6), 934–947.

Stothard, S.E., & Hulme, C. (1995). A comparison of phonological skills in children with reading comprehension difficulties and children with decoding difficulties. *Journal of Child Psychology and Psychiatry, 36*(3), 399–408.

Thompson, G.B., & Johnston, R.S. (2000). Are nonword and other phonological deficits indicative of a failed reading process? *Reading and Writing, 12*(1/2), 63–97.

Vogt, M., & Nagano, P. (2003). Turn it on with light bulb reading! Sound-switching strategies for struggling readers. *The Reading Teacher, 57*, 214–221.

Walczyk, J.J. (2000). The interplay between automatic and control process in reading. *Reading Research Quarterly, 35*(4), 554–566.

Walczyk, J.J., Kelly, K.E., Meche, S.D., & Braud, H. (1999). Time limitations enhance reading comprehension. *Contemporary Educational Psychology, 24*(2), 156–165.

Walczyk, J.J., Marsiglia, C.S., Bryan, K.S., & Naquin, P.J. (2001). Overcoming inefficient reading skills. *Journal of Educational Psychology, 93*(4), 750–757.

Walczyk, J.J., Marsiglia, C.S., Johns, A.K., & Bryan, K.S. (2004). Children's compensations for poorly automated reading skills. *Discourse Processes, 37*(1), 47–66.

Walczyk, J.J., & Taylor, R.W. (1996). How do the efficiencies of reading subcomponents relate to looking back in text? *Journal of Educational Psychology, 88*(3), 537–545.

Walczyk, J.J., Wei, M., Griffith-Ross, D.A., Goubert, S.E., Cooper, A.L., & Zha, P. (2006). *Development of the interplay between automatic processes and cognitive resources in reading.* Manuscript in preparation.

Walker, B.J. (2005). Thinking aloud: Struggling readers often require more than a model. *The Reading Teacher, 58*(7), 688–692.

Winstead, L. (2004). Increasing academic motivation and cognition in reading, writing, and mathematics: Meaning-making strategies. *Educational Research Quarterly, 28*, 29–49.

Wittrock, M. (1986). Students' thought processes. In M.C. Wittrock (Ed.), *Handbook of research on teaching* (3rd ed.). New York: Macmillan.

Yuill, N., & Oakhill, J. (1991). *Children's problems in text comprehension: An experimental investigation.* Cambridge, England: Cambridge University Press.

Questions for Reflection

- The authors note that many struggling readers comprehend better when reading aloud than when reading silently, and they offer a rationale for this behavior. But, in your experience, do you think it is possible that they comprehend better when reading aloud because they have more experiences reading aloud than reading silently? Consider the reading you have struggling readers do. Is oral reading a predominate feature?
- Does low motivation for reading assigned material play a role in your struggling readers' comprehension difficulties? Are there strategies you could use to ameliorate this?
- Do your struggling readers engage in any of the compensatory activities the authors describe? Have you considered those behaviors as possibly facilitating their comprehension? In what ways could you avoid the restrictions on reading the authors outline, and how might that benefit your struggling learners?

Thinking Aloud: Struggling Readers Often Require More Than a Model

Barbara J. Walker

Although thinking aloud to model the active comprehension process has been purported to increase comprehension for all students, this instructional procedure is far from being standard practice in classrooms (Pressley, 2002). Still, teachers ask children questions that have predetermined answers (Cazden, 1988; Durkin, 1978/1979; Pressley, Wharton-McDonald, Hampston, & Echevarria, 1998). Although more teachers ask questions using comprehension processes (i.e., summarizing the story, filling out a story map, using prior knowledge), seldom are the teachers modeling the thinking process *as* students read. Research corroborates that many teachers have difficulty modeling this complex process (Duffy & Roehler, 1989; El-Dinary, Pressley, & Schuder, 1992); therefore, thinking aloud has not become common practice. Because comprehension is a complex process, teachers are mystified when demonstrating how to construct meaning using content knowledge and comprehension strategies. Comprehension is not an overt process but rather an inner self-dialogue about meaning. Thinking aloud makes this internal process observable. Yet, some students have difficulty figuring it out (Block & Israel, 2004); they passively read not expecting the text to make sense.

Even when teachers ask some struggling readers a direct question, they do not respond. Without thinking the students read the words and don't construct meaning. Or, if these struggling readers must respond to a question about text, they say, "I don't know." These readers have learned that if they refuse to respond, someone else will answer. Other students do revise their understanding, but less frequently than their more active peers. Struggling readers often rely on their initial predictions and ignore contradictory information. For example, a third-grade student was reading a selection, "Elmo Learns to Fly" (Margaret, 1975). In the middle section, the text reads "He leaped atop a sun bleached log breathing the fresh air until his great chest was puffed out tight as a drum" (pp. 58–59). Making a prediction, the student said, "Oh, I think he inhales so he could be like a balloon. So he could fly instead of flying with wings, he could inhale like a balloon." From that segment on, the student held on to the balloon prediction, even though the text refers to Elmo as an animal of the pond and marsh. Like this student, many struggling readers are passive when reading.

How Think-Aloud Using Self-Statements Developed

Instructional techniques develop over time with lots of influence from teachers, students, theories, and research. They often start with a problem situation like passive reading. In this type of situation, I decided to develop a way to demonstrate the active thinking process of the reader's mind. Initially, I drew my ideas from psycholinguistic theory (K. Goodman, 1975; Y. Goodman & Burke, 1980), which focused on predicting the author's meaning, and interactive theory (Pearson & Johnson, 1978; Rumelhart, 1976), which focused on shifting between text and prior knowledge. I also studied the work of Vygotsky

Reprinted from Walker, B.J. (2005). Thinking aloud: Struggling readers often require more than a model. *The Reading Teacher, 58*(7), 688–692.

(1978), who proposed that inner dialogue, which coordinates thinking, is developed through social interaction when learning is mediated by more informed others who think aloud, leading learners to verbalize their cognitive processes. When students interact with others they eventually cultivate inner self-directed speech. Building on this theory, Meichenbaum and Asarnow (1979) began teaching children to use self-regulated speech by having adults model self-verbalized regulation of comprehension strategies.

I began by modeling prediction making because it is easy (Pressley, 2002), and readers can be right or wrong as they construct meaning. As one reader in my classroom said, "You can get off track or stay on track, it doesn't matter." My initial attempts to use the theories I had studied were meager at best. As I modeled the prediction process with my fourth-grade students, I found, like other teachers, that thinking aloud was difficult. Teachers predict outcomes by switching between sources automatically and the process is difficult to model. To help students, I demonstrated using my personal knowledge by explicitly pointing to my head and using the text by clearly pointing to the book as I talked.

Models Can Help

After my initial attempts at demonstrating self-talk, I realized that the students needed a structure that they could consistently follow. Therefore, I adapted the self-questions of active thinking together with a format designed for self-instruction (Meichenbaum, 1977). The teacher thinks aloud using the following self-questions, and the students follow the model.

"What must I do? I must predict what might happen. I predict...."

"What's my plan? I must use the text and what I know."

"Does that make sense? Oops! It doesn't. I can change my prediction."

"Did it fit? Yes, I knew it! That sure fits. I am on the right track."

A colleague, who taught struggling seventh-grade readers, implemented the procedure successfully. She found that students in the self-directed questioning group performed better than the read-only group (Mohr, 1984). Using a basal reader, several colleagues and I had third-grade students write down their predictions while they used the questions. We also found that the prediction group performed better than the group that answered teacher-posed questions (Walker, Mohr, Wilson, & Hardgrove, 1986).

Although these procedures worked for many struggling readers, something was still missing. Some struggling readers still remained passive and did not engage in self-directed questioning. So, I began developing self-evaluation sheets to explain the active process after reading stories. The explanation before reading was not enough. These adaptations were influenced by Bandura's (1986) concept of self-efficacy, which refers to people's beliefs about their capabilities to carry out actions required to reach a confident level of achievement (Schunk, 2003). Many struggling readers are not confident and believe they cannot comprehend; they make negative statements about themselves that lower their self-efficacy. Because of repeated failures, struggling readers do not recognize the effective strategies they do use. Instead of learning alternative strategies from their failure, they often give up. Thus, struggling readers do not attribute their comprehension to their own strategic thinking. These readers realize that they could expend effort by reading the words, but they still would not grasp the meaning; thus, they decrease their effort, which in turn reduces feelings of success and diminishes their engagement.

Teachers can make thinking aloud more concrete by writing down self-statements and using self-evaluation sheets (see Figure 1) that discuss strategy use. These techniques can help passive students become more cognizant of a variety of strategies (Walker, 2003). The self-evaluation sheets become tools to open discussion about personal strategy use. At the end of this discussion, the teacher and the students talk about what strategies they might use the next time; in other words, they set goals. In this way, struggling

Figure 1
Self-Evaluation Sheet

When I read,	Not at all	A few times	Sometimes	Most times
I made predictions.				
I used information from the text.				
I used information that I already knew.				
I connected information to see how it fit.				
I said "Oops" and revised a prediction when it didn't fit.				
I said "I knew it" when I was on the right track.				

Today my reading was ____________________ because ____.

readers explain their strategy use and understanding and set personal goals for improving their comprehension. Thinking aloud and strategy instruction have been used effectively for over two decades, and studies have demonstrated that thinking aloud improves comprehension (Brown, Pressley, Van Meter, & Schuder, 1996; Duffy et al., 1987; Mason, 2004; Meichenbaum & Asarnow, 1979; Schunk & Rice, 1991).

Current Think-Aloud Strategies

In most classrooms the teacher selects a short story that is ambiguous, has a plot twist, and is easy to decode so that students focus on comprehension strategies. The teacher divides the story into segments from which multiple predictions could be made. In this way, students can revise and reconfirm their prediction, which in turn involves them in self-talk about constructing meaning.

Figure 2 is a description of the strategy I now use. During this instructional procedure, I make the comprehension process more tangible by writing the key self-statements on a chalkboard. I engage readers in self-assessment using self-evaluation sheets along with analytical conversations about strategy use and meaning.

After students finish reading a story, they complete a self-evaluation sheet and discuss their strategy use. The self-evaluation sheet focuses on evaluation of the prediction process along with conversations about strategy use.

For several summers in a reading center setting, I worked with middle school students who had a passive stance toward comprehension. Although they began to engage in the comprehension process, they needed more active models (more informed others) and someone to discuss their self-evaluation sheets. I added tutors as learners whose role it was to record the students' active process on an evaluation sheet as they participated in understanding the story. After the story was read, the tutors met with a single student and discussed the active comprehension process. One young student reported to me later, "Did you see how excited [the teacher] was when her prediction was on the right track?" This was working; the students were observing the strategies of effective readers, one of which is self-reward. Because of years of failure, passive readers have difficulty getting excited or rewarding themselves for the positive strategies they use (Walker, 1996). Another teacher who had not been able to improve the comprehension scores of her fifth-grade struggling readers decided to use the procedure. She had the volunteer tutors think-aloud as she read stories aloud segment by segment (Shipley, 1990). Afterward, each volunteer discussed the active reading strategies with one student and completed a self-evaluation sheet. The students improved their comprehension as measured by a standardized test.

Figure 2
Self-Questioning Strategy

Modeling predictions

Self-question: "How do I begin?"

Response: "I need to predict what the author is going to say. A good strategy is to look at the title. From the title I predict that...." The teacher models using the title of the story to think aloud about how he or she made a prediction and at the same time writes "I predict" on the middle of the chalkboard.

Modeling sources of information

Self-question 1: "How do I check predictions?"

Response: "To check my prediction, I can think about what I already know or I can look for hints from the author." The teacher writes "I already know that" and "Hints from the author" on the chalkboard.

Self-question 2: "I wonder how it fits together?"

Response: "It fits because I know..., and the author says..., which can connect to support my prediction." The teacher demonstrates how he or she connects the two sources together to support a prediction.

Modeling monitoring

This self-question has three distinctive responses. Usually the teacher uses three different text segments to illustrate them.

Self-question: "Does my prediction make sense?"

Response 1: "Oops, that doesn't make sense. I need to check my thinking. So far, I'm on the right track with...but confused about...." As the teacher models this strategy, he or she writes "Oops" on the right side of the chalkboard. The teacher models self-talk related to making a mistake by saying "It's OK to make a mistake. I can change my prediction as I get more information. Now, I predict...."

Response 2: "Hmmm. Sometimes I am just not sure. Maybe it's.... Or maybe it's...." The teacher models being tentative when predicting by writing "Hmmm" on the middle of the chalkboard.

Response 3: "I knew it. That sure fits. So far I'm on the right track." The teacher models confirming the prediction as he or she writes "I knew it" on the right side of the chalkboard.

Yet, another teacher who was working with high school students with emotional problems used the technique with informational texts. Because the teacher taught many comprehension strategies, she added a last section to the self-evaluation sheet that asked which strategy the students used to construct meaning in the current assignment (L. Wilson, personal communication, September 23, 1993). These students were able to discuss not only the content but also the strategy they had used. I continue to use this technique in my teaching today, and individual case studies consistently demonstrate improved comprehension among students.

More Than a Model

The think-aloud technique used with the self-evaluation sheet (including strategy conversations) promotes the comprehension process as a salient feature of learning. These techniques improved strategy use, promoted self-efficacy, and increased engagement as well as comprehension. Struggling readers in many classrooms and clinics need more than a model; they require someone to think aloud, to model self-statements as they read, to jointly fill out self-evaluation sheets, and to think aloud about strategy use. Through this procedure, struggling readers begin to internalize the comprehension process.

References

Bandura, A. (1986). *Social foundations of thought and action: A social cognitive theory.* Englewood Cliffs, NJ: Prentice Hall.

Block, C., & Israel, S. (2004). The ABCs of performing highly effective think-alouds. *The Reading Teacher, 58,* 154–167.

Brown, R., Pressley, M., Van Meter, P., & Schuder, T. (1996). A quasi-experimental validation of transactional strategies instruction with low-achieving second grade readers. *Journal of Educational Psychology, 88*, 18–37.

Cazden, C.B. (1988). *Classroom discourse: The language of teaching and learning.* Portsmouth, NH: Heinemann.

Duffy, G.G., & Roehler, L.R. (1989). Why strategy instruction is so difficult and what we need to do about it. In C.B. McCormick, G. Miller, & M. Pressley (Eds.), *Cognitive strategy research: From basic research to educational applications* (pp. 133–154). New York: Springer-Verlag.

Duffy, G., Roehler, L., Sivan, E., Rackliffer, G., Book, C., Meloth, M., et al. (1987). Effects of explaining reasoning associated with using reading strategies. *Reading Research Quarterly, 22*, 347–368.

Durkin, D. (1978/1979). What classroom observations reveal about reading comprehension instruction. *Reading Research Quarterly, 14*, 202–224.

El-Dinary, P.B., Pressley, M., & Schuder, T. (1992). Becoming a strategies teachers: An observational and interview study of three teachers learning transactional strategies instruction. In C. Kinzer, & D. Leu (Eds.), *Literacy research: Theory and practice, views from many perspectives* (41st yearbook of the National Reading Conference, pp. 453–462). Chicago: National Reading Conference.

Goodman, K. (1975). The reading process. In S. Smiley & J. Towner (Eds.), *Language and reading* (pp. 19–28). Bellingham: Western Washington State College.

Goodman, Y., & Burke, C. (1980). *Reading strategies: Focus on comprehension.* New York: Holt, Rinehart and Winston.

Margaret, K. (1975). *Witches and whimsies.* Sausalito, CA: In Between Books.

Mason, L.H. (2004). Explicit self-regulated strategy development versus reciprocal questioning: Effects on expository reading comprehension among struggling readers. *Journal of Educational Psychology, 96*, 283–296.

Meichenbaum, D. (1977). *Cognitive behavior modification.* New York: Plenum.

Meichenbaum, D., & Asarnow, J. (1979). Cognitive-behavioral modification and metacognitive development: Implications for the classroom. In P.C. Kendall & S.D. Hollon (Eds.), *Cognitive-behavioral interventions* (pp. 11–35). New York: Academic Press.

Mohr, T. (1984). *The effects of self-questioning on reading comprehension.* Unpublished master's thesis, Oklahoma State University, Stillwater.

Pearson, P.D., & Johnson, D. (1978). *Teaching reading comprehension.* New York: Holt, Rinehart and Winston.

Pressley, M. (2002). *Reading instruction that works: The case for balanced teaching* (2nd ed.). New York: Guilford.

Pressley, M., Wharton-McDonald, R., Mistretta-Hampston, J., & Echevarria, M. (1998). Literacy instruction in 10 fourth- and fifth-grade classrooms in upstate New York. *Scientific Studies of Reading, 2*, 159–191.

Rumelhart, D. (1976). *Toward an interactive model of reading* (Tech. Rep. No. 56). San Diego, CA: Center for Human Information Processing, University of San Diego.

Schunk, D.H. (2003). Self-efficacy for reading and writing: Influence of modeling, goal setting, and self-evaluation. *Reading & Writing Quarterly, 19*, 159–172.

Schunk, D.H., & Rice, J.M. (1991). Learning goals and progress feedback during reading comprehension instruction. *Journal of Reading Behavior, 23*, 251–364.

Shipley, J. (1990). *Evaluating comprehension strategies using Host volunteers.* Unpublished manuscript, Eastern Montana College, Billings.

Vygotsky, L.S. (1978). *Mind in society.* Cambridge, MA: Harvard University Press.

Walker, B.J. (1996, April). *Learned helplessness or why Jamie won't read.* Paper presented at the annual convention of the International Reading Association, New Orleans, LA.

Walker, B.J. (2003). The cultivation of student self-efficacy in reading and writing. *Reading & Writing Quarterly, 19*, 173–187.

Walker, B.J. (2004). *Diagnostic teaching of reading: Techniques for instruction and assessment* (5th ed.). Upper Saddle River, NJ: Pearson, Merrill/Prentice-Hall.

Walker, B.J., Mohr, T., Wilson, L., & Hardgrove, R. (1986, January). *Teaching active comprehension through self-questioning.* Paper presented at the meeting of the Rocky Mountain International Reading Association regional conference, Colorado Springs, Colorado.

Questions for Reflection

- Some struggling readers do not respond when we ask them a question; they almost seem to hope we will skip over them and move on to another student. How do you address this problem? Does this article give you ideas for other approaches to engage your struggling learners?
- Do you see yourself using any of the author's suggested strategies? Which ones would you start with? Why?

Paraphrasing: An Effective Comprehension Strategy

Sharon B. Kletzien

Heather (all names are pseudonyms) looked away from the paragraph and said, "Well, he's just getting ready to go out, but.... I don't remember why; let me look back." She skimmed the paragraph again, "Oh, yeah, he was going to go meet his friend, but his friend isn't really there, so he's not going to find him."

Heather, a fifth-grade student in the West Chester University Reading Center, was practicing paraphrasing, a strategy that students can use to monitor and increase their comprehension. Heather, like many of the students with whom we work in the reading center, reads fluently with accuracy, appropriate rate, and good expression, but after she has read a passage, she has difficulty retelling what she has read and difficulty answering questions about it.

Although paraphrasing has been identified as a strategy that good readers use (Kletzien, 1991, 1992; Kletzien & Dreher, 2004; Meijer, Veenman, & van Hout-Wolters, 2006; Pressley & Afflerbach, 1995), it has not received as much attention as many of the other comprehension strategies, such as visualization, using prior knowledge, or questioning. Yet research into teaching students to use paraphrasing either alone or in conjunction with other strategies (Gajria, Jitendra, Sood, & Sacks, 2007) has demonstrated its benefit. In several intervention studies, paraphrasing has been found to help special education students increase their comprehension (Bakken, Mastropieri, & Scruggs, 1997; Ellis & Graves, 1990; Schumaker & Dreshler, 1992).

Paraphrasing, putting the content into one's own words, is often considered the same as summarizing. Paraphrasing, however, is substantially different from and easier than summarizing. In summaries, readers are expected to reduce the length of a passage by approximately one third through reducing lists into a general statement, selecting a topic sentence or constructing one if there isn't one stated, deleting redundancy, and deleting unimportant information (Brown, Campione, & Day, 1981; Kintsch & van Dijk, 1978). Paraphrasing, on the other hand, does not require that a reader make the distinction between important and unimportant details, find (or create) a topic sentence, or delete redundancy. Summarizing, therefore, is more formal than paraphrasing and requires much more practice to be able to do it well. Students may be able to paraphrase long before they acquire the sophisticated ability to summarize. Indeed, paraphrasing may be seen as a precursor to learning to summarize.

Paraphrasing is different from retelling as well. In retelling, readers are invited to use the words of the author in explaining a passage. In fact, as we work with readers in the reading center, we are interested in whether they use the phrasing and wording of the original text in retelling. In paraphrasing, however, we encourage readers to use their own words and phrasing to "translate" the material to their own way of saying it. Readers may be able to retell without ever actually engaging the content of the passages; they must engage the content if they are paraphrasing.

Paraphrasing encourages the reader to make connections with prior knowledge to access what is already known about the topic and to use words that are part of the reader's knowledge.

Reprinted from Kletzien, S.B. (2009). Paraphrasing: An effective comprehension strategy. *The Reading Teacher, 63*(1), 73–77.

It helps the reader establish retrieval cues that enable integration of what is previously known with what is being read, an important part of comprehension according to Kintsch (1998).

Instructional Sequence

Paraphrasing can be seen as part of the monitoring aspect of metacognition (Meijer et al., 2006). When students understand how and why this strategy works, it becomes part of their metacognitive repertoire and available for independent use. In teaching students to use paraphrasing to monitor comprehension, we make certain that they understand the purpose of the strategy, as well as how to do it.

We follow the Roehler and Duffy (1984) model of strategy instruction; we begin with explanations and modeling of the strategy. As students become adept at using the strategy, we gradually provide less support; thus we scaffold their progress from novice to competent users of the strategy.

In the beginning, we explain that many good readers stop when they are reading, look away from the text, and put what they have just read into their own words. If they are unable to do that, they can look back and reread the text to help them. We explain that this is a good strategy to use to check to see if one has understood the passage. We point out that it is also a good strategy to help readers remember what they read.

We model paraphrasing by using think-alouds with texts that are on the student's instructional level. Because we want to be sure that students understand how the strategy works, we model numerous passages. We use both narrative and expository short passages, making certain that students know why we stop at the end of each paragraph to paraphrase.

During the modeling, we make sure to "not remember" some of the paragraph so that we can model rereading for parts that we either "didn't understand" or "had forgotten." After three or four paragraphs each day, we invite students to participate in the paraphrasing. We paraphrase some of the paragraph and ask students if there is anything else that was in the text. As students begin adding their own paraphrasing, we gradually reduce the number of ideas that we give. After two or three sessions, most of our reading center students take over the paraphrasing completely.

Heather

Heather, a fifth grader, was confident about her reading although her instructional level as determined with the Qualitative Reading Inventory-4 (Leslie & Caldwell, 2005) was third grade. Her oral reading was marked by good word recognition, an appropriate rate, and good expression through the fifth-level passage. When she was asked to retell passages, however, she remembered few of the ideas, and her retelling did not reflect the organization of the passage. She had difficulty answering questions about the passages, especially when they required inferences.

It seemed clear that Heather was not monitoring her comprehension; in fact, it seemed as if she didn't realize that comprehension was the object of reading. Her idea of "good" reading seemed to be oral presentation. When asked what good readers do, she responded that they "said all the words right."

We taught Heather to use paraphrasing to monitor her comprehension. She understood that if she couldn't paraphrase, she should go back to the text and reread to try to clear up her misunderstanding. After the first two weeks of working with the strategy, Heather read *Thunder Cake* by Patricia Polacco (1997). The text read,

> "Hurry now, we haven't got much time. We've got everything but the secret ingredient."
>
> "Three overripe tomatoes and some strawberries," Grandma whispered as she squinted at the list.
>
> I climbed up high on the trellis. The ground looked a long way down. I was scared.
>
> "I'm here, child," she said. Her voice was steady and soft. "You won't fall."
>
> I reached three luscious tomatoes while she picked strawberries. (n.p.)

Heather said, "Um, they needed the secret ingredient, and she had to go up something to get tomatoes and strawberries, but she was scared.

Her grandma told her she wouldn't let her fall, so she got the tomatoes, and the grandma got the strawberries. But I don't understand what she was climbing on, and I don't know why she was getting tomatoes for a cake." At this point, Heather reread the passage but said that she didn't know the meaning of *trellis*. After prompting to think about what it might be based on the context, she decided it must be kind of like a fence because the little girl could climb on it. Even after rereading, she expressed confusion about how the tomatoes were going to be in a cake. This response was quite different from Heather's earlier reading when she seemed unaware of whether or not she had understood. She had begun questioning words and ideas that she didn't understand and seeking to figure them out.

Danny

Not all of our students catch on to paraphrasing as quickly as Heather. For example, Danny, a sixth grader, found it very difficult to put text into his own words. As we began working with Danny, we were convinced that he understood what he was reading because he was able to retell it so effectively. He had some trouble, however, responding to questions that did not use the exact terminology of the text. It seemed obvious to us that he had had a lot of practice with retelling in his reading instruction but that he had not had a lot of experience talking about texts or discussing questions.

Danny had some difficulty with word recognition and read very slowly. After completing passages, however, he was usually able to retell them in great detail, using the exact words and phrases from the text. It seemed that Danny needed to work on automaticity in word recognition to improve his fluency. His instructional level, as measured on the Qualitative Reading Inventory-4, was fourth grade.

Danny was very much interested in sports and wanted to read about football, choosing to read *Emergency Quarterback* by Rich Wallace (2005). At the beginning of our instruction, we focused on developing his fluency, believing that his comprehension was fairly strong and would improve with better automaticity in word recognition. As we talked about the book with him, however, we soon realized that he was not able to discuss the story. He could sometimes repeat sentences in response to direct questions, but he couldn't talk about what was happening in the story nor was he able to make inferences about what he had read. This was not because of a lack of background knowledge because he played football himself and could define the terms used in the book (such as *linebacker, handoff, blitz*) with great enthusiasm. Danny seemed to believe that the point of reading was remembering the exact words, not understanding (or enjoying) the text. When asked what good readers do, Danny's response was that they "remember what they read."

It seemed that Danny was able to remember the actual text, but he didn't integrate it with what he already knew. Kintsch (1998) would consider that Danny formed a textbase. "If readers form only a textbase, they can achieve only a superficial understanding of such texts, sufficient for reproductive recall and recognition, but not for reconstructive recall and inferences" (p. 199).

Our task was to help Danny connect with his prior knowledge and to use that prior knowledge in constructing meaning from what he was reading. He was taught how to use paraphrasing as a means to monitor his comprehension and to make the connections with his prior knowledge. When he first began adding his ideas to the ones that had been modeled, he used the exact phrasing of the text. For example, in the story it states,

> He took a deep breath and called the first play, a simple handoff to Jared between the center and right guard—Sergio and Anthony.
>
> Hoboken had its linebackers packed tight behind the line, ready to exert a lot of pressure. Coach had warned that they were tough to pass against, constantly blitzing. (p. 90)

Danny attempted to paraphrase by saying, "He took a deep breath and called the first play, which was a handoff between the center and guard. Hoboken's linebackers were packed tight behind the line because Coach had warned that they were tough to pass against because they were always blitzing."

We explained to Danny, again, that paraphrasing was putting something in his own words—not just remembering the words of the text. This was difficult for Danny. As he said, "But they say it better than I do." Still, translating the text's language to his own was crucial for him to check his comprehension and connect with his own prior knowledge. If he was unable to "translate" the book language to his own conversational language, it meant that he hadn't really comprehended.

We continued to work with Danny, modeling for him how to put paragraphs and sentences in his own words. His paraphrase of a portion of the story near the end of the book shows how his paraphrasing had changed: "They scored and then they went for the two-point conversion and Jason bobbled it. But then he backed it up to the fifteen with all the defenders on him, and then he broke loose and ran across the field. But then Jason saw the Hoboken safety coming at him, and he saw Miguel open in the end zone, and just when he got hit, he threw a bobbly pass to Miguel, and Miguel caught it and they won." Danny's paraphrasing of the text was conversational; it reflected the text, but it did not use the exact wording and phrasing of the author.

At this point, Danny was able to talk about the story and to get excited about what was happening. He was also much better able to make inferences about the plot and the characters.

Brian

Brian, a seventh-grade budding scientist, provided a different challenge for us. Brian read accurately and fairly quickly through a sixth-grade level. His comprehension seemed relatively strong until he was faced with text that had complex concepts that were new to him. He was particularly interested in weather, especially violent weather such as tornadoes, hurricanes, thunderstorms, and blizzards. He wanted to understand the forces that caused these storms and chose to read *Lightning* by Stephen Kramer (1992), an informational book that explains the causes of thunderstorms and lightning.

Brian found the book somewhat frustrating because he read it with the same speed that he read narratives and other less complex informational books. Because the concepts were new to him and required shifting attention from the text to the illustrations, he needed to read more slowly. It seemed that to Brian slowing down and rereading was an admission that he was not a good reader; his concept of good reading was reading quickly, which was easy enough for him to do with less conceptually challenging material.

One exchange with his teacher illustrated his concerns about reading slowly, even after she had discussed the need for changing speed for more complex ideas:

Teacher: What do you think that's saying?

Brian: That lightning is hot.

Teacher: So we're back to that lightning channel again. I have to reread this.

Brian: It doesn't make any sense to me sometimes.

Teacher: Sometimes when things don't make sense to me, Brian, I have to read it twice.

Brian: And you're a quick reader.

Teacher: But it doesn't matter how quick you read, as long as you understand it.

Brian: Right.

As Brian and his teacher worked through the *Lightning* text, he was encouraged to put the information into his own words, to reread when necessary, and to integrate the illustrations. His understanding of the text and his ability to monitor his comprehension and reread improved dramatically during the three weeks he worked with *Lightning*. Toward the end of the three weeks, he paraphrased one portion:

> Well, it's telling you if you want to count how far lightning is you can always count when you see the lightning: 1, 2, 3, 4, 5. And if it's five seconds that counts as one mile away. And if you count to 20 seconds the lightning is four miles away because 4 times 5 equals 20. And if you count 10 seconds, it's really close and you have to take cover. And if you see lightning far away, you probably won't

hear the thunder because it's probably more than 15 miles away.

Paraphrasing, and explaining that all texts aren't meant to be read with the same speed, was a way to help Brian monitor his comprehension while helping him understand the importance of adjusting his speed.

Paraphrasing and Comprehension

Paraphrasing helps students monitor their understanding and encourages them to access what they already know about a topic. It makes it clear to them that understanding is the goal of reading. Each of the children described in this article each seemed to have a different idea of what "good" reading is. Heather seemed to equate good reading with oral performance; Danny appeared to believe that good reading was recalling the exact words from the text; and Brian seemed to believe that good reading was reading quickly. Each of these children benefited from practice in paraphrasing, a strategy that puts the emphasis on comprehension.

With careful instruction and modeling, focusing on what the strategy is, how to do it, when it is useful, and why it is important, children can learn to monitor their comprehension and take steps to correct it if needed.

References

Bakken, J.P., Mastropieri, M.A., & Scruggs, T.E. (1997). Reading comprehension of expository science material and students with learning disabilities: A comparison of strategies. *Journal of Special Education, 31*(3), 300–324.

Brown, A.L., Campione, J.C., & Day, J.D. (1981). Learning to learn: On training students to learn from texts. *Educational Researcher, 10*(2), 14–21.

Ellis, E.S., & Graves, A.W. (1990). Teaching rural students with learning disabilities: A paraphrasing strategy to increase comprehension of main ideas. *Rural Special Education Quarterly, 10*(2), 2–10.

Gajria, M., Jitendra, A.K., Sood, S., & Sacks, G. (2007). Improving comprehension of expository text in students with LD: A research synthesis. *Journal of Learning Disabilities, 40*(3), 210–225.

Kintsch, W. (1998). *Comprehension: A paradigm for cognition.* New York: Cambridge University Press.

Kintsch, W., & van Dijk, T.A. (1978). Toward a model of text comprehension and production. *Psychological Review, 85*(5), 363–394.

Kletzien, S.B. (1991). Strategy use by good and poor comprehenders reading expository text of differing levels. *Reading Research Quarterly, 26*(1), 67–86.

Kletzien, S.B. (1992). Proficient and less proficient comprehenders' strategy use for different top-level structures. *Journal of Reading Behavior, 24*(2), 191–215.

Kletzien, S.B., & Dreher, M.J. (2004). *Informational text in K–3 classrooms: Helping children read and write.* Newark, DE: International Reading Association.

Leslie, L., & Caldwell, J. (2005). *Qualitative reading inventory-4.* New York: Allyn & Bacon.

Meijer, J., Veenman, M.V.J., & van Hout-Wolters, B.H.A.M. (2006). Metacognitive activities in text-studying and problem-solving: Development of a taxonomy. *Educational Research and Evaluation, 12*(3), 209–237.

Pressley, M., & Afflerbach, P. (1995). *Verbal protocols of reading: The nature of constructively responsive reading.* Hillsdale, NJ: Erlbaum.

Roehler, L.R., & Duffy, G.G. (1984). Direct explanation of comprehension processes. In G.G. Duffy, L.R. Roehler, & J. Mason (Eds.), *Comprehension instruction: Perspectives and suggestions* (pp. 265–280). New York: Longman.

Schumaker, J.B., & Dreshler, D.D. (1992). Validation of learning strategy interventions for students with LD: Results of a programmatic research effort. In B.Y.L. Wong (Ed.), *Contemporary intervention research in literacy disabilities: An international perspective* (pp. 22–46). New York: Springer-Verlag.

Questions for Reflection

- Have you tried using any of the paraphrasing activities described in this article? How did your students respond? How might you include both paraphrasing and summarizing in your teaching to benefit students' comprehension?
- Do you think there are differences in paraphrasing narrative as opposed to expository text? Do you think that use of a range of text types in paraphrasing activities would benefit your struggling learners? How do you decide which texts to use?

Getting the Big Idea: A Neglected Goal for Reading Comprehension

Sean A. Walmsley

American children, according to national surveys, seem to have well-developed basic literacy skills. But they falter when it comes to critical or "thoughtful" literacy (National Center for Education Statistics, 2004). Given the amount of time and attention paid to basic literacy—especially under the aegis of the No Child Left Behind Act of 2001 (2002)—perhaps we shouldn't be surprised by these findings. Indeed, a small study I recently undertook in a rural upstate New York school district suggested that engaging children in "big ideas" is not a common practice. Of 126 teaching or learning episodes observed in K–6 classrooms over a 3-day period, only 4 involved exposing children to or discussing big ideas with them. In most instances, I could not easily have imagined students being engaged in big ideas, either because the teaching or learning activity was focused on something quite specific, like decoding or writing mechanics (where big-idea discussions would not have been appropriate), or because the topic under discussion didn't easily lend itself to big ideas (e.g., having students talk about what they did over the weekend). In other words, I not only observed very few instances where students were engaged in big ideas but also very few in which they easily could have been. In this article, I suggest that it's time to focus again on big ideas.

What Exactly Are Big Ideas and Why Teach Them?

I define a big idea as the main point of a book, magazine article, argument, or film; the moral of a story or the underlying theme of a novel; what an author, poet, speaker, or artist is really trying to communicate; and, finally, the life lessons and deeper understandings a reader, listener, or viewer takes from a text, a work of art, or a performance. In reading, big ideas are associated with whole texts, not parts of them. They are not the same as the main idea of a sentence or paragraph.

One reason to teach U.S. students about big ideas is because they aren't strong in critical literacy. But there are more profound reasons: Understanding big ideas is critical to full participation in work, life, and democracy—especially in the era of the 30-second "in-depth" analysis. For example, the media seem to avoid complex topics. As I write this article, the United States is debating the future of Social Security—surely a big idea—but what do adults, let alone young workers who will be most affected by changes to it, actually know about the issue? As the media become more focused on the trivial, educators need to become more focused on the substantial.

Understanding big ideas also serves children well in many states' English language arts assessments, especially at the high school level. (In my state, New York, questions on the statewide English Regents assessment demand critical analysis and evaluation of big ideas.)

Finally, readers, listeners, and viewers can enter "text" at multiple levels (it is not necessary, as Bloom [1956] suggested, that text must be entered at literal levels before it can be engaged at higher levels). Encouraging children to focus on the big ideas of a text promotes understanding of not only big ideas but also smaller details. In

Reprinted from Walmsley, S.A. (2006, November). Getting the big idea: A neglected goal for reading comprehension. *The Reading Teacher*, 60(3), 281-285. doi: 10.1598/RT.60.3.9

fact, stronger readers routinely use their knowledge of the big ideas to work through and understand the text at sentence and paragraph levels.

Big ideas reveal themselves in different ways. In some cases, they stare the reader in the face. For example, in Cowcher's *Antarctica* (1991), a nonfiction book about the delicate balance between penguins, birds, seals, and humans in Antarctica, the big idea is explicit in the final pages:

> The penguins and the seals have always shared their world with ancient enemies, the skuas and the leopard seals. But these new arrivals [referring to humans] are more dangerous. The seals and penguins cannot tell yet whether they will share or destroy their beautiful Antarctica.... (unpaged)

Fables, especially, wear their big ideas on their sleeves. Some even repeat their big idea at the end of the fable:

> The Crow and the Pitcher (Aesop)
>
> A Crow, half-dead with thirst, came upon a pitcher that had once been full of water; but when the Crow put its beak into the mouth of the pitcher he found that only very little water was left in it and that he could not reach far enough down to get at it. He tried, and he tried, but at last had to give up in despair. Then a thought came to him, and he took a pebble and dropped it into the pitcher. Then he took another pebble and dropped it into the pitcher. Then he took another pebble and dropped that into the pitcher. Then he took another pebble and dropped that into the pitcher. Then he took another pebble and dropped that into the pitcher. Then he took another pebble and dropped that into the pitcher. At last, at last, he saw the water mount up near him, and after casting in a few more pebbles he was able to quench his thirst and save his life. Little by little does the trick.

In most good children's literature, big ideas lie under the surface of the text, revealing themselves indirectly. For example, Trapani's (1998) retelling of *The Itsy Bitsy Spider* recounts the four episodes in which Itsy Bitsy tries, in vain, to climb up the water spout, the kitchen wall, and the yellow pail, but finally climbs a maple tree where she successfully spins her web. Nowhere does Trapani explicitly state the big idea "if at first you don't succeed, try, try again," but that's the unmistakable big idea to which each episode inexorably contributes.

The big ideas of some books are even less transparent—perhaps their authors never really intended them to have big ideas. A good example is Morris's (1993) nonfiction book *Hats, Hats, Hats*, which presents photographs of hats with simple captions (e.g., "Work Hats," "Play Hats"). But as you read this book, you are drawn into big ideas about how different kinds of hats serve different purposes in different situations and especially in different cultures.

Further toward the more obscure end of this scale are texts that present big ideas in opaque ways. For me, despite repeated attempts (on my own, and with expert guidance) to understand Ritchie's exhibit "Proposition Player" (Massachusetts Museum of Modern Art, 2004), I am still hopelessly out of my depth. School children in the middle and upper grades struggle repeatedly with big-idea poems—many of the same ones (e.g., Keats, Wordsworth, Milton) with which I struggled as a child growing up in England.

How Should We Teach Big Ideas?

We need to engage children with big ideas in a variety of ways. We need to infuse big ideas into daily conversation. We need to read fiction, nonfiction, and poetry that express big ideas. We need to have children experience big ideas in a variety of media (art, sculpture, architecture, drama, film) both receptively and expressively. It's hard to understand or discuss big ideas in material that has precious few of them, or in the "content-less" confines of what Schmoker (2001) called the "Crayola curriculum" in which students spend countless hours coloring worksheets. While they are valuable for other purposes, series books (e.g., Famous Five, Boxcar Children, Encyclopedia Brown) are not good sources for big ideas. Nor is "cutesy" poetry. Instead, we should select books and other materials that have what Peterson and Eeds (1990) called "multiple layers of meaning." Their favorite example of a multilayered book was *Tuck Everlasting* (Babbit, 1975). It wouldn't be difficult to select others from the hundreds published each year: the work of Betsy Byars, Cynthia Rylant, Jane Yolen, Gary Paulsen, Eloise Greenfield, and Eve Bunting come immediately to mind. To start with, we should choose fiction, nonfiction, and poetry in which the big ideas are fairly simple and easily accessible. These books need to be read to and with children, and they should be made available for children to read on their own.

We should model, teach, and have children practice strategies for accessing and understanding big ideas. To begin with, modeling might simply consist of telling children what the big idea of a book is before starting to read it aloud. Before reading Trapani's (1998) *The Itsy Bitsy Spider*, a teacher could say,

> Have you ever heard of the expression "If at first you don't succeed, try, try again?" Well, this is a story about a spider who at first didn't succeed, but she tried and tried again. Let's read and find out....

Later, a teacher could explain to children how he or she figured out the big idea of a story or poem. Later still, the teacher might teach children techniques like asking questions or making text-to-self, text-to-world, or text-to-text connections (Keene & Zimmerman, 1997) and show them how to use these techniques independently. Socratic seminars (Adler, 1982; Ball & Brewer, 1996) also provide excellent instructional strategies for teaching students to access, grapple with, and understand big ideas.

One interesting way to build children's understanding of big ideas is to use multiple texts and build understanding within and across them. Here's an example, using two of Kuskin's (1998) poems from her anthology *The Sky Is Always in the Sky* (1998). A teacher might start by sharing "A Bug Sat in a Silver Flower" (p. 29). It's a poem about a little bug thinking "silver thoughts" who is suddenly eaten by a bigger bug. Asking the children what big ideas came to them as they heard or read the poem would probably elicit notions about the food chain: In nature, bigger bugs routinely eat smaller bugs, and smaller bugs in turn eat even smaller ones. They might also raise the point that in nature, not surviving is often a matter of chance—being in the wrong place at the wrong time. I see this daily in the summer at my pond, as the blue heron picks off the goldfish and small bass I so carefully stock. As with Kuskin's smaller bugs, the heron is simply doing to my fish what my fish are doing to smaller creatures like flies or larvae.

Next, the teacher might share another of Kuskin's poems from the same anthology, "Buggity-Buggity Bug" (p. 26). This particular bug was "wandering aimlessly" when all of a sudden, it too met its end, but this time under the shoe of a human being. The teacher can initiate a discussion about the big ideas of this poem. Children can come up with similar ideas as for the first discussion—the notion of being in the wrong place at the wrong time. Some children might latch onto the seemingly careless and thoughtless act of the shoes in relation to the unsuspecting bug underfoot.

Finally, the teacher can ask about the big ideas of the two poems combined. Children might see the difference between what happens to a small bug as part of the food chain as opposed to what happens to some of them as a result of human intervention (intentional or not). In this case, of course, it looks unintentional—careless at worst. But the discussion could easily lead to intentional acts of destruction of bugs by humans, as in the case of pesticides used around the home or garden. What's interesting is how there are big ideas associated with each of the poems individually, but additional ones emerge when the two poems are discussed together.

It always surprises and disappoints me that while so much really good literature is read to children in the early grades, the discussions that take place around this literature so frequently focus on trivial aspects of the books rather than their big ideas. A good example is *Chrysanthemum* (Henkes, 1991), a book about a mouse of the same name who gets teased mercilessly when she goes to school for the first time. The most frequent follow-up activity I see in early primary classrooms involves children doing projects on their names. But *Chrysanthemum* really isn't a book about names, it's a wonderful illustration of the proverb "Don't judge a book by its cover," or the need for children not to be swayed by the opinions of others. It isn't that researching children's names is a bad idea, it's missing the opportunity to broaden and deepen children's understanding of big ideas.

Without such opportunities for critical thought, many children will not develop these understandings, which may not hurt them much during the elementary grades, but will come back to haunt them in secondary school as the conceptual density of material across all subject areas increases.

As teachers, we should be able, by the middle of first grade, to simply pose the question, So, what's the big idea? and have children engage in a discussion of *Chrysanthemum* (Henkes, 1991), or a nonfiction book about recycling, or one of Karla Kuskin's poems about bugs, that engages the big ideas of these works. But we also, as Brown (1991) suggested, ought to be holding regular conversations in classrooms about big ideas in general—conversations about current events, history, science, art, music, politics, environment, and so on—so that children can build up knowledge about these topics, appreciate their importance, and use the knowledge to inform and strengthen their understanding of everything they read, hear, or view.

References

Adler, M. (1982). *The Paideia proposal: An educational manifesto.* New York: Macmillan.

Babbit, N. (1975). *Tuck everlasting.* New York: Farrar, Straus and Giroux.

Ball, W.H., & Brewer, P.F. (1996). Socratic questioning: Then and now. In R.L. Canady & M.D. Retting (Eds.), *Teaching in the block: Strategies for engaging active learners* (pp. 29–31). Larchmont, NY: Eye on Education Press.

Bloom, B.S. (1956). *Taxonomy of educational objectives: The classification of educational goals.* New York: Longman.

Brown, R.G. (1991). *Schools of thought: How the politics of literacy shape thinking in the classroom.* San Francisco: Jossey-Bass.

Cowcher, H. (1991). *Antarctica.* New York: Sunburst.

Henkes, K. (1991). *Chrysanthemum.* New York: Mulberry.

Keene, E.O., & Zimmerman, S. (1997). *Mosaic of thought: Teaching comprehension in a reader's workshop.* Portsmouth, NH: Heinemann.

Kuskin, K. (1998). *The sky is always in the sky.* New York: HarperCollins.

Massachusetts Museum of Modern Art. (2004). *The interventionists: Art in the social sphere.* Cambridge, MA: MIT Press.

Morris, A., & Heyman, K. (1993). *Hats, hats, hats.* New York: Trophy.

National Center for Education Statistics. (2004). Percentage of students, by reading achievement level, grade 4: 1992–2003. *The nation's report card: Reading.* Washington, DC: National Center for Education Statistics, Institute of Education Sciences, U.S. Department of Education. Retrieved March 9, 2005, from http://nces.ed.gov/nationsreportcard/reading/results2003/natachieve-g4.asp

No Child Left Behind Act of 2001, Pub. L. No. 107-110, 115 Stat. 1425 (2002).

Peterson, R., & Eeds, M. (1990). *Grand conversations: Literature groups in action.* New York: Scholastic.

Schmoker, M. (2001). The "Crayola curriculum." *Education Week, 21*(8), 42–44.

Trapani, I. (1998). *The itsy bitsy spider.* New York: Whispering Coyote Press.

Questions for Reflection

- The author describes observing 126 teaching-learning episodes, only 4 of which contained any effort to focus students' attention on big ideas in text. Think about your own reading lessons and those you've observed in colleagues' classrooms. How much attention gets paid to big ideas? Does your experience match the author's?
- Getting the big idea is clearly a primary goal of reading. How can you ensure that this goal is part of your instruction? What effect would that have on your students, particularly your struggling readers?

Scaffolding Students' Comprehension of Text

Kathleen F. Clark and Michael F. Graves

In a first-grade classroom, the teacher carefully monitors students' responses as the class reads Ruth Krauss's *The Carrot Seed* (1945), an informational storybook about a boy planting a carrot seed. The teacher realizes that the children don't understand what the green, fern-like plant they see in the picture has to do with the orange carrots they sometimes have for dinner. She immediately intervenes and, through a series of skillfully chosen questions, leads students to a basic understanding of what growing carrots look like. In another classroom, a group of sixth-grade students is beginning to read Michael Cooper's *Indian School* (1999) as part of a social studies unit. The teacher recognizes that *Indian School* will be a challenge for some of her students and wants to be sure that they all get off to a good start with it. As students begin the first chapter, she provides them with a carefully crafted set of prereading, during-reading, and postreading activities to support their initial understanding of the book. In a third classroom, a fourth-grade teacher is using direct explanation to teach the comprehension strategy of predicting. In doing so, he describes the strategy and how it should be used, models its use and has some students model it, works with students as they begin using the strategy, gradually gives students more and more responsibility for using the strategy independently, and reminds and prompts students to use the strategy over time.

The assistance the teachers provide to aid students' comprehension in these three instances is in some ways quite different. Yet in each case, the teacher relies heavily on the use of instructional scaffolding, one of the most recommended, versatile, and powerful instructional techniques of constructivist teaching. Recent studies of classroom reading instruction have found that, although scaffolding is widely used by some of the best teachers (Taylor, Pearson, Clark, & Walpole, 2000; Wharton-McDonald, Pressley, & Hampston, 1998), it is not characteristic of most teachers (Taylor et al.) and that, when employed, it is typically in support of word recognition (Clark, 2000). Comprehension instruction of any sort is much less frequent than it needs to be (Pressley, 2002a; RAND Reading Study Group, 2002), and agreement about just what we can do to best foster students' comprehension is far from complete (Institute of Education Sciences, 2003). However, there is virtually universal agreement that scaffolding plays an essential and vital role in fostering comprehension (Duffy, 2002; Duke & Pearson, 2002; Palincsar, 2003; Pressley, 2002b). We believe that, because scaffolding is a complex instructional concept and takes many forms, gathering together examples and explanations of various sorts of scaffolding will help to foster its more widespread use. Our purpose here is to give readers a broader perspective of the different roles they can play in using various forms of scaffolding by providing carefully selected examples and descriptions of the forms that scaffolding can take. By so doing, we hope to help teachers construct a deeper understanding of scaffolding, use it more frequently in their classrooms, and thereby improve students' comprehension.

Reprinted from Clark, K.F., & Graves, M.F. (2005). Scaffolding students' comprehension of text. *The Reading Teacher, 58*(6), 570–580.

We begin by considering several definitions of scaffolding, noting the foundations for it, and highlighting reasons why it is effective. Next, we describe three general types of scaffolding and teachers' roles therein and provide examples of each type. Finally, we offer some considerations for making decisions about scaffolding.

What Is Scaffolding?

Wood, Bruner, and Ross (1976) were the first to use the term *scaffolding* in its educational sense. They described scaffolding as a "process that enables a child or novice to solve a problem, carry out a task or achieve a goal which would be beyond his unassisted efforts" (p. 90). Since this initial work, scaffolding has been described as "supported situations in which children can extend current skills and knowledge to a higher level of competence" (Rogoff, 1990, p. 93), "what teachers say and do to enable children to complete complex mental tasks they could not complete without assistance" (Pearson & Fielding, 1991, p. 842), "a process whereby a teacher monitors students' learning carefully and steps in to provide assistance on an as-needed basis" (Wharton-McDonald et al., 1998, p. 116), and as "a temporary supportive structure that teachers create to assist a student or a group of students to accomplish a task that they could not complete alone" (Graves, Watts, & Graves, 1994, p. 44). One of us (Graves & Graves, 2003) has expanded that definition, noting that

> in addition to helping children complete tasks they could not otherwise complete, scaffolding can aid students by helping them to better complete a task, to complete a task with less stress or in less time, or to learn more fully than they would have otherwise. (p. 30)

Pressley (2002b) has provided a particularly rich description, explaining both the metaphor entailed in the term and its educational meaning.

> The scaffolding of a building under construction provides support when the new building cannot stand on its own. As the new structure is completed and becomes freestanding, the scaffolding is removed. So it is with scaffolded adult-child academic interactions. The adult carefully monitors when enough instructional input has been provided to permit the child to make progress toward an academic goal, and thus the adult provides support only when the child needs it. If the child catches on quickly, the adult's responsive instruction will be less detailed than if the child experiences difficulties with the task. (pp. 97–98)

Foundations of Scaffolding

The concept of scaffolding is grounded in Vygotsky's social constructivist view of learning. According to Vygotsky (1978), every mental function in a child's development first appears in collaboration with an adult. The collaboration occurs in what Vygotsky referred to as the zone of proximal development. This is the area between what children can do independently and what they can do with assistance. Over time, given repeated experiences, a child internalizes the collaborative form of the mental processes and is able to engage in them alone or in new contexts.

A related construct that is very helpful in understanding scaffolding is the gradual release of responsibility model (Pearson & Fielding, 1991), a version of which is shown in Figure 1. The model depicts a temporal sequence in which students gradually progress from situations in which the teacher takes the majority of the responsibility for successfully completing a reading task, to situations in which students assume increasing responsibility for reading tasks, and finally to situations in which students take all or nearly all the responsibility for reading tasks. At any point in time, teachers should scaffold students enough so that they do not give up on the task or fail at it but not scaffold them so much that they do not have the opportunity to actively work on the problem themselves.

An Effective Technique

What makes scaffolding so effective is that it enables a teacher to keep a task whole, while students learn to understand and manage the parts,

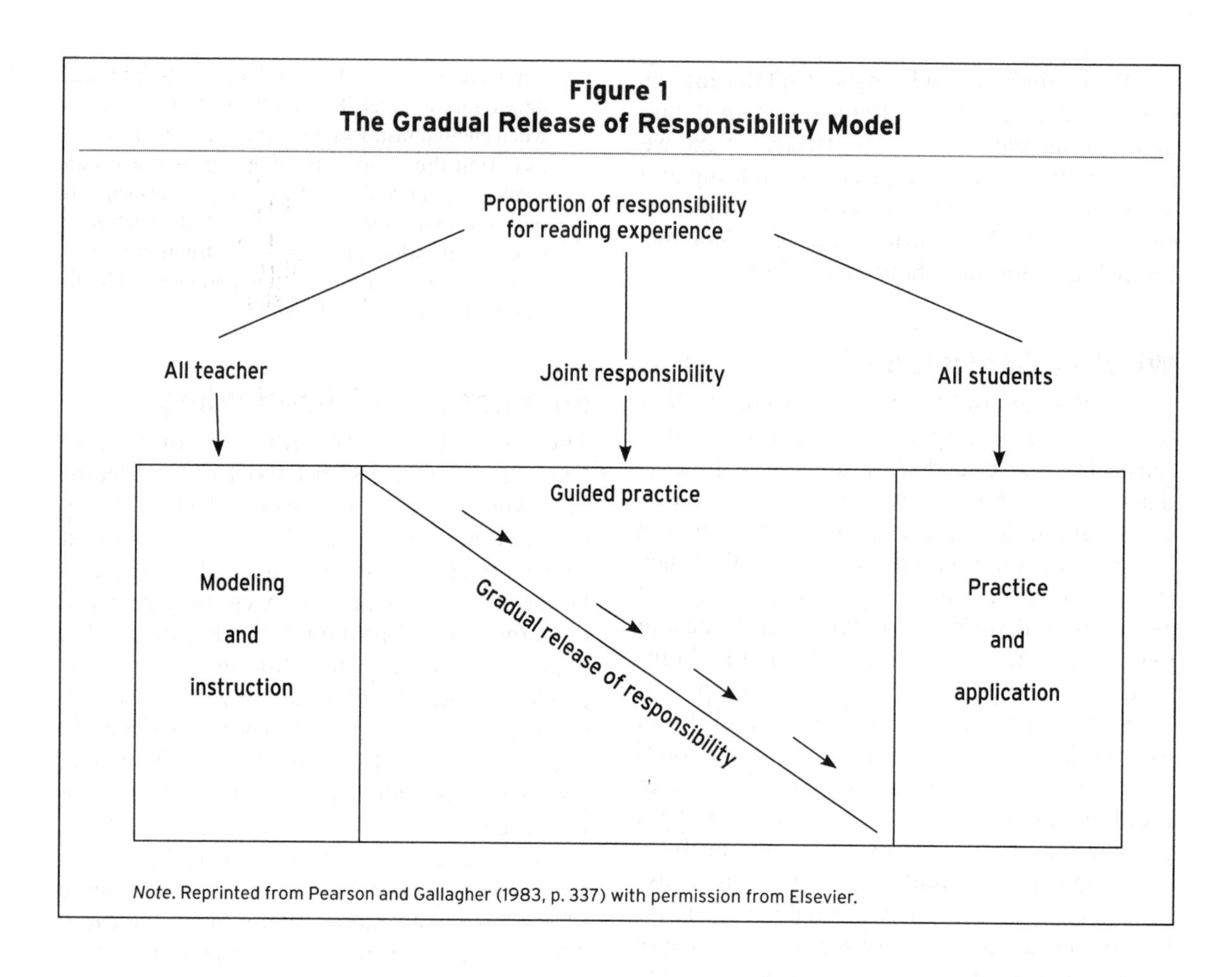

and presents the learner with just the right challenge. Scaffolding integrates multiple aspects of a task into a manageable chunk and permits students to see how they interrelate (Rogoff, 1990). In so doing, it helps students to cope with the complexity of tasks in an authentic manner (Pearson, 1996). Of course, the way that scaffolding is implemented in the classroom depends on students' abilities. Varying levels of support are possible, and the more complex a task is, the more support students will need to accomplish it.

To provide some concrete examples of scaffolding that support students' comprehension and to illustrate the various types, we next describe three types of scaffolding and give two examples of each. These three types are moment-to-moment verbal scaffolding, instructional frameworks that foster content learning, and instructional procedures for teaching reading comprehension strategies.

Moment-to-Moment Verbal Scaffolding

The teacher's role here is to prompt students, ask probing questions, and elaborate student responses in the course of instruction. To effectively scaffold in this way, teachers must call to mind their knowledge of students' instructional histories and ability to apply reading processes (Clark, 2004). In addition, they must consider two things: how their instructional talk moves students closer to the goal and how they can use students' responses to make them more aware of the mental processes in which they are engaged (Gaskins et al., 1997).

The Carrot Seed. In this example, we analyze the instructional scaffolding that a very accomplished teacher one of us observed (Clark, 2000) used with her first-grade students as they worked to make meaning when reading Ruth Krauss's *The Carrot Seed*. The teacher—we'll call her Mrs. Fry—monitors and prompts her students' thought processes and fosters their understanding as they proceed through the text, an informational storybook that complements the class's study of plants in the week's science curriculum. The story revolves around a young boy who plants a carrot seed. Family members repeatedly tell him that it will not come up. Nonetheless, the boy waters it daily. The story concludes with "And then one day a carrot came up." The accompanying illustration, however, is of a green, fern-like plant. There is no sign of a carrot as the students know it. In light of this, the students are understandably confused about what's coming up. Mrs. Fry scaffolds their construction of meaning through careful questioning, and the students come to understand that the part of the carrot plant with which they are familiar, and that they eat, is the root that grows below the ground. In this dialogue, all names are pseudonyms.

Kim: [Reads] And then one day a carrot came up.

Mrs. Fry: [Holding up the picture] Where's the carrot?

Anna: Up?

David: I don't know.

Mrs. Fry: Where's the carrot? Do you see it? [Holds the picture up and points to the plant's sprouting leaves]

Anna: That's the big root.

Mrs. Fry: What's a carrot?

Students: [No response]

Mrs. Fry: Where's the carrot? [Points to the picture]

Pete: In the ground?

Mrs. Fry: So would a carrot be a root?

David: [Shakes head negative]

Mrs. Fry: Aren't roots in the ground?

Students: [Shake heads affirmative]

Mrs. Fry: So do we eat some roots?

Students: [Emphatically] No!

Mrs. Fry: Do we eat carrots?

Students: Yes...yeah.

Mrs. Fry: Is a carrot a root?

Students: Yeah...yeah. [Heads nod affirmative]

Mrs. Fry: We must. The carrot came up.

In the dialogue, Mrs. Fry prompts students to think about the carrot in relation to what they see in the illustration. The first graders experience some confusion as they try to reconcile what they know about a carrot (that it is an orange vegetable) and what they see (the leafy shoots emerging from the ground). Mrs. Fry uses questions to engage their thought processes ("Where's the carrot? Do you see it?"). One child introduces the concept of a root. Building on this connection, Mrs. Fry poses the question "What's a carrot?" The students do not respond, so she points to the picture and refines her question: "Where's the carrot?" One child tentatively offers, "In the ground?" Mrs. Fry affirms this information and poses another question, one that connects the concept of root with that of carrot: "So would a carrot be a root?" One child voices hearty disagreement. Mrs. Fry asks, "Aren't roots in the ground?" The students respond affirmatively, and she pushes their thinking a step further: "So do we eat some roots?" In response to their emphatic negative response, Mrs. Fry asks whether they eat carrots and whether carrots are roots. In this way, through a series of carefully graded questions, students come to refine their understanding of how carrots grow.

The Popcorn Book. In this second example of moment-to-moment scaffolding, Carol Donovan, another very accomplished teacher, scaffolds first graders' efforts as they proceed through Tomie dePaola's *The Popcorn Book* (1978). As Smolkin and Donovan (2002) explained in the chapter from which the following example is taken, the scaffolding Donovan provides demonstrates a procedure they term an *Interactive Read-Aloud*. As they also explain, *The Popcorn Book* is a "dual-purpose book," one that presents two different texts:

> The first, a simple story displayed through cartoon-like characters with speech balloons, is about two brothers who decided to make popcorn. The second is informational; one of the boys wonders why their mother keeps popcorn in the refrigerator, and he reads aloud to his brother from a hefty, encyclopedic tome to find his answer. (p.145)

Our example [taken from Smolkin & Donovan, 2002, pp. 145–146] begins with the text, which the teacher reads aloud, and is followed by comments from the teacher and several students.

Teacher: [Reads] In 1612, French explorers saw some Iroquois people popping corn in clay pots. They would fill the pots with hot sand, throw in some popcorn and stir it with a stick. When the corn popped, it came to the top of the sand and made it easy to get.

Child: Look at the bowl.

Teacher: [Providing an oral commentary on the "story"] Okay, now it's hot enough [for the brothers] to add a few kernels.

Child: What's a kernel?

Child: Like what you pop.

Teacher: It's a seed.

Child: What if you, like, would you think [of] a popcorn seed? Like a popcorn seed. Could you grow popcorn?

Teacher: Oh, excellent, excellent question. Let's read and we'll see if this [book] answers that question, and if not, we'll talk about it at the end.

As you can see by comparing the two examples, Donovan's responses here are somewhat different from those of Mrs. Fry, whose scaffolding prompts were all questions. In this example of moment-to-moment verbal scaffolding, Donovan has just finished reading a segment of text in which the Iroquois procedure for popping corn is described. As the picture is displayed, a child directs the group's attention to the bowl. Donovan comments in a way that focuses readers' attention on a critical element of the popping procedure, the temperature of the sand: "Okay, now it's hot enough to add a few kernels." Then, a child asks the meaning of *kernel*, a word Donovan has used but the child does not understand. Donovan provides the meaning. Given that a kernel is a seed, another student asks if one could grow popcorn. Rather than answer the question, Donovan affirms the question and uses it to set a purpose for reading the next segment of text. Finally, she identifies discussion as a strategy for meaning making following reading. Donovan's instructional actions, focusing attention on salient information, providing relevant information, and identifying a comprehension strategy, scaffold students' comprehension.

Instructional Frameworks That Foster Content Learning

Instructional frameworks that foster content learning are used to guide and improve students' understanding and learning as they read individual texts. The frameworks may or may not include moment-to-moment verbal scaffolding. In scaffolding of this sort, the teacher's role is to structure and orchestrate the reading experience so that students can optimally profit from it. Questioning the Author, or QtA (Beck, McKeown, Worthy, Sandora, & Kucan, 1996), the first framework we discuss, focuses on verbal scaffolding, while the Scaffolded Reading Experience, or SRE (Graves & Graves, 2003), the second framework we consider, includes a variety of types of scaffolding.

Questioning the Author. The intent of QtA is to help students to understand, interpret, and elaborate an author's meaning as they read the text. QtA enables teachers to guide and facilitate students' online or during-reading comprehension as they progress through successive sections of text. Teachers do so by posing certain sorts of questions, called queries. In contrast to more traditional questions that check for understanding of story elements (e.g., Who was involved? What happened first, next, last? How was the problem resolved?), queries enable students to cooperatively construct meaning as they read and reflect on ideas in text. Further, queries are open-ended, permitting multiple, divergent responses and allowing students to participate at their evolving levels of understanding. For example, teachers might ask the following questions:

- What do you think the author means by that?
- How does that connect with what the author has already told us?
- How did the author work that out for us?
- Did the author explain it clearly?
- What's missing?
- What do we need to find out?

Teachers begin their use of QtA by explaining to students that texts are written by ordinary people who are not perfect and who create texts that are not perfect. Consequently, readers need to work hard to figure out what the authors are trying to say. Then members of the class read a text together, with the teacher stopping at critical points to pose queries that invite students to explore and grapple with the meaning of what is written.

The following QtA dialogue [from McKeown, Beck, & Sandora, 1996, pp. 112–113] shows a fifth-grade social studies class studying U.S. history. The class had been working with QtA for some time and is quite skilled in grappling with text ideas. The class is discussing a text segment about the presidency of James Buchanan, a Pennsylvania native. The text indicated that many people believed that Buchanan liked the South better than the North because he believed that it was a person's choice whether or not to have slaves.

Teacher: All right. This paragraph that Tracy just read is really full of important information. What has the author told us in this important paragraph?

Laura: Um, they um think that Buchanan liked the South better because they, he said that it is a person's choice if they want to have slaves or not, so they thought um that he liked the South better than the North.

Teacher: Okay. And what kind of problem then did this cause President Buchanan when they thought that he liked the South better? What kind of problem did that cause?

Janet: Well, maybe um like less people would vote for him because like if he ran for President again, maybe less people would vote for him because like in Pennsylvania we were against slavery and we might have voted for him because he was in Pennsylvania, because he was from Pennsylvania. That may be why they voted for him, but now since we knew that he was for the South, we might not vote for him again.

Teacher: Okay, a little bit of knowledge, then, might change people's minds.

Jamie: I have something to add on to Janet's 'cause I completely agree with her, but I just want to add something on. Um, we might have voted for him because he was from Pennsylvania so we might have thought that since he was from Pennsylvania and Pennsylvania was an antislavery state, that he was also against slavery. But it turns out he wasn't.

Angelica: I agree with the rest of them, except for one that um, like all of a sudden, like someone who would be in Pennsylvania you want to vote for them but then they, wouldn't they be going for the South and then you wouldn't want to vote for them after that.

In this example, the teacher opens the discussion with the query "What has the author told us in this important paragraph?" Laura responds, and the teacher poses another query that furthers the discussion: "What kind of problem did that cause?" Janet contributes her developing understanding, and the teacher synthesizes her point: "Okay, a little bit of knowledge, then, might change people's minds." This scenario illustrates well the sort of scaffolding that takes place during a QtA discussion. The students are focused on the meaning of the text. In keeping with her role of structuring the reading experience, the teacher adroitly directs the discussion but does not dominate it. She leaves plenty of room for student input; the students are the ones who do most of the talking and thinking, and they respond at some length. Finally, they listen to one another and build on one another's responses as they jointly construct meaning for the text.

The Scaffolded Reading Experience. The SRE (Graves & Graves, 2003) is a flexible framework that teachers can use to assist students in understanding, learning from, and enjoying both narrative and expository texts. As in QtA, the teacher's role is to structure and orchestrate the reading experience so that students may optimally comprehend. The SRE has two phases: planning and implementation. During the planning phase, the teacher considers the students who will be doing the reading, the reading selection itself, and the purpose(s) of the reading. On the basis of these considerations, the teacher then creates a set of prereading, during-reading, and postreading activities designed to assist this particular group of students in reaching those purposes. Possible pre-, during-, and postreading activities to consider in creating an SRE are shown in Table 1.

It is important to note that this is a list of *possible* components of an SRE. No single SRE includes all of these activities. As in all scaffolding, SREs should provide enough support that students succeed but not so much support that they do not put in the cognitive effort it takes to learn and grow as readers. SREs vary considerably, depending on the students, reading selections, and their purpose.

Consider as one example an SRE for Robert Coles's *The Story of Ruby Bridges* (1995). This picture-book biography tells the dramatic story of the first black student to attend Frantz Elementary School in New Orleans, Louisiana. The book is appropriate for many third graders and will certainly interest them, but some students will need more assistance in understanding it than others. We show a list of possible activities for the book in Figure 2.

Following are two more sets of activities that illustrate the range of options SREs provide. The first, a substantial SRE, was created for sixth

Table 1
Possible Activities in a Scaffolded Reading Experience

Prereading	During reading	Postreading
Relating the reading to students' lives	Silent reading	Questioning
Motivating	Reading to students	Discussion
Activating and building background knowledge	Supported reading	Writing
Providing text-specific knowledge	Oral reading by students	Drama
Preteaching vocabulary	Modifying the text	Artistic and nonverbal activities
Preteaching concepts		Application and outreach activities
Prequestioning, predicting, and direction setting		Building connections
Suggesting strategies		Reteaching

Figure 2
Scaffolded Reading Experience Activities for *The Story of Ruby Bridges* (Coles, 1995)

Activities in regular type are for students who will find the book relatively easy; those in ***bold italic*** are additional or alternative activities for students who will find the book more of a challenge.

Prereading	Motivating Building background knowledge ***Building text-specific knowledge*** ***Direction setting***
During reading	***Reading to students*** Silent reading
Postreading	Questioning and small-group discussion Writing ***Working with art***

Prereading

- Motivate students by encouraging them to talk about problems they have encountered and how they solved them. They might also talk about some of the obstacles they encountered and what kept them going.
- Build relevant background knowledge by asking students to think about books they have read in which the characters faced a challenge they thought was difficult or impossible but were able to triumph in the end. Then, have students talk about the problems the characters encountered and how they overcame them. If necessary, you can share a few books that exemplify this theme.
- ***Build text-specific knowledge*** for students who need more assistance by previewing the biography. Begin by explaining what a biography is, emphasizing that this is a true story about something that happened to a real person. Introduce the setting, the main characters, and enough of the story line to whet students' appetite for the biography.
- ***Direction setting*** for stronger readers might consist of simply telling students to look for the challenges Ruby faces and how she handles them. ***Direction setting*** for less skilled readers might consist of asking them to look for *one* problem Ruby faces and her solution to that problem.

During reading

- ***Reading some of the story aloud*** can get less skilled readers off to a good start and leave them with a manageable amount of reading to do.
- Silent reading is appropriate for students who can successfully read the book on their own.

Postreading

- Answering questions that get at the essence of the biography in small groups will give all students an opportunity to review the book's important events and issues.
- Writing gives students an opportunity to solidify their understanding of the biography or to respond to it. You will probably want to suggest some topics—tell about the most challenging problem Ruby faced, tell what you admire most about Ruby, or tell how you would have reacted in Ruby's place.
- ***Working with art*** gives students who struggle with writing another way to solidify their understanding of the story or respond to it. Students might draw pictures illustrating significant events in the biography or make collages suggesting their responses to significant events. Of course, artistic activities are often appropriate alternatives for good writers, too.

graders studying the first chapter of Michael Cooper's *Indian School* as part of their social studies work and is designed to help them thoroughly understand the important information presented in the chapter.

SRE activities for *Indian School*

Prereading	Motivating Preteaching vocabulary Questioning
During reading	Reading to students Silent reading

Postreading	Small-group discussion Answering questions Large-group discussion

The second, a much less substantial SRE, might be used with these same sixth graders reading *Frindle* by Andrew Clements (1998) and is designed to help them enjoy this fast-paced and humorous tale.

SRE activities for *Frindle*

Prereading	Motivating
During reading	Silent reading
Postreading	Optional small-group discussion

Again, it should be stressed that these are possible SREs. The scaffolding needed in one situation—what will be most helpful for a particular group of students, a particular text, and a particular purpose or purposes—will often be quite different from the scaffolding needed in another.

Instructional Procedures for Teaching Reading Comprehension Strategies

In addition to guiding their reading of individual texts, it is important to help students become independent readers by providing strategies for use as they read various texts over time. Scaffolding also plays a crucial role in these efforts: The teacher explicitly teaches strategies that foster reading independence, engages students in supported practice with multiple texts, and gradually transfers responsibility for strategy use as students become increasingly able. Here we consider two approaches to teaching comprehension strategies that are strongly supported by research and widely recommended: Direct Explanation of Comprehension Strategies (DECS) and Reciprocal Teaching (RT).

Direct Explanation of Comprehension Strategies. DECS (Duffy, 2002; Duffy et al., 1987) teaches individual strategies in an explicit and very straightforward way. Duke and Pearson (2002) listed the following five components of the procedure and gave a concrete example of the teacher's talk in scaffolding students' learning of the predicting strategy. We include parts of the teacher talk. At some points we have shortened and paraphrased, and, following the example of each components, we have added our comments in brackets.

1. An explicit description of the strategy and when and how it should be used.

   "Predicting is making guesses about what will come next in the text you are reading. You should make predictions a lot when you read. For now, you should stop every two pages that you read and make some predictions."

   [Note how the teacher greatly simplifies the initial task by telling students to make a prediction every two pages.]

2. Teacher and/or student modeling of the strategy in action.

   "I am going to make predictions while I read this book. I will start with just the cover here. Hum...I see a picture of an owl. It looks like he—I think it is a he—is wearing pajamas, and he is carrying a candle. I *predict* that this is going to be a make-believe story because owls do not really wear pajamas and carry candles. I *predict* it is going to be about this owl, and it is going to take place at nighttime."

   [Here the teacher strives to reveal the thought processes that he or she uses in predicting so that students can later use similar processes.]

3. Collaborative use of the strategy in action.

   "So far, I've been doing all the predicting. Now, I want you to make predictions with me. Each of us should stop and think aloud about what might happen next.... Okay, let's hear what you think and why."

   [At this point, the students begin to do some of the work but still have plenty of support from the teacher.]

4. Guided practice using the strategy with gradual release of responsibility.

   [This first example is from an early session, and the teacher is still providing substantial scaffolding by reading along with students and telling them when to make predictions.]

"I have called the three of you together to work on making predictions while you read this and other books. After every few pages I will ask each of you to stop and make predictions. We will talk about our predictions and then read on to see if they come true."

[This second example is from a later session. Students still receive scaffolding, but now it comes from written directions rather than from the teacher, an appropriately less supportive form of scaffolding.]

"Each of you has a chart that lists different pages in your book. When you finish reading a page on the list, stop and make a prediction. Write the prediction in the column that says 'Predictions.' When you get to the next page on the list, check off whether your prediction 'Happened,' 'Will not happen,' or 'Still might happen.' Then make another prediction and write it down."

[Duke & Pearson attribute this technique to Mason & Au, 1986.]

5. Independent use of the strategy.

"It is time for silent reading. As you read today, remember what you have been working on—making predictions while you read. Be sure to make predictions every two or three pages. Ask yourself why you made the predictions you did—what made you think that. Check as you read to see whether your prediction came true. Jamal is passing out predictions bookmarks to remind you."

[Here, students are reading silently by themselves, without the teacher or a worksheet to prompt their predictions. But they are still receiving some scaffolding—the reminder to predict every two or three pages, to think about their predictions,and to check them as well as the bookmark.] (Adapted from Duke & Pearson, 2002, pp. 208–210)

At this point, students have received some excellent instruction and scaffolding and are well on their way to becoming competent with the predicting strategy. However, this should not be the end of the scaffolding. Over time, the teacher will continue to remind students of the importance of predicting, point out different and increasingly challenging texts where the predicting strategy is appropriate, and occasionally discuss with students how their efforts at predicting are progressing.

Reciprocal Teaching. RT (Palincsar & Brown, 1989) is a powerful technique for teaching a coordinated set of four comprehension strategies—questioning, summarizing, clarifying, and predicting. At the heart of RT is a series of dialogues in which the teacher and a small group of students read and discuss a text. Before beginning the dialogues, the teacher directly instructs students on each of the four strategies and evaluates individual students' proficiency with them so that she or he will know how to scaffold each student during the dialogues. Then, as the group progresses through the text segment by segment, the teacher models and guides students through the four strategies. These strategies help students to understand the purposes of reading, activate prior knowledge, focus attention on important content, critically evaluate text, monitor comprehension, and draw and test inferences. The teacher's role in these dialogues is to assist students during reading as they work to comprehend text and to focus and direct the dialogue.

In the following example (see Palincsar & Brown, 1989, for full text), the teacher reads segments of a story about bear cubs to a group of six first graders and guides them through several of the components of RT.

[The teacher reads.] "Baby bear was bigger than his sister and he began to play too rough. His sister jumped onto a tree trunk and climbed quickly upward" (p.33). One of the children interrupts to ask, "What's rough?" Other children come up with possible examples (one suggests something to do with texture; another says "like they beat you up"), then the teacher turns to the text for clarification. The children agree that the second suggestion is what is meant in the text. The teacher replies, "The pinching and hitting, playing too hard, Okay."

The teacher continues reading and comes to a portion of the text where a prediction would be appropriate. She asks the children to predict what happens next. They correctly predict that the tree limb will break and the bear will fall. The teacher reads to confirm the prediction. "He squalled for his mother. Now the mother splashed into the water...." One of the children asks for the meaning of *squalled*. The teacher rereads the sentence, and then asks what the children think the little bear did when he fell. The child who asked the question replies, "Whining and crying," and the teacher confirms that this was a good guess.

In this example, the teacher has guided, modeled, and prompted students as they worked to understand the text. But—in keeping with the essence of scaffolding—she or he has not simply given students the answers. Students have had to do some of the work themselves—questioning, answering questions, and making a prediction—and by repeatedly doing such work, they become increasingly competent with the strategies. As students become more familiar with the strategies, they will take turns assuming the role of the teacher. While the classroom teacher will continue to model and prompt as necessary, he or she will gradually release responsibility for orchestrating and engaging in the strategies to students. Ultimately, the students will assume primary responsibility for employing the strategies as they read.

Flexible and Adaptable Support

As you consider the examples of scaffolding students' comprehension we have presented, you will recognize a lot of similarities as well as a number of differences. Both examples of moment-by-moment verbal scaffolding center on the dialogue between the teacher and a small group of students. Mrs. Fry, however, relied exclusively on asking questions, while Carol Donovan used various sorts of prompts, including focusing attention on critical aspects of text, giving information, using a student's question to set the purpose for reading, and directly identifying a simple comprehension strategy.

The next two examples we presented—the use of the Questioning the Author and Scaffolded Reading Experience instructional frameworks to foster content learning—are quite different from each other. QtA employs a set of queries to prompt students' thinking and discussion as they are reading a text, whereas the SRE gives students various supportive activities to do before, during, and after they read a text. In both cases, however, the goal is the same: to support and improve students' comprehension of a text.

The final two examples we presented—the use of Direct Explanation of Comprehension Strategies and Reciprocal Teaching to teach reading comprehension strategies—are again quite different. DECS teaches individual comprehension strategies through a multifaceted process that includes describing the strategy, modeling it, using it collaboratively, guided practice, and independent use of the strategy. RT teaches the four strategies in a process that includes a relatively short period of instruction on them followed by many small-group dialogues in which the teacher guides students in their use as they collaboratively read segments of a text.

However, while the six examples have similarities and differences, all serve the function of scaffolding—"helping students complete tasks they could not otherwise complete, [and aiding] students by helping them to better complete a task, to complete a task with less stress or in less time, or to learn more fully than they would have otherwise" (Graves & Graves, 2003, p. 30).

In commenting on the sorts of evidence teachers can use in making educational decisions, Stanovich and Stanovich (2003) identified three standards: publication of findings in refereed journals, duplication of results by a number of investigators, and consensus from a body of studies. The use of scaffolding is strongly supported by evidence from all three of these sources. Our goal has been to help readers gain a broader perspective of the different roles they can play in using various forms of scaffolding, more frequently employ scaffolding in their classrooms, and thereby improve students' comprehension. We encourage teachers to add scaffolding to their instructional repertoire. It is a highly flexible and adaptable model of instruction that supports students as they acquire basic skills and higher order thinking processes, allows for explicit instruction within authentic contexts of reading and writing, and enables teachers to differentiate instruction for students of diverse needs. In summary, scaffolding invites students and teachers to collaborate as students become increasingly active readers and thinkers.

References

Clark, K.F. (2000). Instructional scaffolding in reading: A case study of four primary grade teachers (Doctoral dissertation, University of Minnesota, 2000). *Dissertation Abstracts International, 61*, 06A.

Clark, K.F. (2004). What can I say besides "sound it out"? Coaching word recognition in beginning reading. *The Reading Teacher, 57*, 440–449.

Beck, I.L., McKeown, M.G., Worthy, J., Sandora, C.A., & Kucan, L. (1996). Questioning the author: A year-long classroom implementation to engage students with text. *The Elementary School Journal, 96*, 385–414.

Duffy, G.G. (2002). The case for direct explanation of strategies. In C.C. Block & M. Pressley (Eds.), *Comprehension instruction: Research-based best practices* (pp. 28–41). New York: Guilford.

Duffy, G.G., Roehler, L.R., Sivan, E., Rackliffe, G., Book, C., Meloth, M., et al. (1987). Effects of explaining the reasoning associated with using reading strategies. *Reading Research Quarterly, 22*, 347–368.

Duke, N.K., & Pearson, P.D. (2002). Effective practices for developing reading comprehension. In A.E. Farstrup & S.J. Samuels (Eds.), *What research has to say about reading instruction* (3rd ed., pp. 205–242). Newark, DE: International Reading Association.

Gaskins, I.W., Rauch, S., Gensemer, E., Cunicelli, E., O'Hara, C., Six, L., et al. (1997). Scaffolding the development of intelligence among children who are delayed in learning to read. In K. Hogan & M. Pressley (Eds.), *Scaffolding student learning: Instructional approaches and issues* (pp. 43–73). Cambridge, MA: Brookline.

Graves, M.F., & Graves, B.B. (2003). *Scaffolding reading experiences: Designs for student success.* Norwood, MA: Christopher-Gordon.

Graves, M.F., Watts, S., & Graves, B.B. (1994). *Essentials of classroom teaching: Elementary reading.* Boston: Allyn & Bacon.

Institute of Education Sciences. (2003, October 23). *Reading comprehension and reading scale-up research grants* (CFDA No. 84.305). Washington, DC: Author. Retrieved November 15, 2003, from http://ed.gov/programs/edresearch/applicant.html#read04

Mason, J.M., & Au, K. (1986). *Reading instruction for today.* Glenview, IL: Scott Foresman.

McKeown, M.G., Beck, I.L., & Sandora, C.A. (1996). Questioning the author: An approach to developing meaningful classroom discourse. In M.F. Graves, P. van den Broek, & B.M. Taylor (Eds.), *The first R: Every child's right to read* (pp. 97–119). New York: Teachers College Press.

Palincsar, A.S. (2003). Collaborative approaches to comprehension instruction. In A.P. Sweet & C.E. Snow (Eds.), *Rethinking reading comprehension* (pp. 99–114). New York: Guilford.

Palincsar, A.S., & Brown, A.L. (1989). Instruction for self-regulated learning. In L.B. Resnick & L.E. Klopfer (Eds.), *Towards the thinking curriculum: Current cognitive research* (pp. 19–39). Washington, DC: Association for Supervision and Curriculum Development.

Pearson, P.D. (1996). Reclaiming the center. In M.F. Graves, P. van den Broek, & B.M. Taylor (Eds.), *The first R: Every child's right to read* (pp. 259–274). New York: Teachers College Press.

Pearson, P.D., & Fielding, L. (1991). Comprehension instruction. In R. Barr, M.L. Kamil, P. Mosenthal, & P.D. Pearson(Eds.), *Handbook of reading research* (Vol. II, pp. 815–860). Mahwah, NJ: Erlbaum.

Pearson, P.D., & Gallagher, M.C. (1983). The instruction of reading comprehension. *Contemporary Educational Psychology, 8*, 317–344.

Pressley, M. (2002a). Comprehension strategies instruction: A turn-of-the-century status report. In M. Pressley & C.C. Block (Eds.), *Comprehension instruction: Research-based best practices* (pp. 11–27). New York: Guilford.

Pressley, M. (2002b). *Reading instruction that works: The case for balanced teaching* (2nd ed.). New York: Guilford.

RAND Reading Study Group. (2002). *Reading for understanding: Toward an R & D program in reading comprehension.* Santa Monica, CA: RAND Education.

Rogoff, B. (1990). *Apprenticeship in thinking.* New York: Oxford University Press.

Smolkin, L.B., & Donovan, C.A. (2002). "Oh excellent, excellent question!": Developmental differences in comprehension acquisition. In C.C. Block & M. Pressley (Eds.), *Comprehension instruction: Research-based best practices* (pp. 140–157). New York: Guilford.

Stanovich, P.J., & Stanovich, K.E. (2003). *Using research and reason in education: How teachers can use scientifically based research to make curricular decisions.* Washington, DC: National Institute for Literacy.

Taylor, B.M., Pearson, P.D., Clark, K.F., & Walpole, S. (2000). Effective schools and accomplished teachers: Lessons about primary-grade reading instruction in low-income schools. *Elementary School Journal, 101*, 121–165.

Vygotsky, L.S. (1978). *Mind in society: The development of higher psychological processes.* Cambridge, MA: Harvard University Press.

Wharton-McDonald, R., Pressley, M., & Hampston, J.M. (1998). Literacy instruction in nine first-grade classrooms: Teacher characteristics and student achievement. *Elementary School Journal, 99*, 101–128.

Wood, D., Bruner, J.S., & Ross, G. (1976). The role of tutoring in problem solving. *Journal of Child Psychology and Psychiatry, 17*, 89–100.

Children's Books Cited

Clements, A. (1998). *Frindle.* New York: Aladdin.
Coles, R. (1995). *The story of Ruby Bridges.* New York: Scholastic.
Cooper, M.L. (1999). *Indian school: Teaching the white man's way.* New York: Clarion.
dePaola, T. (1978). *The popcorn book.* New York: Holiday House.
Krauss, R. (1945). *The carrot seed.* New York: Harper & Row.

Questions for Reflection

- Many struggling readers have small vocabularies: They simply know the meanings of fewer words than do their more successful peers. Can you imagine how providing the sorts of instructional scaffolding described in this article could benefit these students?
- Duffy and others cited in this article describe scaffolding as quite complicated for teachers to get the hang of. Did the examples and transcripts provided in this article make scaffolding seem like something you could offer in vocabulary lessons for your struggling readers? Are there teachers in your school or district who are accomplished at scaffolding? Could you work with them to improve your own technique?